Introduction to
FRENCH LAW

Introduction to
FRENCH LAW

Professor Brice Dickson

University of Ulster

Parts of Chapters 1–5 incorporate the author's
translation of *Einführung in das Französische Recht*
by Professor Ulrich Hübner of the University of Cologne
and Professor Vlad Constantinesco of the University
of Strasbourg

PITMAN
PUBLISHING

PITMAN PUBLISHING
128 Long Acre, London WC2E 9AN

A Division of Longman Group Limited

First published in Great Britain 1994

© Longman Group Limited 1994

Parts of Chapters 1–5 have been translated and adapted from
Einführung in das Französische Recht
by U. Hübner and V. Constantinesco
© C.H. Beck Verlag 1988

British Library Cataloguing in Publication Data
A CIP catalogue record for this book is available on request from
the British Library.

ISBN 0–273–60140–7

Typeset by Land & Unwin (Data Sciences)
Printed and bound in Great Britain by Bell & Bain, Glasgow

*The Publishers' policy is to use paper manufactured from
sustainable forests.*

CONTENTS

PREFACE

This book was first conceived as a translation into English of what I then felt was the best introductory book available on French law – *Einführung in das Französische Recht* by Ulrich Hübner and Vlad Constantinesco (2nd edn, 1988; Verlag C.H. Beck, Munich). I am grateful to the authors and publishers of that book for permission to incorporate some of my translation of it into the present work, especially the first five chapters.

It quickly became apparent to me, however, that a satisfactory book for an English readership would have to be considerably different from the treatment accorded the subject for German readers. I thus began to use as my models both the published lectures of René David on *English Law and French Law* (1980; Stevens and Sons and Eastern Law House) and the more recent *Droit Anglais*, edited by J.A. Jolowicz (2nd edn, 1992; Dalloz, Paris). My aim was to produce a book which would provide a basic introduction to a wide variety of legal subjects in France, something that would go beyond the texts currently available, confined as they are either to a description of the French legal system as such or to particular legal topics. I wanted something more comprehensive than those books and not as detailed.

Naturally I have had to be selective in my choice of topics. Even within chapters I could not attempt to cover too much ground, for reasons of space as well as lack of expertise. I have therefore confined myself to the areas of law which I think should be of greatest interest to the increasing number of students – not just of law – who are today examining the French system from an English perspective. Amongst the legal topics omitted are social welfare law and environmental law. On the areas covered I have tried to state the law as at 1 January 1994.

I am naturally indebted to a variety of individuals and institutions for their assistance in the writing of this book. The Leverhulme Trust must be thanked for awarding me a European Studentship several years ago: it was this which stimulated my interest in French law and allowed me to develop knowledge and contacts at Parisian Universities. The British Academy also facilitated research there in the late 1980s. More recently it is my past and present employers, the Queen's University of Belfast and the University of Ulster respectively, who should be thanked for their help, financial and otherwise. Students at both campuses have at times been inspirational.

In France thanks are due to the many lawyers and academics who over the years have attempted to answer my queries. Responsibility for any errors which doubtless remain must, unfortunately, rest entirely on my own shoulders. In particular, all the translations of French phrases are my own. Closer to home I must acknowledge the secretarial assistance of

Karen Hamilton, Carol Murtagh, Margaret Trew and Mavis Wilson. Patricia Mallon, my wife, has been tremendously supportive throughout, despite the many hours of isolation the work has entailed. The publishers, in particular Patrick Bond and Elizabeth Tarrant, displayed exceptional patience during the book's long gestation.

Brice Dickson
Jordanstown
February 1994

TABLE OF ENGLISH CASES

TABLE OF FRENCH CASES

Abbreviations for French references:

AJDA:	*Actualité juridique/Droit administratif*
Clunet:	*Journal du droit international*
CE:	*Conseil d'Etat*
Cons const:	*Conseil constitutionnel*
Cour de Cass:	*Cour de Cassation*
D:	*Recueil Dalloz*
JCP:	*Jurisclasseur Périodique*
RFDA:	*Revue française de droit administratif*
S:	*Recueil Sirey*
TC:	*Tribunal des Conflits*

Page references to Bell are to translations of decisions in Bell, *French Constitutional Law* (1992).

TABLE OF ENGLISH LEGISLATION

TABLE OF FRENCH LEGISLATION

Note:
Legislation referred to in the text only briefly in passing is not listed in this Table.

TABLE OF TREATIES

CHAPTER 1

History and sources

INTRODUCTION

For students of English law the three historical events which most mark the development of the English legal system are the Norman Conquest in the 11th century, the initiatives of Henry II in the 13th century and the struggles between Crown and Parliament in the 17th century. Most of the standard features of today's common law were institutionalised in those periods. Even the Industrial Revolution during the 18th and 19th centuries did not affect the basic features of the English legal system so drastically, despite the content of the law changing enormously. The most recent event to have impacted fundamentally on the legal system is the United Kingdom's ratification of the Treaty of Rome, which took effect on 1 January 1973, but it is still too early to say whether the reforms thereby instigated will have as profound an influence as, say, the Glorious Revolution in the 1680s.

In France it is hardly an exaggeration to say that the most cataclysmic event of the past one thousand years was the Revolution at the end of the 18th century. Prior to that, the legal history of the country was as much a history of legal scholarship as of socio-political change. The greatest legacy of the Revolution in legal terms has been the theory and practice of codification, a concept which was staunchly advocated for England in the 19th century by Jeremy Bentham but which, despite more recent support from bodies such as the Criminal Law Revision Committee and the Law Commission, remains alien to the British legal culture.

Le droit ancien

French law forms a part of the family of laws known as the Romano-Germanic family. These share a common origin in ancient Roman law and have developed similar concepts and principles. French law is therefore more easily understood by lawyers in other European countries than by lawyers bred in the Anglo-American tradition. An outline of its historical development is essential to a proper understanding of its present form and content.

As in many other European countries, the law in France prior to its codification in the Napoleonic era was diversified amongst a number of different systems. Although ancient Roman law no longer applied elsewhere in Europe, in the South of France it continued to be used. It was known as the *ius gentium*. Until the 12th century the most important document reflecting the influence of Roman law in Gaul was the *Lex Romana Visigothorum*, sometimes known as the *Breviarium Alaricianum*. This law was named after Alaric II, King of the Visigoths, and was propounded in AD 506. In practice, however, classical Roman law tended to be 'vulgarised', either through being mixed with local customs or through simple ignorance of the original law. Besides, the victorious Germanic tribes remained governed by their own customary law, which around the year 500 was partly committed to writing in documents such as the *Lex Salia* and the *Lex Ripuaria*. At the end of the first millenium, therefore, the law to be applied in France largely depended on the background of the person in question. This system of 'personality of laws' was the Germanic way of doing things. During the rise of the Carolingian Empire in the 9th century it had replaced the principle of 'territoriality', whereby everyone within a particular territory was regulated by the same law (including the so-called Imperial Capitularies).

Gradually, however, with the intermixing of the races, the system of personality of laws became unworkable in France. The multiplicity of local laws was nevertheless hardly reduced, especially as royal decrees tended to lose their validity with the fall of the power of the French King. The law of a particular region became that which previously applied to the predominant race living in that region. Consequently, until the 12th century there was a clear dividing line traversing France roughly in line with the River Loire. In the south of the country the law was mainly based on Roman law and the area was known as *le pays de droit écrit*. This law differed substantially from classical Roman law and from the Roman law of the Digests which was later 'received' in Germany. It was, in fact, a form of customary Roman law. By contrast, in the centre and North of France the people lived under a variety of customary laws originally Germanic, and the area was known as *le pays de droit coutumier*. Here Roman law was resorted to only in order to plug the gaps in customary law or whenever it was viewed as clearly superior to any local customary alternative (as was the case for the law of obligations).

But although there was never a full-blown 'reception' of Roman law, the renaissance of interest in Roman law was still very significant throughout France. At the beginning of the 13th century Justinian's law became more influential in the University of Paris, an institution officially recognised by King Philip Augustus in 1200 and by Pope Innocent III in 1203–6. This was despite the fact that the public teaching of Roman law was actually prohibited at the University until 1679. In 1719, Pope Honorius III again forbade its teaching at the behest of the French Kings, who saw Roman law as the symbol of a pan-European Roman empire. At the same time customary law was making significant progress in Northern France, especially after 1454, when by the Ordinance of Montils-les-Tours Charles

VII ordered all the great customs to be reduced to writing. Although largely ignored at the time, this command was repeated by later kings and publication of most of the regional customs had been achieved by the end of the 17th century, with the Custom of the Duchy of Burgundy (1459–1576), the Custom of Orléans (1509–83), the Custom of Paris (1510–80) and the Custom of Brittany (1539–80) to name but a few. In this way customary law too was scientifically digested, so that by the start of the 16th century French legal science was moving in two directions: on the one hand there was the science of customs, the main advocates of which were Charles Dumoulin (1500–66) and Bertrand d'Argentré (1519–90), who above all attempted to systematise and unify the customs but who also tried to develop principles concerning conflicts of laws; on the other hand there was the science of Roman law, represented by the work of Cujas (1522–90) and Doneau (1527–91), who as practitioners of the 'school of elegance' sought to encapsulate the original spirit of ancient Roman law in their systematic philosophical methods. The centre for the work of such Humanist lawyers was the University of Bourges, though it seems that most French courts remained faithful to the traditional methods of interpreting Roman law devised by the Italian commentator Bartolus (1314–57). Indeed, from the beginning of the 13th to the end of the 15th centuries the South of France was the European focal point for the study and adaptation of Roman law. The various collections of customary laws can in their own small way be justly compared with the 6th-century *Corpus Iuris Civilis* for Roman law and the 12th-century *Corpus Iuris Canonici* for canon law.

The distinction between *droit écrit* and *droit coutumier* survived, in theory, until 1789, but French law *per se* gradually began to emerge as a separate entity during the 17th and 18th centuries. This was partly due to the rising power of the central authorities, whereby further weight was given to the laws made by the King. To a certain extent it was also an expression of political will-power. Important in this context are the *chartes des coutumes* issued under the authority of local *seigneurs* and the ordinances issued under Louis XIV and XV. The *ordonnance civile* of 1667 reformed the law on civil procedure (and remained the basis for this area of law until as recently as the 1970s), while the ordinances on commerce and on the navy, issued by Colbert's Ministry in 1673 and 1681 respectively, had a decisive influence on the later Commercial Code of 1807. Also worthy of note is the *ordonnance criminelle* of 1670. Under Louis XVI and his Minister Daguesseau there were separate laws reforming gifts (1731), wills (1735) and trusts (1747). In the same manner the Age of Enlightenment and of Natural Law saw scholars striving after the harmonisation and development of abstract but rationally based legal principles. Loysel (1536–1617), with his collection of legal maxims in *Institutes Coutumières*, Domat (1625–96), in his major work entitled *Les loix civiles dans leur ordre naturel*, and the comprehensive works of Pothier (1699–1772), especially his *Traité des Obligations*, all had a significant influence on the later *Code civil*.

In pre-Revolutionary France the regional courts, confusingly termed *Parlements*, often had to interpret unclear local customs, and sometimes they issued what are called *arrêts de règlement*, decisions which were intended to be binding on all people in the region, not just on the parties to the case in hand. Many of the principles laid down in these *arrêts de règlements* were incorporated in the commentators' treatises.

Codification

Given the variety of laws existing in France, the need was soon felt for their unification. Nevertheless, it required an ideological and a political impetus to turn this feeling into a reality. The ideological impetus derived from the natural law theory of society which developed during the 18th century and which was based on three main features – rationalism, individualism and radicalism. The main object of attack, of course, was the feudal system, with its attendant dues, inequalities and despotism. It is little wonder, then, that the plan for a codification was first announced during the French Revolution and that the Constitution of 1791 required the drafting of a *Code civil*. The fact that these plans were not fully realised despite three preliminary drafts prepared by Cambacérès was due partly to priority being given to the enactment of constitutional measures and partly to the lack of stable political relationships. However, the Revolution did lead to new laws on various private law matters, namely succession law, family law, parental power and land law; feudal dues on land were abolished, the estates of the Church were confiscated, the division of the population into the three 'estates' of clergy, nobility and citizens was done away with, the legal disabilities of women and illegitimate children were removed, inherited property was made equally divisible among all the heirs (in contrast with the previous system of primogeniture, which favoured the first-born son), and the concepts of divorce and adoption were introduced. These provisions reflected the new spirit of the age and were in turn to influence the provisions of the eventual *Code civil*. Collectively they are known as *droit intermédiaire*, the law applying in the period between the Revolution in 1789 and the rise to power of Napoleon in 1799.

After relationships had been settled, Napoleon, as First Consul, set up a Commission in August 1800 consisting of four important magistrates – Tronchet and Bigot-Préameneu from the north of the country, and Portalis and Maleville from the south. Within four months this body had prepared a preliminary draft. After giving the courts all of three months to submit their views, and after listening to the debates in the *Conseil d'Etat* under Napoleon's chairmanship, the Commission reworked the draft. The document overcame the opposition of the *Tribunat* – or at any rate was withdrawn from its consideration by Napoleon – and became the *Code civil des Français* on 21 March 1804.

The Code is particularly noteworthy for the way in which it combines traditional legal principles with new ideas of the day. This gives it the appearance not of a set of revolutionary laws but of a statute book designed for the ordinary citizen. The lack of any real break with tradition (apart from the abolition of feudal tenure) was guaranteed by the composition of the Commission, whose members were thoroughly steeped in *droit ancien*, but who, when they were faced with contradictory customary law, succeeded in arriving at compromises. They were able to reform family law in a way which differentiated it sharply from both canon law and the revolutionary laws, as well as to integrate succession law and land law in a way which distinguished them from a feudal law approach. The Commission's work has not only survived 10 French Constitutions – only one of which (the Charter of 1814) actually altered the *Code civil* (by banning divorce). Today, despite all the social changes that have taken place, it still forms the basis of French civil law, even if in some parts, such as landlord and tenant law, credit security law and insurance law, several additional regulations have had to be inserted. In so far as the *Code civil* was unsystematically structured and over-rooted in the past, this is probably because the drafting Commission's chief concern was to resolve differences between the various regions of France rather than to create a wholly new and coherent system.

The Napoleonic law-making process had a decisive impact on the French legal system beyond the *Code civil*, even if in many fields a number of amendments have since had to be made. The Code of Civil Procedure of 1806 has been altered on many occasions, most noticeably in 1958 and in 1975. The Commercial Code of 1807 has had to be significantly reformed to take account of economic developments. The company law statute of 1867 has been amended by a statute of 29 July 1966, competition law (1955) by a statute of 13 July 1967, the laws on commercial dealings (1935) and on maritime matters by statutes of 3 January 1967 and 7 July 1967. The Criminal Code of 1810 was altered on numerous occasions by the insertion of new provisions and was not completely replaced until the new *Code pénal* in 1992 came into force on 1 March 1994. The *Code de l'instruction criminelle* of 1808 was replaced in 1958 by a Code of Criminal Procedure; this was significantly supplemented by the *nouveau Code de procédure pénale* passed by Parliament in 1992.

Public law was an important area of law which escaped the codification process, even though numerous institutions of today's French administrative system were already in place during the days of Napoleon I. At the beginning of the 19th century administrative law was not sufficiently developed in any country to be susceptible to codification.

SOURCES OF LAW

As French law is mostly codified, the primary source of law is obviously statute law. However, this has not prevented much discussion about the theory of sources, especially about the extent to which case law is a source of law. The debate is connected with the jurisprudential controversy over the nature of law and with constitutional theories concerning the separation of powers. In this respect French law is very different from common law systems, where it is now taken for granted that the two main sources of law are Parliament and the judges. In France, much more so than in England, the Constitution is a source of law, while the judges, playing a much reduced role compared with their counterparts in England, create law only in exceptional circumstances. In particular, the peculiarities of French law lie in the importance of its constitutional norms and in the formal distinction it makes between statutes (*lois*) and regulations (*règlements*). All of these documents are often referred to as written law (*droit écrit*) in an attempt to distinguish their contents from legal customs, decisions in cases and opinions of academics. This is a more modern usage of the terms *droit écrit* and *droit coutumier*. The nature of each of these legal sources will now be considered in turn.

Constitutional norms

Although the French Constitution qualifies as the highest ranking legal norm, it has always been regarded as too unstable and abstract a source of law to be given an overriding significance. Too unstable because France has had a large number of constitutions throughout its history. The 'immutability' which a constitution ought to enjoy has therefore been considerably tempered. Constitutions have been viewed as abstract – as removed from legal realities – because in France there has never been any real control over the 'constitutionality' of statutes: no judge can be asked to determine whether a statute does or does not conform with the Constitution. This considerably reduces the effectiveness of the Constitution and differentiates it from, say, the Constitutions of Germany or the United States. France has therefore not accepted Montesquieu's notion of checks and balances to control power but instead adheres to Rousseau's idea of the sovereignty of the people. Parliament represents the will of the people and is for that reason just and sovereign; any 'control' of Parliament is superfluous. Moreover, in France there is a deep-seated fear of judicial power and a suspicion that judicial control through the Constitution might lead to the judiciary becoming the most powerful institution in the state. The absence of any constitutional court such as the US Supreme Court is also partly explained by the manner in which the French state is structured: in a unified state the constitutional control of powers and duties is not as important as in a federal state.

However, in recent years some reappraisal of the constitutional balance of powers has been necessitated by the blossoming of the *Conseil constitutionnel*, created in 1958. This is a fundamentally important development. As the *Conseil constitutionnel* can declare a statute to be unconstitutional, precedence must now clearly be given to the Constitution rather than to statute law. The *Conseil* has also accorded constitutional status to the rights and freedoms which are mentioned in the Preamble to the 1946 Constitution or in other statutes. It calls these *principes fondamentaux reconnus par les lois de la République*. This means, in turn, that for the first time in French constitutional history account has been taken of the Preamble to the Declaration of the Rights of Man and of the Citizen, dating from 1789. By recognising that any society in which rights are not guaranteed does not have a Constitution, the *Conseil constitutionnel* has acquired for itself a significance comparable to that of the US Supreme Court. This development coincides with the tendency in European nations (now both Western and Eastern) to adapt themselves to the model of states governed by the 'rule of law'. A further explanation for the increase in the authoritativeness of the French Constitution lies in the case law of the administrative courts since 1958. In relation to the control of regulations this case law has deduced various 'general principles' from the Constitution.

Statutes

A statute (*loi*) was traditionally defined, on a formal level, as a general and impersonal measure voted upon by Parliament. Parliament was omnipotent. Article 34 of the 1958 Constitution broke with this tradition by conferring only a limited set of powers on Parliament. This was because of bad experiences during the Fourth Republic, when the government was frequently rendered almost completely incompetent to deal with matters because it was constantly obstructed by Parliament. Today the French Parliament has power to legislate only upon those matters which are seen as particularly important for the state or which particularly affect individuals; apart from this it is the government which, by Article 37, has the power to make all other laws. The regulations issued by the government in exercise of this power are known as *règlements autonomes*, to distinguish them from the regulations which provide further details on matters already legislated for by a Parliamentary statute (*règlements d'exécution des lois*). The former traditional definition of a statute must therefore now be limited by an important criterion: it must be a measure which falls squarely within the topics mentioned in Article 34 of the Constitution. The division of law-making powers created by the Constitution is further examined in Chapter 3.

It must be said, however, that developments since 1958 do not mean that there has been some kind of 'legal revolution' in France. It remains true that there is no really substantive difference between a statute and a regulation, only a functional difference: while a statute sets out the main principles regulating a certain matter (Parliament keeping to the scope of its remit in Article 34), a regulation will provide for its own implementation and application. In this connection a second point is important: whenever Parliament's measure cannot exclude the intervention of government law-making powers the distinction between a *règlement autonome* and a regulation implementing a statute has to be abandoned; the *pouvoir règlementaire* then has a unity which cannot be divided.

A statute, unlike a *règlement*, must be officially promulgated by the President of the Republic; it is published in France's *Journal Officiel* (JO) and comes into force the following day unless containing a provision to the contrary.

Regulations

A *règlement* is the generic term for the general impersonal measures taken by an administrative authority. Included would be *décrets* issued by the President or by the Prime Minister and *arrêtés* issued by government Ministers, regional prefects or mayors. It is to be noted, however, that *décrets* and *arrêtés* are not always regulations; they can also be 'single' acts. But in the French system all regulations are still *actes administratifs* and as such can be judicially reviewed. This was formerly disputed in relation to the *règlements autonomes* issued under Article 37 of the Constitution: it was argued that these were in effect statutes issued by the government and so were not examinable in courts. The *Conseil d'Etat*, however, has decided that they do fall within its jurisdiction: *règlements autonomes* are not statutes and must conform with the Constitution as well as with the 'general principles' deduced therefrom by the *Conseil d'Etat*. The other type of regulations – those which implement and apply statutes – are fully subordinate to statute law.

Ordonnances

Besides changing the scope of statute law, the 1958 Constitution introduced a novel feature by providing in Article 38 for the possibility of Parliament delegating its law-making powers to the government:

> *Le Gouvernement peut, pour l'exécution de son programme, demander au Parlement l'autorisation de prendre par ordonnances, pendant un délai limité, des mesures qui sont normalement du domaine de la loi.*

> (The government may, in order to carry out its programme, ask Parliament for authority to issue ordonnances, for a limited period only, taking measures which are normally taken by statute law.)

The Parliamentary authorisation for *ordonnances* is termed *une loi d'habilitation* and during its lifetime Parliament loses the right to pass its own statutes on the areas in question (Article 41). This distinguishes *ordonnances* from the otherwise similar *décrets-lois* which were issued during the Fourth Republic. The *ordonnances* come into force as soon as they are published but lapse if a statute ratifying them is not laid before Parliament within the period stipulated in the *loi d'habilitation*. Prior to ratification the *ordonnances* have the status of *règlements* and as such they can be challenged before the *Conseil d'Etat* as being *ultra vires* (*recours en annulation pour excès de pouvoir*). Once ratified they acquire a status equivalent to *lois* and are therefore immune from challenge in the administrative courts. Proposed *lois d'habilitation* can of course be referred to the *Conseil constitutionnel*, and in recent cases this Council has been prepared to indicate what conditions must be adhered to if subsequent *ordonnances* are to comply with the Constitution.

Governments have had recourse to Article 38 on many occasions: in the period 1960 to 1990 a total of 23 *lois d'habilitation* were issued, resulting in over 150 *ordonnances*. The periods for which they have been permitted range from one month to three and a half years (this last being to enable the government to issue *ordonnances* on EC matters between 1966 and 1970). Only about one-third of the *ordonnances* have been subsequently ratified by Parliament.

The significance of written law

Written law (the Constitution, *lois*, *règlements* and *ordonnances*) is the most important source of law for both civil and criminal matters in France. As far as penalties for breaking the criminal law are concerned (except those for minor summary offences, known as *contraventions*), these must be provided for by statute law, in line with the principle which is basic to all systems based on the rule of law, namely *nulla poena sine lege* (no penalty unless there is a statute on the matter). There is therefore little room for 'interpretation' of the law in this context.

Even in matters of civil law there seems to be complete adherence to the principle that decisions must always be based on one or more statutory texts. But here there is wider scope for interpreting and 'discovering' the law, processes for which all the techniques familiar to lawyers in common law systems can be used (e.g. arguments based on grammar, history, purpose or analogy). This applies as much to matters governed entirely by the *Code civil* as to matters which are only partly regulated by legislation (such as employment law). The same can be said regarding public law which, although it contains numerous statutes, decrees and regulations, leaves many basic questions – those of general administrative law – unregulated by any written law. It nevertheless remains true that France's concentration on written law and its concomitant reluctance expressly to confer law-making powers on judges, have altered the very conception of law in France. It has certainly made the development of the law less dependent on procedural niceties – something which bedevilled English law in the 19th century and which in many respects still does (e.g. the distinction between legal and equitable rules).

French legislative provisions also differ from English legislative provisions in that, while some of them have always to be obeyed (*lois impératives* or *lois d'ordre public*), others permit individuals to opt out of their application (*lois supplétives*). This is a distinction drawn in other European countries also: the Germans, for instance, talk of *zwingendes Recht* and *nachgiebiges Recht*. While judges in England sometimes interpret statutes in such a way as to result in their non-applicability, the system as a whole does not formally recognise the same distinction.

General and fundamental legal principles

As already mentioned, general principles of law (*principes généraux du droit*) are significant in French law, especially with respect to the judicial control of *règlements autonomes*. As these are not subordinate to any statute there was doubt as to the standards against which they should be measured. The task was eventually given to general principles of law such as the principle of equality or the right to a fair hearing. These are the creation of the *Conseil d'Etat*, but because they find their origin in legislative texts they cannot honestly be cited as fully-fledged examples of judge-made law. It should be noted, however, that Parliament does not need to heed these principles whenever it is enacting statutes: they serve only to control *règlements autonomes*. In the hierarchy of legal sources in France, general principles of law can therefore be said to occupy a place below statutes but above regulations. The *Conseil constitutionnel*, however, has on several occasions applied a similar category of legal norm – *principes fondamentaux reconnus par les lois de la République*. These do have a constitutional status and several of them overlap with the general principles favoured by the *Conseil d'Etat*.

Case law

The role of case law (*jurisprudence*) as a source of law in France can be examined under two heads: on the one hand there is the question whether decisions in cases can create law; on the other hand there is the question whether such law as is created has any binding effect for the future.

The first of these questions has both a theoretical and a practical aspect to it. Legal theorists – and not just legal positivists – mostly deny altogether that case law is a source of law, relying for support on the principle of separation of powers. But even if one has the greatest respect for that principle it cannot be gainsaid that French case law *has* already created new legal rules, in the area of civil law as well as public law. The generally worded provisions of the *Code civil* and the consequent freedom given to judges to interpret and apply those provisions have made possible the development of new rules and have without doubt been responsible for the Code's ability to come to terms with the social, technical and economic developments since Napoleon's day. The most obvious example of this is the growth of tort law.

It was not until 1896 that judges 'discovered' Article 1384(1) of the *Code civil*, yet today it is undoubtedly one of the most significant provisions in the Code. It has been developed into a basis for 'no fault' product liability, the generality of which has no comparison in any other legal system. In a similar way case law has, as the Code requires, excluded agreements benefiting third parties from the scope of tort liability, but on many occasions has allowed those who are affected by such agreements to sue in contract law. In many areas case law has pushed developments which Parliament has later endorsed, as with the law of 1898 on liability for accidents at work. There is therefore no doubt that case law does have creative powers in civil law. This is even clearer in areas where there are no legislative provisions. The law concerning strikes is mostly the work of the *Cour de Cassation*, while the rules on administrative acts and on compensation for public wrongs are based on decisions of the *Conseil d'Etat*.

The second question concerning case law – whether it can have any binding effect – also sees a certain discrepancy between theory and practice. Unlike the rule of *stare decisis* in Anglo-American law, French courts are in principle not bound by any previous judgments. But in fact the lower courts, as well as the higher ones and the *Cour de Cassation* itself, do generally follow the precedents of the highest courts, deviating from them only occasionally. The core sentences of basic decisions are frequently cited in subsequent cases as if they were legislative texts. These *règles de droit* are at a more abstract level than the *ratio decidendi* of an English case and do not operate in the same inflexible manner; often, though, the judges will go out of their way to 'distinguish' the case before them from an established *règle de droit*.

It is worth remembering at this point that decisions of the *Conseil constitutionnel*, which cannot be challenged in any other court, are binding on both the government and the judiciary (Article 62 of the Constitution). Constitutional case law is likewise unambiguously superior to case law emanating from the ordinary or administrative courts.

The form of French judgments is startling for Anglo-American lawyers (as well as for many European lawyers). The sentences all begin with either '*attendu que*' (given that) or '*considérant que*' (in view of) and the judgment ends with the actual decision. The facts of the case and the reasons for the decision, which are not explicitly separated, are packed together in subordinate sentences, although this does not seriously affect the comprehensibility of the text, partly because the French language (like English, but unlike German) does not invert the verb and subject in subordinate sentences. Also noteworthy is the brevity of the decisions issued by the highest courts. The judgments of the *Cour de Cassation* and *Conseil d'Etat* are often only 10 or 12 lines long; they do not contain any discussion of theories and doctrinal opinions but simply set out the solution to the case somewhat like a formula.

Customary law

Immediately after the 19th century codifications, French legal doctrine denied the existence of any customary law, but today its validity is fully accepted. Custom can be used to supplement statutory provisions (*consuetudo secundum legem*), even to contradict them, as with the custom that a married woman has the right to use her husband's surname (*consuetudo praeter legem*), but it cannot be used to invalidate them, except in a few particular instances, as where the *Code civil* appears to prohibit charging interest on interest even on a current account (Article 1154 of the *Code civil*). Some French legal writers also classify trade practices as part of customary law, while others see them merely as proto-customs. In general, however, although custom was the only source of law in parts of France during the era of the *droit ancien*, today it plays a wholly subordinate role.

International law and domestic law

Unlike the United Kingdom, France adopts a 'monist' approach to international law. This means that it gives priority to international law over internal domestic French law. But once again it is necessary to distinguish between the theory and judicial practice in this regard.

The Constitution itself points unambiguously to the pre-eminence of international law as a source of law. According to Article 55:

> *Les traités ou accords régulièrement ratifiés ou approuvés ont, dès leur publication, une autorité supérieure à celle des lois, sous réserve, pour chaque accord ou traité, de son application par l'autre partie.*

> (Treaties or agreements properly ratified or approved have, as soon as they are published, a higher authority than stautes, provided that the convention or treaty is applied by the other party.)

When Article 55 speaks of ratification it is referring to an act of the President (Article 52, which also confers on the President the power to *negotiate* treaties); when it speaks of approval it apparently means acceptance by the Prime Minister. Article 53 provides that certain types of treaty (e.g. those which alter statute law or relate to an international organisation) must be ratified or approved by a statute (*en vertu d'une loi*) and the treaty cannot come into force until this is done. Article 54 permits the *Conseil constitutionnel* to declare that an international agreement entered into by France violates the French Constitution; in this event ratification or approval cannot take effect until the Constitution has been amended. This is precisely what occurred in 1992, when the *Conseil constitutionnel* decided that the Maastricht Treaty on European Union violated the Constitution in so far as it envisaged (for example) the creation of a single European currency. A *loi constitutionnelle* was therefore enacted to amend the Constitution and, for good measure, ratification was submitted to the people for approval in a referendum.

The *Conseil constitutionnelle* is competent only to judge the constitutionality of a treaty *before* it is ratified. Once ratification has occurred it is *functus officio*. In 1975, for instance, the Council refused to give a ruling on whether a proposed statute on abortion was in conflict with the European Convention on Human Rights (which France had ratified the year before). However, the *Cour de Cassation* has not held itself aloof in this manner. Later in 1975 it decided that EC law must take priority over a French statute on import duties even though the latter was enacted after France's adherence to the Treaty of Rome in 1957 (the *Cafés Jacques Vabre* case). In *Nicolo* (1989) the *Conseil d'Etat* reached a similar conclusion, despite its earlier inclination to prefer the maxim *lex posterior derogat legi priori*.

In a similar vein the French courts restrict themselves when interpreting international treaties. The task is seen as a function of the government. If the possibility of a breach of an international agreement arises incidentally in a court case the judge must adjourn the case and submit the question to the Minister for Foreign Affairs, unless he or she holds the agreement to be unambiguous and not requiring any interpretation. This again demonstrates that in practice French judges are not always prepared to admit the preeminence of international law.

Academic opinion

It would be wrong to underestimate the significance of academic opinion (*doctrine*) as a source of French law. Although it does not qualify as a source in the strict sense of the word, it has decisively influenced the case law in many fields, such as private international law (*see* Chapter 14). This is comparable to the role of academic opinion in other European legal systems: its function is to provide a critique of the case law and to analyse it systematically. In Anglo-American legal systems not so great an influence is attributed to such work. The French approach can perhaps be distinguished from some other European approaches in that it focuses more on the practical aspects of law, a feature which is evidenced to a certain extent by the type and slant of academic publications. Notes on decided cases play a large role in France, while long commentaries such as are found in Germany are rare. In general the place of commentaries is taken by practitioner encyclopaedias (*répertoires*) and by textbooks (*manuels, traités*).

Legal literature

Collections of legislation

The official collection of legislation is known as the Official Journal (*Journal Officiel*: JO), which is published daily. More precisely this should be referred to as the Official Journal for Statutes and Regulations (JO – *Lois et décrets*), as proceedings in Parliament are also published under the title of the Official Journal, and of course one should not confuse either of these with the *Journal Officiel* of the European Union. The daily issues of the JO – *Lois et décrets* are bound into several volumes for each year. Chronological and subject-matter indexes facilitate the search for legislation, as does the legislation's own numbering system. Thus, if a statute is cited as *loi n° 60–336 du 14 mars 1960, JO 1960, 1192*, the first set of figures (before the hyphen) indicates the year in which the legislation was passed (1960), the second set indicates the legislation's number within that year's consecutive list, and the JO reference indicates that the text of the legislation is to be found at page 1192 of the 1960 volume(s) of the Official Journal.

As already explained, France still owes its five main codes, albeit sometimes extensively amended, to the codification process which occurred in Napoleonic times. These are the *Code civil*, the *Code de commerce*, the *Code pénal*, the *Code de procédure civile* and the *Code de procédure pénal*. All are republished each year by Dalloz in an updated form. Other publishers (e.g. Litec) also produce versions. The modern codes contain many other relevant legislative provisions as well as references to the most important judicial decisions which have interpreted the legislative provisions, but there is no commentary as such. France used to have such commentaries in the 19th century, during the so-called 'exegetical' period, but very few exist today.

Besides these modern versions of early codes there are other codes which are simply collections of all the relevant legislative texts relating to a particular field of law, usually brought together as a result of a government decree codifying the existing legislative provisions. Thus, Dalloz publishes such volumes as the *Code administratif*, the *Codes des baux et de la copropriété* (dealing with leases and co-ownership), the *Code de la construction et de l'habitation*, the *Code électoral*, the *Code de l'environnement*, the *Code général des impôts* (for taxes), the *Code rural et Code forestier* (for agricultural land and forests), the *Code de la santé publique, de la famille et de l'aide sociale*, the *Code de la sécurité sociale*, the *Code des sociétés* (for companies), the *Code du travail* (for employment law) and the *Code de l'urbanisme* (for town planning). The *Code du travail* is reissued annually by Dalloz but all the others are republished less regularly. Other publishers produce codes which are not usually the result of a government codification decree but which are nevertheless extremely convenient compilations. An example is Litec's *Code des hôtels, restaurants et débits de boissons*, compiled by Elisabeth Cristini (1986). The publishers of the *Journal Officiel* also produce codes such as the *Code de la route* (on road traffic law), the *Code de l'aviation civile*, the *Code des communes* (for local government law), the *Code des marchés publics* (for public procurement law) and the *Code des tribunaux administratifs et des cours administratives d'appel*. Most of these are the result of *lois* enabling the codification to occur and they are prepared by the *Commission supérieure de codification*, a standing body charged with overseeing the whole codification process. Its most recent products are the *Code de la propriété intellectuelle* (1992) and the *Code de la consommation* (1993), both of which so far only comprise *une partie législative* – the *partie réglementaire* is to follow in due course.

It can be appreciated that, taken together, these codes represent the vast bulk of legislation applicable in France today. The nearest English equivalent is the 100-plus volumes of *Statutes in Force*, a publication bought by few law libraries let alone by private practitioners or students.

Collections of case law

In France collections of case law (*recueils de jurisprudence*) are in practice almost as important as collections of legislation. There are 'official' collections such as the *Bulletin des arrêts de la Cour de Cassation*, which has a series for decisions of the criminal division of that court and another for the civil divisions, and the *Recueil des arrêts du Conseil d'Etat et du Tribunal des Conflits* (known as the *Recueil Lebon* after a former editor), which every two months publishes the leading decisions in administrative law, including some taken by the *tribunaux administratifs* and by the *Cour de discipline budgétaire*, but without many comments.

Two classic legal journals – *Dalloz* and *Sirey* – are used by lawyers more often than the official collections just mentioned; in 1964 they merged under the title *Recueil Dalloz*. Also important are the *Jurisclasseur Périodique – Semaine Juridique* (JCP) and the *Gazette du Palais* (Gaz. Pal. or GP). The model form for these journals is a division into three parts, each of which is separately paginated. There is the articles section, *Chroniques* (cited as I or Chr.), the case law section, *Jurisprudence* (cited as II or J.) and the legislation section (cited as III or L.). Cases are cited on the basis of the name of the deciding court and the date; place names alone signify a *Cour d'appel* decision for that area. In reports of administrative law cases it is customary to cite the name of the plaintiff after the date of the decision. Thus, *Cass. 23 mars 1892, D.1892 II, 131* refers to a decision of the *Cour de Cassation* taken on 23 March 1892 and reported in the second part of the *Dalloz* journal for 1892 at page 131. In the JCP, however, the final number is not a reference to a page but to an item: thus *T.C. 28 mars 1955, Effimief, JCP 1955 II, n° 8786* means a decision of the *Tribunal des Conflits* taken on 28 March 1955 and reported in the second part of the *Jurisclasseur* for 1955 at para. 8786; *Effimief* is the name of the plaintiff in the dispute. The collections contain indexes listing dates, the subject-matter dealt with and the names of the parties; sometimes there are also brief summaries of the cases and a list of key phrases. Some European countries report cases without once mentioning the names of the parties, the lawyers or the judges, but in France the parties' names *are* given in the judgment itself and the names of the lawyers and judges are supplied at the end of the judgment. Immediately after most law reports there will be case-notes (*notes, observations*) written by distinguished academics.

For some time now France, like England, has been publishing casebooks containing the most important cases relating to particular fields of law. Litec publishes annual collections of cases decided by the *tribunaux administratifs* and the *cours administratives d'appel*, and in 1991 it produced a book summarising all the decisions of the *Tribunal des Conflits* and of the *Conseil d'Etat* between 1985 and 1989 (edited by Daniel Chabanol). Even the *Que Sais-Je?* series now has a volume containing 77 decisions of the *Conseil constitutionnel* (edited by Philippe Ardant, 1990). Some publishing houses produce collections of leading decisions in particular areas of law; these include H. Capitant, F. Terré and Y. Lequette, *Les grands arrêts de la jurisprudence civile* (9th edn, 1991); D. Vidal, *Grands arrêts du droit des affaires* (1992); L. Favoreu and L. Philip, *Les grandes décisions du Conseil constitutionnel* (7th edn, 1993); M. Long, P. Weil, G. Braibant, P. Delvolvé and B. Genevois, *Les grands arrêts de la jurisprudence administrative* (10th edn, 1993); J. Pradel and A. Varinard, *Grands arrêts du droit criminel* (3rd edn, 1992; 2 vols) and, an unusual one, C. Debbasch, *Les grands arrêts du droit de l'audiovisuel* (1991), a casebook on broadcasting law. All of these casebooks contain commentaries by well-known academics and provide an excellent overview of their subject. They can be cited as '*G.A.Nr . . .*' (*Grands Arrêts*, number . . .).

Encyclopaedias

In France legal encyclopaedias (*répertoires*) and digests (*jurisclasseurs*) have now largely taken the place of comprehensive commentaries on the law. Practitioners, or anyone wanting to obtain clear information on a certain point, cannot easily do without these works. They are published in a loose-leaf format and are compiled by a group of experts who explain the law on the basis of a thorough and on-going analysis of case law. There are encyclopaedias and digests for nearly every legal field – civil law, commercial law, administrative law, tax law, international law, etc.

Textbooks

The French draw a distinction between *traités* (textbooks) and *manuels* (handbooks). The former contain comprehensive explanations of an area of law and should be used with some caution because, being so wide-ranging, not many new editions are published and they are therefore sometimes out of date. *Manuels* are a shorter form of textbook mainly aimed at law students; they are frequently updated because they are relatively superficial in their coverage. Books of basic principles (*mémentos*) set out the main points of a subject, allowing students to gain an initial insight into a new area. There are also legal books in the 'What Do I Know?' series (*Que Sais-Je?*), each of which is usually less than 128 pages in length.

Five main publishers share the market for legal literature: Presses Universitaires de France (PUF), with its *Themis* series, Dalloz, with its *Précis Dalloz*, Librairie Générale de Droit et de Jurisprudence (LGDJ), Litec and Montchrestien.

Journals

As well as the journals already mentioned, which reproduce and discuss reported cases, there are a large number of other periodicals specialising in academic articles with a wider scope but also containing summaries of relevant case law developments. Examples include the *Revue trimestrielle de droit civil* (cited as *Rev. trim. 1991, 310*), the *Revue trimestrielle de droit commercial et de droit économique* (cited as *Rev. trim. dr. com. 1991, 156*), the *Revue française de droit constitutionnel* (since 1990) and the *Revue du droit public et de la science politique en France et à l'étranger* (since 1983). Nearly every area of law now has at least one journal devoted exclusively to its study and there are also, of course, important journals published in French on EC (now EU) law (e.g. the *Revue du marché commun* and the *Revue trimestrielle de droit européen*). A *revue trimestrielle* appears three times a year. Other journals appear at all manner of intervals.

FURTHER READING

A country's legal history exercises a definite but rarely articulated influence on contemporary practitioners and commentators, if not at a conscious level then at a subconscious one. It is wise, therefore, for all students of French law to familiarise themselves with the principal features of the relevant history. This will help them to understand how and why French lawyers currently reason. The most accessible detailed account in English of French legal history is contained in *An Introduction to European Legal History* by O.F. Robinson, T.D. Fergus and W.M. Gordon (2nd edn, 1994). Also useful are *An Introduction to the Civil Law*, Chapter 1, by K.W. Ryan (Australia, 1963); Brissaud, *The Continental Legal History Series* (1968), vol. 1, Chapter 3; *An Introduction to Comparative Law* (2nd edn, 1987), Chapter 7, by K. Zweigert and H. Kötz; *The French Legal System* (1993), Chapter 1, by C. Dadomo and S. Farran; and West *et al.*, *The French Legal System: An Introduction* (1992). *See also* Maillet, 'The Historical Significance of French Codifications' (1970) 44 *Tulane Law Review* 681. The classic works on French legal history are by Olivier and Martin, *Histoire du droit français des origines à la Révolution* (1948); Glasson, *Histoire du droit et des institutions de la France* (8 vols, 1887 to 1903); Imbert,

Sautel and Boulet, *Histoire des institutions et des faits sociaux* (2 vols, 1957 to 1970); and Ousliac and Malafosse, *Histoire du droit privé* (3 vols, 1963 to 1971).

For a discussion of views on sources of law, see especially Gény, *Méthode d'interprétation et sources en droit privé positif* (reprint of 2nd edn, 1954) and, putting forward a different position, Boulanger, 'Notations sur le pouvoir créateur de la jurisprudence civile' (1961) *Rev. trim. dr. civ.* 417. A fascinating comparison of contrasting legislative techniques is provided by Dale (ed.), *British and French Statutory Drafting: The proceedings of the Franco-British Conference of 7 and 8 April 1986* (Institute of Advanced Legal Studies, London).

The best source of help with difficult French legal terminology is the *Dictionnaire Commerce Droit Finance* compiled by Robert Herbst and Alan Readett, a three-volume publication, each volume leading with a different language (English, German, French). Volume 1 is in its fourth edition (1985); volume 3 in its second edition (1982). Each has about 1,000 pages of excellent definitions and synonyms. More accessible in every sense is *Dictionnaire Economique et Juridique Français-Anglais/Anglais-Français* by J. Baleyte, A. Kurgansky, C. Laroche and J. Spindler (3rd edn, 1992). Most convenient one-language guides, which are popular even with French law students, are *Lexique de termes juridiques* by R. Guillien, J. Vincent, S. Guinchard and G. Montagnier (9th edn, 1993) and *Vocabulaire juridique* by F. de Fontette (4th edn, 1994).

CHAPTER 2

Courts and lawyers

THE JURISDICTION OF FRENCH COURTS

In France there are certain organisational principles applying to all courts which are intended to provide important guarantees for persons seeking justice. First and foremost is the principle of the independence of the judge (*neutralité du juge*), a concept which encapsulates the non-partisanship of the judicial function and which is also demanded by Article 6(1) of the European Convention on Human Rights and Fundamental Freedoms. It entails the judge not taking the initiative on matters and simply giving an affirmative or negative decision on the questions with which he or she is confronted: the judge must not stray beyond those questions but must not ignore them either. Independence also means that the government must not interfere in any judicial activity, though as far as French judges who act as prosecutors are concerned (*magistrats du parquet*) the principle is severely limited, notably by the duty placed on these officials to enforce the law. In administrative law disputes, where the procedure is again more inquisitorial than adversarial, the judges often go out of their way to assist the plaintiff so as to lessen the inequalities which would otherwise exist *vis-à-vis* the administration. In purely civil law cases, where the procedure tends to be adversarial, there is less scope for a judge to come to the aid of one of the parties.

In order to ensure a fair trial the principles of adversarial procedure (*procédure contradictoire*) and defence rights (*droits de la défense*) are adhered to. The former means that defendants must have the right to discovery, the right to a fair hearing and the right not to be subjected to a default judgment unless they have been properly summoned to court. All trials and judgments must take place in public, except when there is a danger to security or public order (*huis clos*). A further guarantee for litigants is the right to appeal, either to a higher court on facts and law (*appel*) or to the *Cour de Cassation* on questions of law alone (*pourvoi en cassation*). Even before a judge begins to hear a case a litigant may apply to have the judge disqualified (*récusation*), perhaps on account of some connection between the judge and the matter in hand. The judge may also of his or her own motion declare an interest in the proceedings and decline to hear them (*déport*).

The French legal system makes a basic distinction between ordinary courts (for both civil and criminal matters) and administrative courts. Within the ordinary court system (*l'ordre judiciaire*) France uses several specialist courts but does not carry this specialisation through to the appeal court level. There has also been in existence for many years a *Tribunal des Conflits*, the function of which is to allocate matters to ordinary or administrative courts if there is a dispute on that point. England, of course, has a unitary court system: it does not separate out administrative matters for discrete treatment, though calls for it to do so are frequently voiced.

The first instance 'ordinary' courts

Civil law courts

Civil law courts operate on three levels: first instance courts (*juridictions du premier degré*), appeal courts (*juridictions d'appel*), and the *Cour de Cassation*. Their composition, functions and powers are governed by provisions which are collected together in the *Code de l'organisation judiciaire*.

First instance courts either have a general jurisdiction (*compétence de droit commun*) or a specialised jurisdiction (*compétence d'attribution* or *compétence d'exception*). The court with general jurisdiction is the *tribunal de grande instance*, which, since a reforming law in 1958, is usually located in the main town of each *département*, though today all but 32 *départements* have two or more such *tribunaux*. There are 175 in mainland France and six in French overseas territories; before 1958 there was a total of 351. In English terms the *tribunal de grande instance* is equivalent to something between the High Court and (especially after their jurisdiction was enlarged by the Courts and Legal Services Act 1990) the county courts. The main difference, perhaps, is that it has a criminal as well as a civil jurisdiction, but no appellate jurisdiction. When acting in a criminal capacity it is known as the *tribunal/chambre correctionnel*. Being a *juridiction de droit commun*, the *tribunal de grande instance* is competent to hear all disputes unless they have been specially reserved for another court. Each *tribunal* has a president and at least two other judges; many of them will have several divisions (*chambres*), with corresponding vice presidents. Normally they sit in benches of three (*formation collégiale*). In 1990 all the *tribunaux de grande instance* in France dealt with a total of 463,000 cases, some 10 per cent more than the 1985 figure. However, in the same five-year period the average duration of a case, from the date when proceedings were lodged with the court to the date of its decision, fell from about 50 to 42 weeks.

The *tribunal d'instance* is, technically speaking, one of the specialist courts, being roughly comparable to a magistrates' court in England. It is the successor to the ancient institution known as *le juge de paix*, created for each canton during the Revolution and abolished in 1958. England, of course, still retains the office of Justice of the Peace, dating back to at least 1361. There is usually one *tribunal d'instance* for every *arrondissement*, the administrative unit into which *départements* are divided, and, unlike all other courts in France, it is staffed by only one judge (*statuant à juge unique*), seconded for the purpose for three years at a time from the *département's tribunal de grande instance*. There are, in all, 473 *tribunaux d'instance*. On the civil side a *tribunal d'instance* can, generally speaking, hear disputes which involve no more than 30,000 francs (about £3,600). Only if the amount exceeds 13,000 francs (about £1,500) can there be an appeal (as distinct from a *pourvoi en cassation*, which can never be denied); this may be compared with the jurisdiction of a district judge in England's so-called small claims court, where disputes involving less than £1,000 can be heard, and against whose decisions it is likewise almost impossible to appeal. And as with the small claims court it is, as a general rule, the location of the defendant's residence which dictates the place at which a claim to a *tribunal d'instance* must be brought. The *tribunaux d'instance* also deal with disputes over voting rights at elections and, since 1988, with arrangements concerning the protection of minors. In 1990 more than 501,000 civil cases were disposed of in the *tribunaux d'instance*, a rise of nearly one-third over the 1985 figure. Again there was a reduction in the average duration of cases, from about 22 to 19 weeks. More than 30,000 arrangements concerning minors were submitted for approval. In 1988, the last year when Presidential and Parliamentary elections occurred, there were no fewer than 154,000 disputes over voting rights.

In addition to the *tribunaux de grande instance* and the *tribunaux d'instance* there are several other specialist courts or judges, such as the *juge des expropriations*, who deals with compulsory acquisition of property, and the *juge des tutelles*, who deals with wards of court. The president of the *tribunal de grande instance*, sitting alone, has special powers to deal with urgent matters. The specialist courts often use the services of non-legal experts sitting as judges, a practice known in French as *échevinage*, the courts being referred to as *juridictions échevinales*. Criminal cases involving defendants under 18 years of age are heard either by the *juge des enfants* or by the *tribunal pour enfants*. The former cannot deprive a minor of his or her liberty but can order certain educative measures to be taken; of the latter there are 131 in France, each consisting of two lay assessors and a judge seconded from the *tribunal de grande instance*. *Tribunaux pour enfants* deal with cases where a more serious punishment should be imposed, though no minor who is under 16 years of age can be given the same penalty as an adult might incur for the crime in question. The *Commission d'indemnisation des victimes d'infractions* (CIVI) was created in 1977 in order to allow compensation to be awarded to victims of serious unsolved crimes; it comprises two judges from the *tribunal de grande instance* and one person with a special interest in the problems of victims.

The bodies dealing with individual employment law disputes are known as the *conseils de prud'hommes* (councils of wise men!), an institution originating in the Lyons area. These are the French equivalent of England's industrial tribunals. Since reforms were introduced in 1979 there are now 282 *conseils*; they exist in each *département* and have five divisions depending on the type of employment in question; usually a division has eight judges. Each *conseil* comprises a minimum of two elected representatives of employers (*employeurs*) and two of employees (*salariés*). They sit with an even number of adjudicators (*le principe de la parité*), the chairperson's role alternating. If no majority decision can be reached the *conseil* can ask the president of the local *tribunal d'instance* to determine the matter one way or the other. Before adjudicating on labour law disputes these *conseils* attempt conciliations, in which capacity they sit in private as *bureaux de conciliation* comprising two assessors, one an employee and the other an employer. Disputes involving public sector employers, and all collective employment disputes, are excluded from the jurisdiction of the *conseils*, as are disputes about social security matters or injuries at work. Appeals lie to a *cour d'appel*, unless the amount in dispute is less than 18,200 francs (about £2,200). Each year the *conseils de prud'hommes* resolve approximately 150,000 cases.

The oldest of the specialist courts are the commercial law courts (*tribunaux de commerce*). These have no direct counterpart in England's legal system (nor indeed in France's overseas territories). There is usually one *tribunal de commerce* in each *arrondissement* and they are staffed by at least three lay adjudicators (*juges consulaires*), who are elected to their posts by fellow commercial traders and may serve continuously for up to 14 years. The adjudicators must be at least 30 years old and have been registered as traders (*commerçants*) for at least five years. In accordance with Articles 631 to 641 of the *Code de commerce*, the *tribunaux* deal with all legal disputes connected with commercial transactions, including bankruptcy petitions. As with civil cases in the *tribunaux d'instance*, for disputes involving less than 13,000 francs (about £1,500) there is no appeal to a higher court. In 1987, however, a *Commission nationale de discipline* was created to deal with cases where members of the commercial courts misbehave. In 1990 the *tribunaux de commerce* disposed of more than 283,000 cases.

Disputes regarding agricultural tenancies are the concern of the 413 *tribunaux paritaires des baux ruraux*, which are usually linked to the local *tribunaux d'instance*, a judge from which presides over four assessors, two elected by landlords (*bailleurs*) and two by tenants (*preneurs*). In part, the jurisdiction of these *tribunaux* equates with that of the Lands Tribunal in England. As with labour law disputes, there must be an official attempt at conciliation before the court will hear the case.

Likewise, social security disputes are initially dealt with by one of the 110 *tribunaux des affaires de sécurité sociale* (formerly known as *commissions de première instance de sécurité sociale*), which comprise two lay assessors and a judge from the local *cour d'appel*. In England the parallel body would be the social security appeal tribunals. The assessors represent both sides of the employment relationship and the court is presided over by a judge from the local *tribunal de grande instance*. Appeals, except in cases where less than 13,000 francs is in dispute, lie to a *cour d'appel*. In 1989 these social security courts handled more than 112,000 cases; many more such disputes were dealt with by regional social security bodies which are not courts at all.

Criminal law courts

In France criminal law courts are divided into those which investigate offences (*juridictions d'instruction*) and those which pass judgment in cases (*juridictions de jugement*). This reflects the traditional role given to judges in criminal investigations in France. The *juridictions d'instruction* are the *juges d'instruction* and the *chambres d'accusation*. The former are judges from the local *tribunal de grande instance*, seconded for three-year periods to conduct investigations into serious criminal offences. Because of their former power to detain suspects indefinitely during an investigation they are considered to be very powerful individuals and are sardonically nicknamed *les petits juges*. The *chambres d'accusation* are a division of the *cours d'appel* and their main function is to hear appeals against orders made by the *juges d'instruction*. In addition they decide whether cases involving serious offences should be sent to the *cour d'assises* for trial, they supervise extradition proceedings and the rehabilitation of offenders, and they serve as the disciplinary body for police officers responsible for investigating crimes.

The first instance courts which pass judgment on criminal cases are the *tribunaux de police*. There are currently 454 of these throughout France, including those in the largest cities of Paris, Lyons and Marseilles, where they are independent of the local *tribunaux d'instance*. Only the most minor of crimes (*contraventions*) can be dealt with in *tribunaux de police*, the maximum penalty being a fine of 12,000 francs (about £1,450) and/or two months' imprisonment. The competent court is usually that of the *arrondissement* where the crime was committed, although sometimes the place of residence of the defendant can be used as the location for the trial. More serious offences (*délits*) are tried by the *tribunaux correctionnels*, which form part of the *tribunaux de grande instance* in each area. They normally comprise three judges, although the *Code de procédure pénale* allows a single judge to hear certain designated cases, such as car insurance fraud. Appeals from the *tribunaux de police* and the *tribunaux correctionnels* lie to the *cours d'appel*. For persons under 18 there are specialist courts: in each *département* there is at least one *tribunal pour enfants* for minor offences (the presiding judge is referred to as the *juge des enfants* and is assisted by two lay judges) and the *cour d'assises des mineurs* (with three judges and nine jurors) to try serious offences (*crimes*) committed by young people aged 16 or 17.

The *cours d'assises* deal with the most serious category of offences, known as *crimes*. There is at least one in every *département* and it comprises three judges, at least one of whom (the president of the court) must be drawn from the *cour d'appel*. At present there are 99 such courts. Together with these judges sit nine jurors (*jurés*), who must be aged at least 23. As in England there are categories of persons who are either disqualified from jury service (e.g. persons who have served a prison sentence of one month or more) or exempt therefrom (e.g. members of the police and army); unlike in England most professionals, such as doctors and teachers, are not exempt. The defence can peremptorily challenge up to five persons initially selected for jury service, and the prosecution four; there is no longer such a right in English law, all challenges now having to be for cause. Once empanelled the jurors assist the judges to determine not only whether the defendant is guilty or innocent but also, if guilty, what the sentence should be. The latter decision can be by a simple majority (except in cases where a very high prison sentence is being imposed), but the former must be by a majority of at least eight to four. In the 1980s the *Code de procédure pénale* was altered on two occasions so as to dispense with jurors when defendants are being tried for military crimes, crimes against state security or terrorist offences, and in 1992 the jurisdiction of this special *cour d'assise* was extended to cover drug-trafficking offences. In such cases jurors are replaced by a panel of six assessors, all professional judges. France has abolished what in English law are known as courts-martial (*tribunaux permanents des forces armées*) but can re-establish them in wartime. Meanwhile soldiers accused of criminal activities are tried in the ordinary criminal courts. In all cases there can be no appeal against a decision of the *cour d'assises*, although a *pourvoi en cassation* can still be taken to the *Cour de Cassation*.

For the sake of completeness it is necessary to mention France's High Court of Justice (*La Haute Cour de Justice*), a body whose function is to try the President for treason. For this to happen both the *Assemblée Nationale* and the *Sénat* must pass a motion to that effect; an investigation (*l'instruction*) is then conducted by five judges from the *Cour de Cassation*, but 24 'judges' who are members of Parliament then decide on guilt and the appropriate sentence. The court's existence is provided for by Articles 67 and 68 of the Constitution, supplemented by statute. In theory the United Kingdom Parliament retains the power to convert itself into a High Court in order to try people for treason but as no use has been made of this power for 300 years it can now be considered dead.

Prior to a constitutional amendment in 1993 this Court also had power to try members of the government for serious crimes. Now a *Cour de Justice de la République* has been formed for this purpose, mainly in order to make it easier to hold ministers accountable to individual citizens. Its creation was largely prompted by a scandal surrounding the use of HIV-infected blood by the national transfusion service. The *Cour de Justice* consists of 12

Parliamentarians – six from each chamber – and three judges from the *Cour de Cassation*, one of whom serves as the presiding member. What is perhaps most startling to an English lawyer is that any individual can petition a committee of the court (*une commission des requêtes*) if he or she feels aggrieved by a crime committed by a member of the government; proceedings can also be started by the *procureur général* at the *Cour de Cassation*. If the court decides that the application is admissible it will try it in conformity with the ordinary criminal law.

The appellate 'ordinary' courts

The only second instance court in France is the *cour d'appel*, which hears both civil and criminal cases and where the judges are referred to as *conseillers*. There are currently 30 of these appeal courts in France (and three in overseas territories), each having several divisions (*chambres*) and each dealing with appeals from several *départements*. Special divisions of the court have been created to hear appeals from the specialist first instance courts. Criminal appeals will be dealt with by a division known as the *chambre des appels correctionnels*, with cases involving juvenile defendants going to a *chambre spéciale*. As mentioned earlier, there is also a *chambre d'accusation*, which reviews the decisions of *juges d'instruction* in serious criminal cases before they are passed on for trial in the *cour d'assises*. In all there are more than 1,100 *conseillers* employed in *cours d'appel*; in 1990 they disposed of some 169,000 civil cases, the biggest number coming from *tribunaux de grande instance*, together with some 50,000 criminal cases involving more than 70,000 defendants.

At the head of the ordinary court structure stands the *Cour de Cassation*, comprising five civil law divisions (*chambres civiles*) and one criminal law division (*chambre criminelle*), all sitting in Paris. The five civil law divisions consist of three which each deal with one or more specific areas of civil law, one which deals with financial and commercial matters, and one which focuses on social welfare issues. Usually five judges hear each case, as in the Appellate Committee of the House of Lords in the United Kingdom. A *chambre mixte* is created, consisting of at least 13 judges drawn from at least three of the divisions, when the case cuts across the court's divisions or when there are already conflicting decisions on the point from different divisions. The main function of the *Cour de Cassation* is to ensure that the law is uniformly applied throughout the French court system. Like the House of Lords, it hears only questions of law, not questions of fact, so the French do not view it as a court of third instance, or as an appeal court. It does not 're-judge' a case but decides whether to quash a judgment which has been challenged before it. The closest English analogy is probably judicial review in the Divisional Court. A *pourvoi en cassation* alleges that a decision was 'illegal' (*violation de la loi* in criminal cases, *non-conforme à la loi* in civil cases), but rather than applying its view of the law to the dispute before it, the *Cour de Cassation* refers the case back (*renvoi*) to another court of second instance (i.e. one of the *cours d'appel*). That court is not bound to follow what the *Cour de Cassation* has said; it retains control over decisions of fact in the case. If the *cour d'appel* chooses not to follow the *Cour de Cassation*, the case then comes before the full *Cour de Cassation* (25 judges representing all six divisions, sitting *en Assemblée plénière*), the decision of which *is* then binding on the *cour d'appel* to which it is remitted. In 1990 the *Cour de Cassation* disposed of nearly 19,000 civil and commercial cases and over 7,000 criminal cases; the decision was quashed (*cassé*) in nearly 20 per cent of the former but in only about 7 per cent of the latter.

The administrative courts

In France there are significant differences between the ways in which the administrative courts and the ordinary courts are organised. The highest administrative court is the *Conseil d'Etat*, which has a great variety of functions. In addition there are numerous specialist courts which are subject to the control of the *Conseil d'Etat*.

The *Conseil d'Etat* was originally (in the 1790s) a body which served to advise the government in its law-making functions. Later it became ministerial custom to abide by the conclusions reached in the *Conseil d'Etat*'s debates, especially when it was hearing complaints from private persons against the administration. In this way it also developed into a court. Today the *Conseil d'Etat* still exercises both functions, as a consultative body and as a judicial body. In addition it assists with the drafting of government Bills before they are presented to Parliament. The laws presently governing it allow for six divisions (*sections*), five of which have advisory tasks on financial matters, public works, home affairs, social issues and research. The sixth division hears disputes (*section du contentieux*) and is further sub-divided into 10 sub-divisions (*sous-sections*). The members of the *Conseil d'Etat* likewise serve not only as judges: the 250 or so *conseillers, maîtres de requêtes* and *auditeurs*, who are all part of the *grands corps d'Etat*, often take on key positions in the administration after serving in the *section du contentieux*; while attached to the *Conseil* they belong to both the judicial and one of the administrative divisions. When they adjudicate cases they usually sit in benches of five, although the more important cases can be heard by a bench of 13 senior *conseillers* (*l'assemblée du contentieux*) or by 17 less senior judges (*section du contentieux en formation de jugement*). Nominally the president of the *Conseil d'Etat* is the Prime Minister; in practice the body is headed by its vice president.

When dealing with disputes the *maîtres de requêtes* and *auditeurs* serve as *commissaires du gouvernement*. Despite their title these very important persons do not represent the government's interests in the case but instead compile an impartial and thorough report on the facts and issues in the dispute, a report which ends with suggestions as to how the dispute should be decided (the so-called *conclusions*). A similar role is performed by the *avocat général* in the *Cour de Cassation*.

The *Conseil d'Etat* is a court of first instance, an appeal court and a court of *cassation* all rolled into one. Its first instance activities include judicial review (*recours en annulation*) of *décrets* and of the administrative decisions taken by national professional bodies or public corporations and disputes concerning regional and European elections.

The most important of the courts for which the *Conseil d'Etat* is an appeal court are the *tribunaux administratifs*, though some appeals from these *tribunaux* go instead to the recently created *cours administratives d'appel*. It was only when a decree was issued in 1953 that the *tribunaux administratifs* replaced the *conseils de préfecture* and acquired general jurisdiction over administrative cases, subject to disputes being specifically allocated to other bodies. Since then, therefore, in most administrative law cases there has been the chance of two court hearings, whereas before 1953 the *Conseil d'Etat* was to a large extent the only competent court. Besides their adjudicatory function the *tribunaux administratifs*, like the *Conseil d'Etat* itself, have certain advisory functions, although these are quite limited. With the exceptions of Paris and overseas territories, the geographical competence of each of the *tribunaux administratifs* extends over several *départements*, there being 26 in all. Each court, besides having a president, has several judges (*conseillers*) working within it, one of whom takes on the role of *commissaire du gouvernement*; each case is heard by a bench of three judges, although the president is empowered to hear certain procedural matters as a single judge. The cases heard in the *tribunaux administratifs* which can still be appealed directly to the *Conseil d'Etat* are those concerning local election disputes (it has already been noted that Parliamentary and Presidential election disputes are dealt with initially by the *tribunaux d'instance* and regional and European election disputes directly by the *Conseil d'Etat*) and those alleging that administrative regulations are *ultra vires* (*recours pour excès de pouvoir*). Other decisions by the *tribunaux administratifs* can be appealed to the *cours administratives d'appel*.

The *cours administratives d'appel* have existed since the beginning of 1989. Only five of them were created (in Paris, Bordeaux, Lyons, Nancy and Nantes), their purpose being to reduce the workload otherwise falling on the *Conseil d'Etat*. Each has either three or four divisions, every case being heard by either four or six *conseillers*, the president again having power to act alone when dealing with interlocutory applications. There is no further right of appeal from the *cour administrative d'appel* – only the right to apply to the *Conseil d'Etat* to have a decision quashed for being contrary to law (*recours en cassation*).

The *Conseil d'Etat* is also an appeal court for several specialist courts such as the overseas courts (*conseils du contentieux des territoires d'outre mer*), the admiralty court (*conseil des prises maritimes*) and the war veterans tribunal (*jury national des marchés de guerre*). There are even more courts for which the *Conseil d'Etat* serves as a court of *cassation*, again mostly with a very specialised and limited jurisdiction. Worth mentioning in particular is the Court of Accounts (*Cour des comptes*), which is not really a court at all because, like the National Audit Office in England (headed by the Comptroller and Auditor General), it checks the administration's accounting procedures. The *Cour des comptes* itself acts as an appeal court for the 22 regional bodies which monitor local expenditure (the *chambres régionales des comptes*). If officials breach the accounting regulations they can be brought before the *Cour de discipline budgétaire*, against the decisions of which there can again be a complaint to the *Conseil d'Etat* as a court of *cassation*. Also relevant here are the disciplinary courts of certain professional organisations, such as those regulating doctors, architects and accountants. In this guise the *Conseil d'Etat* performs a function which in the United Kingdom is carried out by the Judicial Committee of the Privy Council. A further body in this context which has been much in the news recently is the *Commission de recours des réfugiés*, which handles requests for asylum from refugees. When it is acting as a court of *cassation* the *Conseil d'Etat* appoints a committee of three judges to decide whether the case is admissible before subjecting it to a full hearing; this compares with the procedure used in the European Commission of Human Rights in Strasbourg and to an extent with the function performed by the Appeal (as opposed to the Appellate) Committee of the House of Lords in the United Kingdom.

The *Tribunal des Conflits*

France set up its *Tribunal des Conflits* as early as 1872. Its function is to decide disputes concerning which of the two sets of courts is competent to hear a particular case. It consists of nine members, three elected from their own membership by each of the *Conseil d'Etat* and the *Cour de Cassation*, and two others, plus deputies, selected by those chosen six. The members sit for a renewable term of three years. In addition the Minister for Justice is a member *ex officio*: he or she acts as the nominal president and has a casting vote in the event of a stalemate within the *tribunal*, though this rarely happens given that cases are usually heard by a bench of three members. The body hears cases in three sets of circumstances:

(a) where both sets of courts appear to have competence in the matter,
(b) where neither does, and
(c) where the two sets of courts already appear to have issued irreconcilable decisions on the topic in question.

The first of these situations is known as one where there is a 'positive' conflict. The *Tribunal des Conflits* protects the administration from inroads being made on its jurisdiction by the ordinary courts: the administrative courts can remove a case from the ordinary civil law courts (though not the criminal law courts), while the ordinary courts are not permitted to invoke like protection. The action is set in motion by the local prefect, who submits an invitation to the ordinary court to decline to hear the case (*déclinatoire de compétence*). If the ordinary court nevertheless declares itself competent the prefect can then issue an *arrêté de conflit*, which suspends the proceedings before the ordinary court until the *Tribunal des Conflits* has decided the jurisdictional point.

The second situation is known as one where there is a 'negative' conflict. If both sets of courts declare themselves unable to deal with the case the party affected is allowed to petition the *Tribunal des Conflits*. In addition, since 1960 any court which has declared itself incompetent can invoke the opinion of the *Tribunal des Conflits* straightaway.

Only where there are irreconcilable decisions relating to an issue (*conflit de décisions au fond entraînant déni de justice*) can the *Tribunal des Conflits* itself decide the case. This was settled at the conclusion of the *Rosay* case in 1932. Monsieur Rosay was injured while travelling as a passenger in a car which collided with an army lorry. The civil law courts rejected the action against the keeper of the car and the administrative law courts rejected the action against the administrative authorities. As it had been proved that the accident was neither the fault of the injured party nor due to any act of God, the two decisions amounted to a denial of a judicial remedy. As a result legislation was passed in 1932 permitting the victim to bring his or her case directly to the *Tribunal des Conflits* within two months for a final decision on the matter.

In 1990 the *Tribunal des Conflits* disposed of 44 cases, 30 of which were submitted to the *Tribunal* by lower courts under the 1960 reforms.

Delimiting the two jurisdictions

As in other European countries, the existence of two sets of courts in France has led to difficulties in drawing lines of demarcation between them. There is no statute which stipulates the kinds of disputes which are reserved for administrative or for ordinary courts. It has been left to case law and academics to draw up demarcation criteria. A comparable task has recently had to be undertaken by English courts in order to define the situations in which seeking the public law remedy of judicial review is more appropriate than submitting a private law claim. French law tends to let the matter be decided in accordance with the type of law involved in the case, thereby mixing the criteria for deciding what is part of administrative law with those for deciding whether administrative courts should deal with a matter. It is no surprise, therefore, that the key concepts of French administrative law –

puissance publique and *service public* (*see* Chapter 4) – have come to form part of the criteria on the jurisdictional issue as well.

Despite the prohibition against this dating from a statute of 1790, France was already beginning to develop judicial control over administrative authorities during the 19th century. This control was gradually extended to keep pace with the increase in administrative functions. As a reaction against this, at the beginning of the 19th century the *Conseil d'Etat* completely forbade the civil courts from ordering the state to pay money to a claimant (*théorie de l'Etat débiteur*). Later a distinction was drawn between *actes d'autorité* (actions carried out in the exercise of an authority) and *actes de gestion* (managerial actions), with the notion of *puissance publique* coming to the fore. But in 1873, in the *Blanco* case, the notion of *service public* was stressed instead. That was a case where a tort had been committed during the exercise of a public service (it was another road accident) and the jurisdiction of the administrative courts was affirmed. Subsequently the 'school of public service' (represented by writers such as Duguit and Jèze) wielded a noticeable influence on the case law. The theory has nevertheless been criticised and many decisions can be explained only by applying the tests of *puissance publique* or *gestion privée*; these suggest that administrative courts should have jurisdiction in all cases where there has been an exercise of public power rather than of private management, whether in the context of a public service or not.

Today one must be satisfied with a formula which says that administrative courts are to be used for disputes which are concerned with relationships in public law (*rapports de droit public*), or which relate to situations or powers which are different from those involving private individuals. Excluded altogether from judicial control, whether by administrative courts or ordinary courts, are international disputes (e.g. those involving a foreign public body) and constitutional wrangles (e.g. those concerning the relationship between Parliament and the government). Disputes between citizens, including claims based on *voie de fait* (i.e. excessive use of force by a state official) or involving privately run 'public' services, are dealt with by ordinary courts. French law also adheres to the theory based on *bloc de compétence*, whereby any part of the activity associated with a public or private organisation will be regulated in accordance with the nature of the whole enterprise.

As regards incidental matters arising during a case, French law distinguishes between the position in civil and criminal courts. Civil courts can interpret regulations but cannot check their conformity with statute law (i.e. whether they are *ultra vires* or not). Criminal courts, on the other hand, have an unqualified right to interpret and check the validity of regulations and administrative acts. This is because of the principle that criminal trials ought not to be delayed. It must be noted, moreover, that administrative courts are able to deal with actions concerning liability for official acts and compensation claims. By statute, however, all vehicle accidents are now excluded from this general rule, being subjected instead to the civil courts. If the facts in *Blanco* were to recur, the result would now go the other way. This division of labour based on the area of law involved in a dispute avoids over-complicating an important legal field. Other statutes have allocated disputes over indirect taxation and confiscation to the ordinary courts.

It is clear even from this brief outline that in France the demarcation between ordinary courts and administrative courts is far from straightforward. This is often put forward as a good reason for not creating a special set of administrative courts in a common law country such as the United Kingdom. It may well be, however, that the demarcation problems are an acceptable price to pay for effective control over the administration by specialised bodies.

LAWYERS IN FRANCE

Judges and procurators

French judges differ from their counterparts in the United Kingdom in that they are usually members of a career judiciary rather than former legal practitioners. A few practitioners (and legal academics) are now appointed, but the majority still qualify as judges after studying at the national training school for the judiciary in Bordeaux (the *Ecole nationale de la magistrature*). When they graduate from there they are assigned either to be 'sitting judges' (*magistrats du siège*, i.e. judges who actually hear and decide cases) or 'standing judges' (*magistrats du parquet* or *magistrats debouts*, i.e. judges who act as prosecutors). Judges who serve in the administrative courts are mostly recruited from the prestigious training school for public administrators, the *Ecole nationale d'administration* (graduates of which are sometimes nicknamed *énarques*). Under recent decentralisation plans this famous establishment, the *alma mater* of many Presidents and Prime Ministers, is to be transferred from Paris to Strasbourg.

Articles 64 to 66 of the Constitution make special provision for *l'autorité judiciaire* (not, be it noted, *le pouvoir judiciaire* – the choice of term is deliberate). Article 64 denotes the President of the Republic as the guarantor of the independence of judicial authority but says that he or she is to be assisted in this by a body called the *Conseil supérieur de la magistrature*. The *magistrats du siège*, it adds, are to have security of tenure (*sont inamovibles*). The *Conseil supérieur* was the subject of a constitutional amendment in 1993. Its members are no longer appointed solely by the President of the Republic and its jurisdiction has been extended to cover *magistrats du parquet* as well as *magistrats du siège*. When sitting to deal with the former it comprises the President, the Minister for Justice, one *conseiller* appointed by the *Conseil d'Etat*, three public persons (not MPs or judges) appointed by the President and by the two Presidents of the National

Assembly and Senate, one *magistrat du siège* and five *magistrats du parquet*. When sitting to deal with *magistrats du siège* it has five such judges in its make-up and only one *magistrat du parquet*. Apart from acting as the disciplinary body for all judges, in which capacity it is presided over by the first President or the *procureur général* of the *Cour de Cassation* depending on the type of judge being disciplined, it nominates judges to be high-ranking members of the *Cour de Cassation*, first presidents of the *cours d'appel* and first presidents of the *tribunaux de grande instance*, as well as giving its collective view on the persons nominated for other judicial roles by the Minister for Justice.

It is clear that existing members of the judiciary can easily exercise an influence over who should be appointed to or promoted within their own body (though this influence would not be as strong as in England). Judges do not have as distinct a status in France as they have in the United Kingdom because there is a traditional distrust of judicial power dating from pre-Revolutionary days. The link with the government is even plainer as regards administrative judges, because these *can* be displaced. But French judges have not allowed this organisational structure to become an instrument of political power which may be wielded against them. The development of judicial review and the positions taken by the *Conseil d'Etat* suffice to prove this. As well as that, in practice personalities tend to be more important than organisational structures, even if these personalities are not in the public eye in the same way as they may be in the United Kingdom. The Constitution, moreover, in Article 66, acknowledges the special position of the judiciary by charging it with the reponsibility of guarding individual liberty and by declaring that no one can be arbitrarily detained, by a judge or anyone else (*nul ne peut être arbitrairement détenu*).

As a result of both statutory provision and decisions of the *Conseil d'Etat* and the *Conseil constitutionnel*, judges serving in the administrative courts have been granted almost as great a degree of protection against government interference with their activities as judges in the ordinary courts. The *Conseil supérieur des tribunaux administratifs et cours administratives d'appel* performs similar functions to those of the *Conseil supérieur de la magistrature*, though its existence is not expressly guaranteed by the Constitution. For all judges, of course, there is a ban on openly engaging in political activity. Many of them do, however, belong to a trade union and have been known to take 'industrial action' in order to seek improvements to their conditions of service. Given the size of the judiciary it is not unheard of for members to be disciplined for failing to adhere to the expected standards of behaviour.

The *magistrats debout* (also known as *le parquet* or *le ministère public*) represent the government in cases before the ordinary courts. They are not as independent as the judges, their chief task being to prosecute crimes and in civil cases to intervene as an interested party or even, if the case concerns a matter of public policy, as a main party. In this latter role they bear comparison with the Official Solicitor and the *amicus curiae* in English courts. Most countries with a system of law derived from ancient Roman law have a similar type of official, sometimes called in English a procurator. In Scotland the office of the procurator-fiscal is analogous.

Auxiliary lawyers

'Auxiliary' lawyers (*auxiliaires de justice*) are those persons who, while not being judges, are regularly involved in the administration of justice. They can be categorised as follows:

(a) **Greffiers** (court clerks) are officials who perform a variety of important functions in order to assist the smooth running of the court system. They help the judges with the organisation of papers, they preserve and serve copies of important documents and they deal with correspondence, pieces of research and the collection of statistics. They are responsible for the maintenance of the court register (*le répertoire général*), which records the details of all the cases processed, as well as for the documents connected with each individual case (*dossiers*). Since reforms introduced in 1967, *greffiers* have been recognised not as private practitioners in possession of an 'office' which could be transferred at a price to new incumbents (*officiers ministériels*), but as civil servants working as court officials (*fonctionnaires*). The chief clerk in each court is now designated the *greffier en chef*; he or she is responsible for running the administrative offices of the court (the *secrétariat greffe*). In 1990 there were 6,208 *greffiers* employed in the French legal system, a number which has remained fairly static for over a decade.

(b) **Huissiers de justice** (process-servers/bailiffs) are mainly people who serve documents on litigants and enforce judgments. They are still *officiers ministériels*, with their own 'office' (*charge*); some work together in a professional partnership (*société civile professionnelle*). Today they also operate a debt recovery service and conduct factual inquiries on behalf of the parties or the court itself. In 1990 there were 3,055 *huissiers*, almost half of whom were working as sole practitioners.

(c) **Notaires** (notaries) are again *officiers ministériels*. They act as obligatory authenticators and preservers of important documents, such as deeds transferring land, and are employed to draw up other papers such as wills. In addition they sometimes administer the estates of people who have died. Like other *officiers ministériels* notaries cannot engage in activities incompatible with their profession, such as money-lending or the representation of clients in court, but they may give legal advice on a wide variety of matters. Their national governing body is the *Conseil supérieur du*

notariat. To become a *notaire* an applicant must pass a rigorous series of examinations and undergo a two-year apprenticeship. In 1990 there were 7,500 *notaires*, slightly over one-third working as sole practitioners and the remainder in groups.

(d) **Avocats and avoués,** terms very roughly translatable as barristers and solicitors, were members of separate professions in France until a statute of 31 December 1971. The role of an *avoué* – another *officier ministériel* – was to conduct the procedural steps prior to the trial of a civil case in a *tribunal de grande instance*, a process known as *postulation*. The 1971 statute allowed *avocats* to carry out this function in addition to their own traditional functions of representing clients in court (*plaidoirie*) and giving legal advice; today the only *avoués* are those attached to the *cours d'appel*. Also incorporated in the new unified body of private practitioners, all entitled to call themselves *avocats*, were the *agréés* – lawyers who dealt with cases before commercial courts – but excluded from the reforms were the *conseils juridiques*, persons giving legal advice, drafting legal documents or even representing clients before non-judicial bodies and the *tribunaux de commerce*, but not qualified as *avocats* or as *notaires*; many of these worked as in-house para-legals for companies or formed themselves into companies, acquiring an expertise in commercial or taxation issues which they were allowed to advertise. A *conseil juridique* could be an employed lawyer, whereas all *avocats* had to be self-employed, even if working in a partnership. As it was a requirement that one be a French national before being able to qualify as an *avocat*, most foreign lawyers practising in France did so as *conseils juridiques*. The effect of a statute passed on 31 December 1990, which came into force on 1 January 1992, was to complete the merger of the legal professions by allowing the 5,000 or so registered *conseils juridiques* to practise as *avocats* and permitting the 18,000 or so *avocats* to do all types of work previously performed by *conseils juridiques*. The only advocates who are not included in the new profession are those 60 individuals who practise exclusively in the country's supreme courts – the *Cour de Cassation*, the *Conseil d'Etat* and the *Tribunal des Conflits*; they are named *avocats aux conseils* and, like *notaires* and the former *avoués*, they hold their office as a *charge*, something which can be sold when they retire.

For the first time in France it is now a criminal offence to give legal advice or draft legal documents for reward unless one is a member of a regulated professional organisation. Those who are such members must have a degree in law and be insured against losses resulting from their professional negligence. Naturally, therefore, the para-legal advice sector is nothing like as vibrant in France as it is in England. Regulations have been published laying down the conditions which a non-French person must satisfy before being able to practise as an *avocat*; as is to be expected, these are more generous to other EC nationals than to non-EC nationals.

Avocats are organised on the basis of local bar associations (*barreaux*), the president being a *bâtonnier* elected for two years. The council of each *barreau* (*le conseil de l'ordre*) serves as the disciplinary body for the *avocats* in the locality, appeals against its decisions lying to the area *cour d'appel*. A national body, the *conseil national du barreau*, seeks to harmonise local standards and to represent the profession in its dealings with the government. Another law at the end of 1990 permitted *avocats* to band together into new types of 'professional' companies, whether public, private or semi-private; these can be joined by non-lawyers, such as accountants, thereby equipping them to serve as multi-disciplinary practices in the age of the Single European Market. *Avocats*, like the former *conseils juridiques*, *can* now be employed by other *avocats* and certified as specialists in particular legal fields, though whatever the structures within which they work they retain a personal responsibility for the clients they represent.

It is only comparatively recently that French lawyers have been able to provide services in return for state-funded legal aid. In 1851 a system of *assistance judiciaire* was introduced whereby lawyers were expected to undertake work for poor clients *pro bono*, i.e. for no remuneration at all. Eventually, in 1972, a statutory scheme called *aide judiciaire* was set up. This spread the burden of supporting poor litigants across the whole legal spectrum but was applicable only for matters going to court. From 1 January 1992, however, a scheme named *aide juridique* replaced *aide judiciaire*. This does extend to non-litigation matters, being available for advice and assistance too. It can be used in all courts and in all legal areas, whether contentious or non-contentious. Each local *barreau* receives annual funding from the government to pay for the scheme in its area, and naturally only those litigants whose resources fall below a certain level (at the moment about £600 per month) can qualify. Those with a higher income can qualify but must pay a contribution towards the legal costs. Although there are complaints in England that the legal aid schemes there are not as comprehensive as they should be, they are still, on the whole, more generous than in France.

The education of lawyers

French legal education differs considerably from the British system in both the academic and the professional stages. Education within the universities is the responsibility of the former Faculties of Law (*Facultés de droit*), which since 1968 have been called 'units of teaching and research' (*unités d'enseignement et de recherches*: UER). After two years (*premier cycle*), holders of a school-leaving certificate (*baccalauréat*) who pass their examinations obtain a diploma of general university studies (*diplôme d'études universitaires générales*: DEUG) in law. After a third year, a degree (*licence*) is conferred and, after a fourth year, a masters (*maîtrise*), marking the end of the *deuxième cycle*. Students who do not have a school-leaving certificate can spend two years studying for a Certificate in Law (*capacité en droit*). Much more so than their English counterparts, students of law in France will study non-legal subjects to contextualise their knowledge of hard law. It is common for them to take courses in economics, politics, sociology or public administration.

Instruction at university level takes the form of lectures (*cours*) and tutorials (*travaux dirigés*), at any rate for the main subjects. In a student's third and fourth year he or she can begin to specialise in, say, public law or private law. Courses tend to be devoted to particular legal subjects and at the end of each academic year there are written and oral examinations set by the same professors and lecturers who ran the courses. This should mean that a student is almost certain to pass provided he or she gets to grips with the material taught in class, but in practice there is a very high fall-out and failure rate, certainly compared with the experience of university law departments in the United Kingdom. The written and oral examinations are university examinations and passing them is a precondition to proceeding to the next year of studies. The examinations take place annually in early summer, with resits in the autumn. Some of the examinations allow students five hours to write their answers. If a student fails the first-year examinations on four occasions he or she must leave that particular UER.

After obtaining a masters degree a student at a university can obtain one of two alternative further diplomas. A Diploma of Specialised Higher Studies (*diplôme d'études supérieures spécialisées*: DESS) provides training in a specialist branch of the law (e.g. construction law or banking law) and preparation for a future career. A Diploma of Advanced Studies (*diplôme d'études approfondies*: DEA), on the other hand, has more to do with helping a person gain promotion within his or her profession: in fact a DEA is often a *sine qua non* for advancement. In France doctorates are obtained by comparatively few people, such as those who want to seek a teaching position in third-level education. A doctoral thesis would be comparable to that required in Britain for a PhD; it leads to a 'state' doctorate, *un doctorat d'Etat*. This is also available to foreigners who have law degrees, though it is easier for them to obtain a university doctorate, *un doctorat d'Université*, which is specially designed for non-French scholars.

Post-university legal education, as one would expect, is more closely geared to professional legal practice. Anyone wanting to qualify as a judge must complete a three-year training programme at the national training school for the judiciary in Bordeaux (*École nationale de la magistrature*); access to this is usually on the basis of a competition between degree-holders. To be able to practise as an *avocat*, after the reforms of 1971 and 1990, a student needs not only a masters in law (*maîtrise*) but also a Certificate in Professional Legal Aptitude (*certificat d'aptitude à la profession d'avocat*: CAPA). Again, access is through an entrance examination; the course entails one year's training at a professional training centre (*centre de formation professionnelle*), rounded off by an examination for the Certificate. Most of the training centres are connected to the law departments in universities. A qualified *avocat* will then be registered in the list of apprentice lawyers (*avocats stagiaires*). He or she can use the title *avocat* and has all of the rights of such a person, except that he or she must practise in the office of a fully qualified lawyer. Only after a minimum of two years will the new *avocat* be registered in the list of fully qualified lawyers (*avocats inscrits au tableau*).

By sitting further tests a person with a degree in law can apply directly for a position in the public service, or for one of the few and highly sought after places at the elite National School of Administration (*Ecole nationale d'administration*). The latter will ensure him or her a place in the ranks of one of the state's *grands corps*, i.e. the *Conseil d'Etat*, the *Cour des comptes*, the *Inspection des Finances*, the Ministry of Foreign Affairs, etc.

Teaching positions in university law departments are obtained by means of a competition, *un concours d'aggrégation*. Applicants must have two Diplomas of Advanced Studies as well as a doctorate. Emphasis is placed not so much on an applicant's research capabilities, which will be clear from the doctoral thesis, as on his or her teaching abilities. Usually four lectures have to be given in front of the selection panel (*jury d'aggrégation*), all within a short period and to some extent prepared without the aid of any books. After each round of lectures some candidates are eliminated, until there are only as many candidates as there are vacancies. The lectures are each delivered according to a traditional plan, which French legal scholars tend to adhere to meticulously: there will be an introduction and then two parts, each with two sub-parts. This rather Cartesian approach to the presentation of knowledge is a feature of the whole of French law and legal education. The approach is much more systematic and deductive than that adopted in English law, which in comparison is very casuistic.

FURTHER READING

Excellent accounts in English of the French court system and legal professions can be found in Chapter 3 of *The French Legal System: An Introduction*, by Andrew West *et al.* (1992) and in Chapters 3 and 4 of *The French Legal System*, by Christian Dadamo and Susan Farran (1993). Also very useful are Chapters 6 and 7 of *An English Reader's Guide to the French Legal System*, by Martin Weston (1991). Further details about the administrative courts can be found in *French Administrative Law* (4th edn, 1993) by Neville Brown and John Bell. A much shorter description of the ordinary courts is supplied in Barry Nicholas, *The French Law of Contract* (2nd edn, 1992), at pp. 7–12. For a quasi-political assessment of French judges, see Dallis Radamaker, 'The Courts in France' in *The Political Role of Law Courts in Modern Democracies*, Jerold Waltman and Kenneth Holland (eds) (1988), and for a detailed description of the training system see Nagourney, 'Legal Education in France' (1981) 5 Comp Law Ybk 45. Recent changes affecting the legal professions are discussed by Roger Smith in 'Reforms without resources' (1993) New LJ 1200.

The books published in France do not tend to use the phrase *système de droit* in their title; instead the material is discussed in works such as *La justice et ses institutions* by Jean Vincent, Serge Guinchard, Gabriel Montagnier and André Varinard (3rd edn, 1991), *Institutions judiciaires* by R. Perrot (5th edn, 1991) and *Droit judiciaire privé* by L. Cadiet (1992). In the *Que Sais-Je?* series there are succinct accounts in *Les magistrats* by Georges Boyer-Chammard (1985) and *Le notariat* by Jean Riouffol and Françoise Rico (2nd edn, 1992). Books claiming to be an introduction to law (e.g. *Introduction au droit*, by B. Starck, H. Roland and L. Boyer, 1991) are not similar to books published in England with this kind of title (e.g. *Introduction to English Law* by Philip James, 12th edn, 1989): the latter usually give potted accounts of a variety of branches of law such as contract law, tort law, land law and criminal law, while the former are more jurisprudential in their approach – closer to English books on legal reasoning.

Constitutional law

INTRODUCTION

Apart from the fact that France has a written Constitution while the United Kingdom does not, what is meant by *droit constitutionnel* in France is not what is meant by constitutional law in England. In France the term embraces all the rules governing the organisation of the state, while in England these are more likely to be explained in books on public administration, government or politics. The English, moreover, tend to include within constitutional law the protection of civil liberties, whereas in France, mainly for historical rather than pedagogical reasons, *libertés publiques* are studied separately, sometimes as part of public law. The French also distinguish more sharply than do the English between constitutional and administrative law, largely because in France constitutional law has naturally been seen as the body of rules explaining the *written* Constitution whereas administrative law has long been recognised as very much a branch of law in its own right, with its own courts, judges and distinct rules. In England administrative law has been accepted as a separate legal subject only in the last 30 years or so and is a long way from acquiring its own specialised courts.

In both nations the constitutional history of the society has left deep impressions on present-day theory and practice. And both countries can be said to be currently experiencing considerable constitutional tension: in France this is a result of the increased activity of the *Conseil constitutionnel* which, although it cannot declare statutes to be unconstitutional once they have been made, is staking a claim for itself, along with the *Conseil d'Etat*, as the creator and upholder of fundamental human rights in France. In England the tension stems from widespread dissatisfaction regarding the absence of a written constitution, the need for greater autonomy for the regions, calls for a Bill of Rights and pressure for a fairer voting system.

CONSTITUTIONAL HISTORY

A knowledge of French constitutional history is essential for an understanding of today's constitutional realities. Not without justification,

France since 1789 has been referred to as a constitutional 'laboratory' where different systems have been tested. On the other hand, certain principles have developed which indicate some continuity of thought down the centuries.

Since 1789 there have been, in all, 14 Constitutions in France. The constitutional monarchies drew up several of them (in 1791, 1814 and 1830), naturally conferring considerable power on the Monarch or Emperor but limiting this power by giving responsibilities to the people's assemblies. The experiences derived from these régimes gradually led to a Parliamentary system, in which the government separated itself more and more from the Head of State and relied instead on a Parliamentary majority. Meanwhile there were many Constitutions which embodied a republican system of government (in 1793, 1795, 1799, 1848, 1875, 1946, and 1958), and which (at least until 1875) represented a reaction against a constitutional monarchy. They differed as to what alternative system to establish, ranging from Parliamentary supremacy, where Parliament's powers were greatly increased (as in the 1793 draft) to a presidential system of government, which presupposes a strict separation of powers among organs of the state (as in 1848). Even the 1795 Constitution favoured an over-exact division of labour in this respect. Between those alternatives there were various forms of Parliamentary government.

France has also experienced systems of government which depend heavily on the presence of one particular 'man of foresight', in whose hands all power is concentrated. This was the case for the Constitutions of 1799, 1801 and 1803 prepared for Napoleon I's First Empire and for the 1852 Constitution during Napoleon III's Second Empire. It also applies to the 1958 Constitution *vis-à-vis* de Gaulle. Democratic imperialism and populist democracies have each played an important role in French constitutional tradition, even if only in a negative respect, i.e. as regimes which limited freedoms and led to subjugation. In this context we should also mention the Vichy regime of 1940–41, headed by Marshal Pétain.

So during the last two hundred years France has experienced almost every form of government, each Constitution lasting for an average of about 14 years. The changes are partly explained by the fact that there was a desire to devise the most satisfactory system and a will to increase as much as possible citizen participation in public affairs. But there was also a certain inconstancy at work, and it can be argued that variety was possible only because continuity was preserved through other means, often difficult to detect.

One of the principles lying at the heart of the process of constitutional evolution is that of national unity, and as formulated in numerous constitutional texts the idea of *unité nationale* has had important consequences. However, because it expresses a homogeneous and rational concept of national identity, the focus on unity tends to deny to members of society any right to be different, to autonomy or eccentricity, and presents society as the sum of identical and interchangeable individuals. Any attack on this unity, even if in fact it is largely fictitious, is viewed as endangering the nation and leading to splits within it.

The need for national unity also helps to explain the unitary nature of the French state, manifested until very recently by the centralisation of administrative authority. Although Parliament undertook a deep-seated reform of administrative structures during the 1980s, in an effort to decentralise them, the unitary character of the state is still apparent in the fact that the decentralised administrative authorities (with the exception of those in overseas territories) have been organised along the lines of a nationally imposed model. The gap between a unitary decentralised state and a federal state has not been bridged.

Another key concept which runs through French constitutional history is 'sovereignty'. In its French form this notion has scarcely changed in character since it was first devised in the late Middle Ages by the Crown-appointed legal scholars who saw it as a means of strengthening the authority of the King and guaranteeing the kingdom's independence from outside influences. For this reason sovereignty is still a central concept of French public law, as the case law of the *Conseil constitutionnel* illustrates. Maintaining and protecting it means that any transfer of sovereignty to international institutions is considered a breach of its inalienability and indivisibility. Any limitations on sovereignty are accepted only if they in fact help to bolster it. A comparable attitude is to be found in the United Kingdom, which has always maintained a rather ambivalent stance concerning the transfer of sovereignty to organs of the European Community. But the distinction between sovereignty of the people and national sovereignty has been a constant discussion point in French constitutional history. The notion of popular sovereignty entails general elections and the right to vote. The notion of national sovereignty, on the other hand, is a liberal idea which entails a weighted electoral system and the right to be represented. France has opted for the latter concept of sovereignty, though this of course is tempered by resort to general elections (only since 1945 for women) and to occasional referenda.

Lastly, we should note the significant progress which the French have made in moving towards a political system which seeks to unite liberalism with democracy. Protection of citizens against state power and increased participation by citizens in the exercise of state power are both constant themes of modern French constitutional history. Allied to these themes is the notion of republicanism: even courts such as the *Conseil d'Etat* and the *Conseil constitutionnel* frequently cite this concept – without defining it more precisely – as one of the basic principles upon which today's French state is founded. It is encapsulated in part of Article 2 of the 1958 Constitution, which provides that well-known motto (*devise*) for the country: *liberté, égalité, fraternité*. Article 2 also states that the country's guiding principle (*son principe*) is government of the people, by the people, for the people, and that the Republic is indivisible, secular, democratic and 'social'.

France's constitutional indivisibility has not prevented it from granting independence to some of its previous colonies, most notably Algeria in 1962, but it works against greater autonomy for its four overseas *départements* (French Guiana (*Guyane*), Guadeloupe, Martinique and La Réunion: total population around 1.25 million) and its six overseas territories (French Antarctic Territories, Mayotte, New Caledonia, Polynesia, St Pierre et Miquelon, and Wallis and Futuna: total population around 400,000). These overseas areas are sometimes known, for short, as *les DOM-TOM* (*les départements d'outre-mer et les territoires d'outre-mer*). Even the Corsican people have encountered difficulty in achieving a special status for themselves.

THE 1958 CONSTITUTION

To appreciate the significance of the current French Constitution it is first important to recall some historical events which occurred after the Second World War. The 1946 Constitution of the Fourth Republic, which had been approved by a plebiscite, created a classic Parliamentary system in which Parliament had greater power than the government. This was intended to reverse the position which had prevailed during the inter-war years, when Parliament had delegated many of its law-making powers, through enabling statutes called *lois d'habilitation*, to the government, which then issued *décrets-lois*. The system of proportional representation which was in place in 1946 ensured that there was a precise representation of public opinion but meant that Parliament was made up of a number of different political parties. This led to unstable coalition governments, which indeed became the hallmark of the Fourth Republic. One governmental crisis followed another and public opinion found this state of uncertainty increasingly unacceptable. During the crisis in Algeria General de Gaulle was asked to head the government (13 May 1958), with the statute of 3 June 1958 empowering the government to take all measures necessary to set the nation back on its feet (*le redressment de la nation*). On the same day the power to alter the Constitution was transferred from Parliament to the government, which then had the task of presenting a new constitutional draft and setting up a consultative committee (*comité consultatif*), mainly comprising Members of Parliament. On 28 September 1958, 67.7 per cent of those eligible to vote approved the new constitutional draft, and when it was promulgated on 5 October it became the Constitution of the Fifth Republic.

Before examining the main features of the 1958 Constitution it is helpful to review the pressures and influences to which the constitution-making process was subjected. The pressures are clearly reflected in the 'mandate' which Parliament gave to the government of General de Gaulle on 3 June

1958 in accordance with Article 90 of the 1946 Constitution. The terms of reference were comparatively broad, indicating how the term 'Constitution' was understood at this time:

(a) the legislature and the executive had to be based upon general suffrage;
(b) the separation of powers had to be enshrined in such a way as to make the government and Parliament independent of each other and separately responsible for their own areas of responsibilities;
(c) the government had to be answerable to Parliament;
(d) the power of the judiciary had to be independent;
(e) the Constitution had to regulate the relations between the Republic and its 'members', the people.

But even if the government's tasks were informed by the principles of democracy, separation of powers and Parliamentarianism, they were still also subject to the influence of the constitutional thinking of particular individuals forming part of the government. The influence of General de Gaulle is often viewed as the only dominating factor. The real picture, however, is more complex. General de Gaulle first gave concrete expression to his constitutional views in his famous speech at Bayeux on 16 June 1946. That is where he set down the main points which the 1958 Constitution was to develop: state recovery, a renewal of state institutions, a balance between freedom of expression and the need to guarantee continued national security, a bicameral Parliament, strict separation of powers, and an overarching role for the Head of State as a guarantor of national independence.

Although de Gaulle's influence was important and the lineaments of his philosophy were clearly integrated into the architecture of the 1958 Constitution, there was still room for the impact of others. The hand of the Minister for Justice, Michel Debré, is apparent in the 'rationalisation' of Parliament's powers and in the limiting and re-organising of the legislature. Henri Capitant should also be mentioned: seizing upon the arguments of Carré de Malberg, he successfully lobbied for the incorporation of a provision on referenda, one of the obvious techniques of 'direct' democracy.

The 1958 Constitution at present contains a Preamble and 89 Articles, which are divided among 15 titles (*titres*). These titles deal respectively with national sovereignty (Arts 2–4), the President (Arts 5–19), the government (Arts 20–23), Parliament (Arts 24–33), relations between Parliament and the government (Arts 34–51), international agreements (Arts 52–55), the *Conseil constitutionnel* (Arts 56–63), judicial authority (Arts 64–66), the *Haute Cour de Justice* and the *Cour de Justice de la République* (Arts 67–68), the *Conseil économique et social* (Arts 69–71), local authorities (Arts 72–76), the French Community (Arts 77–87), associate nation agreements (Art. 88), the European Community and European Union (Arts 88.1–88.4), and constitutional amendments (Art. 89).

Constitutional amendments

The procedure for amending the Constitution is set out in Article 89 (*De la révision*). It confers the power of initiating an amendment both on the President (at the suggestion of the Prime Minister) and on MPs. Both chambers of Parliament must approve the amendment and it must then be submitted to a referendum, unless (being an amendment emanating from the President) the President decides to submit it instead to Parliament meeting in congress at Versailles (*en Congrès*), in which case it must be approved by three-fifths of the votes cast. No amendment can be considered if it affects the integrity of the French territory or the republican form of government.

The Constitution has been amended on only seven occasions since 1958, but some of these are of fundamental significance. Both the referendum procedure and the congress procedure have been used. In addition, despite the apparent exclusivity of Article 89, amendments have occurred through 'ordinary' referenda. This was the case in 1962 when a statute approved in a referendum (*loi référendaire*) altered the Constitution so as to allow for the direct election of the Head of State. This measure bestowed an unambiguous legitimacy upon the President of the Republic and established his precedence in political life. It also shifted the equilibrium between the government and Parliament so that more power became vested in the former. It certainly helped to turn France's political system into one which is more obviously based on a Presidency.

Another important change to the Constitution did not initially seem to be so: the constitutional amendment of 29 October 1974 (effected *en Congrès*) made it easier to invoke the powers of the *Conseil constitutionnel*. Besides the existing four invoking authorities – the President of the Republic, the Prime Minister and the Presidents of the National Assembly and the Senate – the 1974 law allowed 60 Senators or Members of Parliament (*députés*) to refer matters to the *Conseil*. Since then the Parliamentary opposition has used this right frequently, in order to have differences of opinion between themselves and the majority in Parliament resolved by constitutional judges. Indeed, the right to invoke the *Conseil* has helped to give the opposition a constitutional role and has endowed the *Conseil* itself with a judicial function with political consequences.

In 1992 the Constitution was amended by the insertion of new provisions (Arts 88.1–88.4) allowing France to ratify the Maastricht Treaty and, a year later, amidst allegations of corruption on the part of certain Ministers, an amendment was passed strengthening the independence of the judiciary by changing the composition of the *Conseil supérieur de la magistrature* and making it easier to prosecute members of the government. Other suggested amendments have failed to see the light of day. President de Gaulle held a referendum in 1969 on his proposals to create new regional governments and alter the status of the *Sénat*: soon after losing the vote the President resigned. In 1984 President Mitterrand proposed an amendment allowing recourse to a referendum for statutes which affect *libertés publiques*, but the proposal failed to obtain Senate support.

In December 1992 President Mitterrand set up a committee to consider what amendments should be made to the Constitution (*comité consultatif pour la révision de la Constitution*). It was chaired by Georges Vedel, a former member of the *Conseil constitutionnel* and ex-Dean of the Faculty of Law at the Sorbonne; the other 14 members were judges, professors of law or politics, or former government Ministers (including Pierre Mauroy, an ex-Prime Minister). The President himself suggested to the committee what parts of the Constitution were in need of reform and even went as far as making his own recommendations, two of which he had unsuccessfully sought to implement in earlier years (requiring referenda to be held for statutes affecting fundamental civil liberties and permitting individual citizens to petition the *Conseil constitutionnel* if they considered that a statute violated their freedoms). As if this were not enough to differentiate the French way of instigating reforms from the English (contrast, for example, the bland remit of the Royal Commission on Criminal Justice, 1991–93), the President asked the committee to submit its report within the next 10 weeks! He told the presidents of the National Assembly and Senate that the purposes of the committee were to ensure a better balance of powers between the government and Parliament, to reinforce the independence of the judiciary and to strengthen citizens' rights.

The committee just managed to deliver its 70-page report within the given deadline. It recommended a whole series of changes to the 1958 Constitution and produced a draft of the proposed new document. In essence the recommendations served three main goals: a clearer definition of executive power, a more dynamic role for Parliament, and greater involvement of the ordinary citizenry. More precisely it reached the following conclusions:

1 There should be no change to the presidential term of office (seven years, renewable once).

2 The *Conseil constitutionnel* should be given the power to decide when the conditions necessary for the exercise of emergency powers under Article 16 no longer apply.

3 The text should make it clear that while the President has overall responsibility for the direction of national defence, the Prime Minister has responsibility for *organising* the national defence.

4 After a new government has been formed it should seek a vote of confidence in the National Assembly within 15 days.

5 Express provision should be made in the Constitution for the appointment of the *médiateur* (ombudsman).

6 Members of the government should be banned not just from being MPs but also from being the heads of local authorities.

7 A new court should be established to try members of the government for criminal offences.

8 Every year the government should arrange a Parliamentary debate on the social welfare budget and Parliament should always be given the opportunity to debate the allocation of French troops to a foreign conflict.

9 Both the National Assembly and the Senate, instead of the government, should be given the right to dictate the agenda for one of their sittings each week.

10 There should be provision made for up to eight Parliamentary Commissions in each chamber (at present there are six), one of which should be devoted to European Union affairs.

11 A minority of the members in each chamber of Parliament should be allowed to insist upon the creation of commissions of inquiry to look into the management of public services or to assess public policies.

12 The provision on the independence of the judiciary (Article 64) should be extended to embrace the prosecuting authorities (*les magistrats du siège*), and the composition and powers of the *Conseil supérieur de la magistrature* should be revised.

13 Express constitutional protection should be accorded to privacy, personal dignity and the right to communicate.

14 The *Conseil constitutionnel* should be given the power to strike down statutes which violate the fundamental rights accorded to each person by the Constitution; it should be open both to individuals and to courts to ask the *Conseil* to take such a decision (but this reform should be delayed for two years to allow Parliament to examine and revise existing statutes).

15 Referenda should be permissible *vis-à-vis* proposed statutes which may affect fundamental freedoms, and the right to call a referendum should be extended to one-fifth of the members of Parliament provided they are supported by one-tenth of the electorate. All proposed referenda should first be checked by the *Conseil constitutionnel*, which would mean that no longer could a referendum itself be used to change the Constitution (as de Gaulle tried to do, successfully, in 1962 and, unsuccessfully, in 1969).

16 The Constitution's provisions on the French Community should be repealed but provisions should be inserted describing the new decentralised local authorities set up in 1982.

17 In order to avoid one of the chambers of Parliament permanently blocking a proposed constitutional amendment, provision should be made for allowing the President to submit the text in question to a referendum provided it has been approved by at least three-fifths of the votes cast in either chamber.

Although most of the above recommendations command cross-party political support, it may be some time before all or many of them are implemented. However, in July 1993, in the wake of the scandal surrounding the supply of HIV-infected blood by the national transfusion service, the two chambers of Parliament did amend the Constitution by altering the composition and powers of the *Conseil supérieur de la magistrature* (*see* Chapter 2) and by creating a new *Cour de Justice de la République* to try members of the government for criminal offences (*see* Chapter 2).

Parliament

Parliament has two chambers, the National Assembly and the Senate, the main functions of both being to enact statutes and control the activities of the government. The National Assembly has 577 members (22 representing overseas areas) – smaller than the United Kingdom's 651-member House of Commons. It is directly elected every five years. By Article 34 of the Constitution the election system is regulated by Parliamentary statutes (*lois*). After experimenting with proportional representation (introduced by a statute dated 10 July 1985) France reverted a year later to a two-round majority voting system (*scrutin majoritaire à deux tours*). As a result a certain degree of governmental stability was restored. The two-round electoral system ensures increased representation for the strongest parties. In the first round only a person who wins an absolute majority of the votes is elected at that point; if no candidate achieves this majority there is then a second round of voting to allow the electorate to choose between the top two candidates in the first round.

Senators (of whom there are 322, including 26 representing overseas areas) are elected for nine years, one-third of the seats being renewed every three years. The election takes place within an electoral college comprising the members of the National Assembly for the *département* in question and the local representatives at district, city, *département* and regional level. The voting system differs according to the number of senatorial seats allocated to each *département*: the two-round majority voting system is used for *départements* with four seats or fewer, while in the other *départements* a system of proportional representation applies. The powers of the Senate are much less extensive than those of the National Assembly, but, like the still more undemocratic House of Lords in the United Kingdom, it has survived attempts to reform or even abolish it. President de Gaulle submitted a reform proposal to a referendum in 1969, but the people rejected it, a result which led to the President's resignation.

Although the 1958 Constitution established a bicameral system with a National Assembly and a Senate, the appearance of equality within this system does not reflect reality. Both chambers have equal rights concerning constitutional reforms (Article 89) and laws affecting the fundamental rights of the Senate (Article 46); acceptance of the relevant statutes in those areas depends on the agreement of both chambers. By contrast, a modified rule applies to 'simple' and 'financial' statutes (Article 45): if, after two attempts, the National Assembly and Senate cannot agree on the text of a Bill, the government has a discretion to set up a joint commission, comprising seven members of the National Assembly and seven Senators, charged with the task of working out a compromise statute for submission to both chambers; if an agreement can still not be reached (or if the joint commission cannot even agree a compromise text), the National Assembly, where of course the government will have a majority, has the final say over which text should be adopted.

The nature of the relationship between the two chambers of Parliament illustrates clearly the Constitution's desire to 'rationalise' Parliament's role. The government's position has been strengthened, in that it can either rely on the support of a majority in the National Assembly when enacting statutes or prevent the approval of a draft statute which it finds unacceptable by blocking it in the Senate.

The executive

The executive also consists of two branches – the President of the Republic and the government, the head of which is the Prime Minister. The 1958 Constitution originally provided for the President to be elected by the 'Congress', i.e. by the National Assembly, the Senate and local councils, but since the 1962 referendum the same system of direct, general, two-round majority voting has been used for Presidential as well as Parliamentary elections. François Mitterrand was elected in 1981 and re-elected in 1988. He is only the fourth person to hold the office, the others being Charles de Gaulle (1959–69), Georges Pompidou (1969–74: he died in office) and Valéry Giscard-d'Estaing (1974–81). The President stays in office for seven years; he appoints the Prime Minister and also – after taking the advice of the Prime Minister – the members of the government (Article 8(2) of the Constitution). There are currently 48 persons in the government – 30 Ministers and 18 Secretaries of State (*Secrétaires d'Etat*). (In the French system a Secretary of State is subordinate to a Minister, the reverse of the position in Britain.)

The presence of two branches within the executive is not something new, either in French constitutional history or in general constitutional theory. However, the way in which this duality operates under the 1958 Constitution is specific to the Fifth French Republic and has given rise to some problems. The Head of State, elected by direct general suffrage, has certain responsibilities which are carried out without any other body's involvement; his powers are laid down in Articles 5–19 of the Constitution. Amongst these are the right to call a referendum (Article 11), the right to dissolve the National Assembly (Article 12) and the power to issue emergency laws (Article 16). His function is summed up in Article 5:

Le Président de la République veille au respect de la Constitution. Il assure, par son arbitrage, le fonctionnement régulier des pouvoirs publics ainsi que la continuité de l'Etat. Il est le garant de l'indépendance nationale, de l'intégrité du territoire, du respect des accords de Communauté et des traités.

(The President of the Republic guards the Constitution. He ensures, through his brokerage, the proper functioning of public powers and the continuity of the state. He is the guarantor of national independence, of territorial integrity, and of respect for Community agreements and treaties.)

The Prime Minister does not necessarily have to be a member of Parliament (Georges Pompidou was not when appointed Prime Minister in 1962), or even the head of any particular political grouping (Raymond Barre was not in 1976), though of course the President will not completely ignore the make-up of the National Assembly when making a choice. In 1986 President Mitterrand chose a political opponent, Jacques Chirac, because he was the leader of the largest political party returned in the general election of that year. In 1993 Chirac turned down the honour, deferring to his colleague Edouard Balladur; his reason for doing so was his professed desire to prepare his campaign for the Presidential elections in 1995.

The existence of unfettered Presidential powers strengthens the political responsibilities of the Head of State and turns the President into the dominant branch of the executive: this is often referred to as the 'unequal duality' of the system (*le dualisme inégalitaire*). On the other hand, if one examines the administrative responsibilities of the separate branches of the executive one sees that it is the Prime Minister who has the stronger effectiveness in everyday political affairs.

There are also attempts within the Constitution to set limits on the powers and responsibilities of the heads of the executive. The President, as an elected office-holder, has to carry out the programme which he has put before the electorate (Article 6), while the Prime Minister, as an appointed official, must lead the government (Article 21). It is the government which decides what the nation's policies should be and how they should be implemented (Article 20). Putting this division of labour in a different way: any function which is not expressly reserved to the President (such as foreign affairs and defence) is within the Prime Minister's sphere of competence. But ambiguities can still arise: Article 15, for instance, says that the President is the commander-in-chief of the armed forces and that he is to preside at meetings of the national defence committee, but Article 21 says that the Prime Minister is responsible for the national defence. By a decree issued in 1964 President De Gaulle ensured that control of France's nuclear arsenal is specifically conferred upon the President. Each period of the Fifth Republic has given rise to a different balance of power between the President and the Prime Minister, but the pre-eminent position of the President has never been seriously questioned, even in the two-year periods of *cohabitation* between a socialist President and a right-of-centre government following the elections of March 1986 and March 1993.

There is even a sharing of powers when it comes to issuing emergency laws. The government's Cabinet (*conseil de ministres*) is able to declare both a state of siege (*état de siège*) and a state of emergency (*état d'urgence*); the former is mentioned in the Constitution itself (Article 36), while the latter is provided for by a 1955 statute amended in 1960. Each of these *états* can endure for more than 12 days only if Parliamentary approval is granted, but while they last they confer greater powers on the civilian authorities or transfer these to military personnel. The last occasion on which either was resorted to in mainland France was in 1961, when there was an attempted *coup d'état*; a state of emergency was declared in New Caledonia during race riots in 1985. The President, on the other hand, as already noted, also has power to rule by emergency decree. Article 16 permits him to do so if the country's institutions, independence, indivisibility or international obligations are seriously and immediately threatened and if the proper functioning of public constitutional powers has been interrupted. The measures the President can take are those which are required by the circumstances (*exigées par les circonstances*), though he must first consult with the Prime Minister, the Presidents of the National Assembly and Senate and the *Conseil constitutionnel*. The power was last invoked in 1961, again during the Algerian crisis, when de Gaulle operated under it for nearly six months. In a well-known decision of the *Conseil d'Etat* arising out of a challenge to one of de Gaulle's decisions taken during this period, it was held that matters which would otherwise have been legislated for by Parliament (here it was the creation of new courts, staffed by military personnel) could not be challenged in the administrative courts just because they were taken by the President acting under Article 16 (the *Rubin de Servens* case, 1962). In the United Kingdom, emergency laws can be issued only by, or under the authority of, Parliament, though the government's control over Parliament will usually ensure that it gets its way on the matter. If an emergency law is contrary to one of the UK's international obligations the government can issue a notice 'derogating' from the treaty in question, as has indeed occurred in relation to the seven-day detention power conferred by the Prevention of Terrorism Act, considered by the European Court of Human Rights as being in breach of the European Convention on Human Rights and Fundamental Freedoms (the *Brogan* case, 1988). A subsequent challenge to the notice of derogation failed, on the ground that the notice satisfied the preconditions laid down in Article 15 of the Convention (*Brannigan and McBride* v *UK*, 1993).

Relations between the executive and the legislature

As already explained in Chapter 1, Article 34 of the Constitution limits the law-making ability of Parliament to the topics there mentioned. For topics not there mentioned the government has a general regulation-making power (*un pouvoir réglementaire*: Article 37). The adoption of this division of labour was presaged by an opinion of the *Conseil d'Etat* in 1953, sought by the government of the day in the face of its increasing powerlessness *vis-à-vis* Parliament. The division also applies to work within Parliament. The government is in control of the daily order of business in each chamber (Article 48): it can usually defeat proposed amendments to statutes through using the 'block vote' procedure (*vote bloqué*) and it can object to a proposed statute on the ground that according to Article 34 Parliament does not have the power to pass such a law (Article 41), while Parliament cannot do this in relation to a proposed government regulation which it thinks deals with a topic which can only be legislated for by statute. The dominant presence of the governing party in the National Assembly assures the executive its power base, even when there is friction between the government and representatives in the Senate.

The strengthening of the executive is also apparent in other provisions of the 1958 Constitution. Article 23, for instance, prohibits government Ministers from simultaneously serving as members of the National Assembly (*le principe d'incompatibilité*), a principle which is supposed to keep political life clean but which detracts from the Parliamentary character of the system and is in direct contrast with the constitutional convention within the United Kingdom. Also relevant to the pre-eminence of the executive is the way in which members of the government are appointed. The National Assembly, unlike during the Fourth Republic, has now no say in this matter. The Prime Minister and the other Ministers are not elected by Parliament but appointed and dismissed by the President (Article 8), though in the case of Ministers this is only after the President has consulted the Prime Minister on the matter. As regards their ability to control the government, members of the National Assembly and the Senate have the right to ask written or oral questions and to instigate debates; by Article 48(2) one session per week in each chamber must be set aside for Parliamentary questions. They also, most importantly perhaps, have the final say over whether to adopt the government's proposed budget.

A final indication of the executive's strength is the position regarding votes of no confidence and dissolution motions. The procedures for votes of no confidence (Article 49) are complicated. First of all the signatures of one-tenth of the members of the National Assembly are required. A vote is successful only if it achieves an absolute majority within the Assembly, and only the votes of those who support the no confidence motion are counted – abstentions are taken to be part of the pro-government vote. Such strict preconditions mean that only one vote of no confidence has been successful since 1958 (the one in 1962 which led to the resignation of the first cabinet of Prime Minister Pompidou). As opposed to this, the government can seize the initiative to ask for a vote of confidence. It has never had to resort to this, since after their appointment all governments have been presumed to have the confidence of Parliament. This is made particularly clear by Article 49(3) of the Constitution, which provides that, if the government ties a vote of confidence to a vote on a draft statute, the draft is taken to have been approved unless a motion of no confidence is tabled and is successful. In this way a statute can be approved without the actual agreement of the Assembly.

Against this imbalance in favour of the government must be placed the presidential right to dissolve the *Assemblée Nationale* (but not the *Sénat*) (Article 12). Before exercising this power the President must consult with the Prime Minister and with the Presidents of the National Assembly and the Senate, but none of these people has a veto on the matter. Even though the National Assembly may be supportive of the government the President can dissolve it if he wishes to see it replaced for his own political reasons. When viewed in this light the power of dissolution seems more akin to a device in a monarchical system of government than in a Parliamentary system. So far it has been exercised on three occasions: on 5 October 1962 (after the vote of no confidence in Pompidou's government), on 30 May 1968 (to put an end to the May 1968 crisis), and on 22 May 1981 (to allow for a new National Assembly to be elected in line with the party background of the new socialist President, François Mitterrand, elected on 10 May 1981). Its use in such circumstances – without the fetters imposed during the days of the Third and Fourth Republics – testifies further to the enhanced role of the executive *vis-à-vis* Parliament. One constraint, imposed by Article 12, is that no further dissolution can occur within a period of 12 months following the general election after a dissolution; this election must itself take place between 20 and 40 days after the dissolution.

The position of the *Conseil constitutionnel*

The significance of the *Conseil constitutionnel*, a body governed by Articles 56–63 of the Constitution, was not immediately appreciated by legal experts in 1958. Its most important function was thought to be the demarcation of statute law from regulatory law, defining the respective areas of competence of Parliament and government. Today the *Conseil* is regarded as the supervisor of all constitutional activities, as the arbiter between the majority and opposition parties within Parliament, and as the national body protecting human rights.

The Constitution confers eight functions on the *Conseil constitutionnel*:

1 to declare that *règlements* coming into force after the 1958 Constitution are in fact dealing with matters which are within the government's law-making competence and are therefore able to be amended by the government after seeking the view of the *Conseil d'Etat* (Article 37(2));

2 to decide disputes between the government and a chamber of Parliament whenever the former objects to a proposed legislative provision on the ground that it is not within the competence of Parliament to make (Article 41);

3 to decide whether an international obligation accepted by France contains a provision contrary to the French Constitution, but only if asked to do so by the President, the Prime Minister or the President of the National Assembly or Senate (Article 54);

4 to supervise the election of the President (Article 58);

5 to decide disputes concerning the persons properly elected to the National Assembly and the Senate (Article 59);

6 to supervise the holding of referenda (Article 60);

7 to examine all new *lois organiques* and rules of Parliamentary procedure to ensure that they conform with the Constitution (Article 61(1)); the term *loi organique* is not defined in the Constitution but on 19 occasions a statute is described as such; one can deduce that the term refers to statutes which set out in detail the way in which public authorities (*pouvoirs publics*) are to operate;

8 to examine any other proposed *lois* to ensure that they conform with the Constitution, but only if asked to do so by the President, the Prime Minister, the Presidents of the National Assembly or the Senate, or (since 1974) 60 members of the National Assembly or the Senate.

According to a recent study of the *Conseil constitutionnel*, by early 1992 it had taken 167 decisions on *règlements* submitted for its consideration under Article 37(2), rejected four proposed legislative provisions under Article 41 on the ground that they were not within Parliament's law-making competence, ruled on four occasions upon the compatibility of an international obligation with the French Constitution, and decided that four elected Parliamentarians were in fact ineligible for election, while a further nine were undertaking activities incompatible with their work as Parliamentarians.

A PARLIAMENTARY OR A PRESIDENTIAL DEMOCRACY?

In view of all the points already mentioned, it is not easy to characterise the Fifth Republic's political system. Is it a Parliamentary democracy or a Presidential one? This question has been asked many times but has not yet been satisfactorily answered.

Perhaps by seeking to classify the system one tends to distort the reality. Certainly it is difficult to pigeon-hole the Fifth Republic into one of the classic categories, which is doubtless why one commentator, Jacques Georgel, has invented an entirely new label, that of *démonarchie*; others refer to the situation as one of 'dyarchy'. When seeking to do so one must above all take account of the facts that the President is directly elected and that referenda are used. The introduction of direct Presidential elections in 1962 certainly changed the character of the Constitution by shifting the balance even further away from the Prime Minister and towards the President. Both President and National Assembly can say they are directly chosen by the people: each can claim to have the trust of the electorate. Such double democratic legitimacy is a hallmark of a Presidential democracy, as in the United States of America, but such a system also calls for a strict separation of powers between the executive and the legislature, which is *not* a feature of the Fifth Republic's Constitution. The double legitimacy has numerous consequences, the most important of which is that the government has to enjoy the confidence of two masters – the Head of State as well as Parliament. That the confidence of the President plays the more important role is apparent from the resignation of the cabinet of Mr Chaban-Delmas in July 1972, since shortly beforehand Parliament had expressly voiced its support for the government.

To this extent the Fifth Republic reminds many commentators of 'dualist' Parliamentarianism – that which developed during the Monarchy of 1830–48, when the government needed the confidence both of the Orleanist King and of Parliament. But to label the Fifth Republic in this way gives too little attention to another important phenomenon, the holding of referenda (Article 11). It is not just the existence of the institution which is significant but rather the use that has been made of it by the President. It is through referenda that changes to the Constitution have been introduced (Article 89). Above all the personal intervention of the President, who openly links his own political fate to the result of the vote, has turned referenda more into votes on his own performance than on the issue in question. This was certainly the case with the referendum in September 1992 on ratification of the Treaty of European Union, signed at Maastricht in December 1991. The narrow 'yes' vote ensured that President Mitterrand could remain in power for at least the time being.

The result of the 1986 Parliamentary elections led for the first time to there being a President of a different political persuasion from that of the majority in the National Assembly. The new situation, referred to as 'cohabitation' and lasting from March 1986 to May 1988, turned out not to be damaging to the Constitution, in spite of a few hiccups. A further bout of cohabitation from 1993 to 1995 looks like being equally manageable. The 1958 Constitution, which permits such political musical chairs, survived these problems and is stronger as a result.

POLITICAL PARTIES

The functioning of the French Constitution is largely in the hands of the political parties of the day. A brief survey of the recent history and present status of the main parties is therefore appropriate.

Article 4 of the 1958 Constitution expressly recognises political parties:

Les partis et groupements politiques concourent à l'expression du suffrage. Ils se forment et exercent leur activité librement. Ils doivent respecter les principes de la souveraineté nationale et de la démocratie.

(Political parties and groupings compete for electors' votes. They can be created and act freely. They must observe the principles of national sovereignty and of democracy.)

But there is no statute which more precisely regulates the organisation and rights of parties. They simply have the status of 'clubs' in the sense of the 1901 statute on associations. For a long time the identifying feature of political parties in France was their multiplicity. In many commentators' eyes this was an expression of the French national character, with its emphasis on individuality and independent judgement. But the work of Duverger has shown it to be the result of the electoral system. The Fourth Republic's system of proportional representation (PR) led to a splintering of the parties because it allowed for all nuances and tendencies in public opinion to be represented in Parliament, there being no threshold of votes to be reached, as with Germany's 5 per cent rule. By way of contrast, a majority voting system, as in England, tends almost inevitably to lead to a two-party system, or at any rate to a bi-polarisation of political forces. These hypotheses are largely confirmed by the experiences of the Fifth Republic. Despite the adoption of a PR voting system in 1985, a majority government was still elected at the subsequent general election. The change back to a majority voting system took place immediately afterwards.

The two most important streams of leftist thought in France are represented by the Socialist Party (*Parti Socialiste*: PS) and the Communist Party (*Parti Communiste Français*: PCF). After a pact in 1972, when a third party known as the 'Movement of the Radical Left' (*Mouvement des Radicaux de Gauche*: MRG) was formed, they followed a common strategy for a while; besides embracing an agreement over candidates this encompassed a common programme for government. After this strategy had achieved notable successes in the Parliamentary elections of 1973 and in the local elections of 1976 and 1977, it came to an end with the failure of the discussions between the leaders of the three parties in September 1977. The split continued until 1981, when the Communist Party put forward its general secretary, Georges Marchais, as a candidate in the Presidential election, standing against François Mitterrand, First Secretary of the Socialist Party. The latter, of course, won the election. For the Parliamentary elections on 14 and 21 June 1981 the parties came together again, though under different arrangements. Four Communist Party representatives entered Prime Minister Mauroy's second government, even though the Socialist Party had won an absolute majority of the Parliamentary seats (270 out of

491) and therefore did not need to rely upon the support of the 44 communist members.

Consisting as it did of different political elements, the government encountered severe difficulties. In July 1984 the worsening economic situation resulting from external factors led to the communists leaving the government when Laurent Fabius replaced Pierre Mauroy as Prime Minister. Each political grouping was struggling with its own problems. The communists, who had to come to terms with a diminishing degree of support in the country (11 per cent in the 1984 European Parliament elections), fell back to their oppositional role as a watchdog of the government's performance. The socialist parties – the PS and the MRG – appeared as representatives of a pragmatic and realistic standpoint, rejecting ideological sectarianism, turning away from links with Marxism and laying the basis for a possible future 'social democratic' party comparable to the SPD in Germany or the Labour Party in Britain. When the left lost its majority in 1986 (the combined leftist seats fell from 327 to just 251) it had to reorientate itself. This it managed to do by 1988, when its tally of seats rose to 302 (19 more than the number required for a majority in the Assembly).

In the elections of March 1993, however, the left suffered a humiliating defeat. Their tally of seats fell to a paltry 91, the same number as had been won in June 1968; only 24 seats went to members of the *Parti Communiste*, its poorest showing since 1958. Clearly the left is once again on the defensive in France, fighting for its very survival. It is not expected to do well either in the elections for the European Parliament in 1994, or in the Presidential election the following year.

As far as the right is concerned, there are two main political groupings and several smaller ones. The Gaullist political tradition is perpetuated by the Republican Alignment (*Rassemblement pour la République*: RPR), which in 1976 emerged as the political successor to the Union for the Defence of the Republic (*Union pour la Défense de la République*: UDR). Its general secretary is Jacques Chirac. Remaining faithful to its traditional philosophy of maintaining a staunchly independent nationalism and a strong respect for state authority, the RPR has had to throw in its lot with other groupings at election times. The most prominent of its partners is the Union for French Democracy (*Union pour la Démocratie Française*: UDF), to which in turn several groups belong, all supportive of President Giscard d'Estaing in the 1970s – notably the Republican Party (*Parti Républicain*: PR), the Centre for Social Democrats (*Centre des Démocrats-Sociaux*: CDS), and the Radicals. The UDF symbolises a movement of the right which is more liberal than conservative, and therefore more modern than the rival grouping of Chirac. From the formation of the Fifth Republic until 1973 the Gaullists were a significantly stronger political force than their more centrist rivals. From then until 1993 the UDF gained considerable ground, actually winning 131 seats in the 1988 elections as opposed to the Gaullists' 130. By

1993, however, the pendulum had swung back towards the RPR, which in the March election took 242 seats compared with the UDF's 207.

Lastly, there is the National Front (*Front National*: FN), with Le Pen at its head. This party tries to stir up unrest among a section of the public over the number of foreigners in France (especially those from the states of North Africa, the Maghreb), and its concentration on the themes of public order, security, unemployment and immigration have led it to adopt the catchphrase 'France for the French' (*La France aux Français*). In 1984 the National Front won seats in the European Parliament and the system of proportional representation also helped it to win no fewer than 35 seats in the National Assembly in the elections of March 1986. In 1988, however, its representation fell to just one, and even this was lost in 1993. Various non-aligned right-wing parties did, however, win 37 seats in 1993, making the overall left/right ratio 91:486. There is also an ecology party in France (*Les Verts*), but it has yet to succeed in electing a *député*.

FURTHER READING

The text of most of the French Constitution is reproduced in English in John Bell's *French Constitutional Law* (1992), pp. 245–61, and at pp. 265–9 he gives an English version of the 1958 *Ordonnance* on the organisation and operation of the *Conseil constitutionnel*. Bell's book contains a wealth of information on how the Constitution operates, particularly in the realm of guaranteed freedoms; it also has 85 pages mainly devoted to extracts from decisions by the *Conseil constitutionnel*. A much more manageable account of French constitutional law is provided in Chapter 6 of *English Law and French Law*, by René David (1980). For accounts of the political context within which the constitutional arangements function, see Vincent Wright, *The Government and Politics of France* (3rd edn, 1989), and J.E.S. Hayward, *Governing France: The One and Indivisible Republic* (2nd edn, 1983). There are several good accounts of the influence of the *Conseil constitutionnel*; amongst them are M. Harrison, 'The French Constitutional Council: A Study in Institutional Change' (1990) 38 *Political Studies* 603, and Cummins, 'The General Principles of Law, Separation of Powers and Theories of Judicial Decision in France' (1986) 35 *International and Comparative Law Quarterly* 594.

For the text of the various French Constitutions, see P. Pactet, *Textes de droit constitutionnel* (2nd edn, 1992). The seminal work on constitutional history is Deslandres, *Histoire constitutionnelle de la France de 1789 à 1870* (2 vols; 1932), but see too Marcel Morabito and Daniel Bournaud, *Histoire constitutionnelle et politique de la France* (2nd edn, 1992). Works on constitutional law usually contain short introductions to constitutional history and ideas. A useful work of reference is the *Dictionnaire de la Constitution*, by Raymond Barillon and others (4th edn, 1986). The 1958 Constitution, or extracts therefrom, can be found (in French) in West *et al.*, *The French Legal System: An Introduction* (1992) at pp. 177–88, and in Kahn-Freund, Lévy and Rudden, *A Source-book on French Law* (3rd edn, 1991), at pp. 28–43; in the remainder of Chapter 1 the latter also contains many extracts from constitutionally important cases.

On the 1958 Constitution in particular, see Burdeau, Hamon and Troper, *Droit constitutionnel* (23rd edn, 1993); J. Gicquel, *Droit constitutionnel et institutions politiques* (12th edn, 1993); Leclercq, *Institutions politiques et droit constitutionnel* (8th edn, 1993); P. Pactet, *Institutions politiques, Droit constitutionnel* (11th edn, 1992); Ardant, *Institutions politiques et droit constitutionnel* (5th edn, 1993); and Turpin, *Droit constitutionnel* (1992). For an interesting critique of the modern Constitution and proposals for reform, see Bernard Chantebout, *La Constitution Française: Propos pour un débat* (1992). This must now be supplemented by the Vedel Report: *Propositions pour une révision de la Constitution: Rapport au Président de la République* (1993), on which see O. Passelecq, 'La philosophie du rapport Vedel' (1993) 14 *Rev. fr. du dr. const.* and *La révision de la Constitution* (1993), a collection of essays published by the Association française des constitutionnalistes. Two succinct specific works are *Le Conseil constitutionnel*, by P. Avril and J. Gicquel (1992), and *Le Conseil constitutionnel*, by H. Roussillon (2nd edn, 1994). The Council is also the subject of a collection of essays in the journal *Pouvoirs* (no. 13, 1991). For the role of the Conseil in EU affairs, see Peter Oliver, 'The French Constitution and the Treaty of Maastricht' (1994) 43 *International and Comparative Law Quarterly* 1.

Relevant journals include *Revue du droit public et de la science politique en France et à l'étranger*, *Revue politique et parlementaire*, *Revue française de science politique*, *L'année politique*, *Revue française de droit constitutionnel*, *Revue française d'études constitutionnelles et politiques* and *Pouvoirs*.

CHAPTER 4

Administrative law

CHARACTERISTICS OF FRENCH ADMINISTRATIVE LAW

The origins of French administrative law – the distinct set of legal rules governing bodies and activities in the public sector – go back to the French Revolution of 1789. In an important departure from the scheme of things during the period of the *ancien régime*, a statute of 16 and 29 August 1790 established the basic division of jurisdictions by removing from the ordinary courts any right to decide disputes between citizens and the administration; this right was seen as belonging to the administration itself. The Constitution of the Year VIII (1799) created the *Conseil d'Etat* which, as described in Chapter 2, later developed into the chief court for administrative matters. Legal rules slowly began to form and became the most important basis for French administrative law.

Unlike civil law or criminal law, administrative law in France is not codified. This does not mean that it is composed only of case law – statutes and regulations have become increasingly significant. But these legislative texts are widely dispersed. Although attempts have been made to aggregate some of the provisions (for instance in the Code of Local Administration, *Code de l'administration communale*, the Road Traffic Code, *Code de la route* and the Forestry Code, *Code forestier*), there is still no full-blown codification in this area. Administrative law is therefore largely judge-made law (*droit prétorien*). It is nevertheless a flexible system, tailored for particular circumstances and in a state of constant development. This enables it to strike a balance between the administrator's need for efficiency and the citizen's need for protection. The price paid for this is a degree of legal uncertainty, perhaps most graphically manifested by the laconic phrases of the judgments issued by administrative courts.

The judicial input into French administrative law has made it a complex and highly nuanced system. Complex, because in matters where no legislative provisions exist, the whole of the relevant case law must be examined. It is not always easy to calculate the meaning of decisions (several decisions on similar questions might contradict one another, or the same solutions might have been applied to different sets of facts), their relative value (which decision takes precedence?) and their scope (are they applicable to the case in hand?). All of this entails some uncertainty and can be the cause of subtly differentiated expert comments (such as those concerning the notion of *service public industriel et commercial*). But in the last 20 years or so the number of pertinent statutes and regulations has greatly increased. This is viewed by most French lawyers as a progressive development, since written law is more acceptable than judge-made law because of its clarity, certainty, accessibility and stability. Administrative law has, some might say, now left its developmental period behind it. However, some people still have doubts about the value of this change. For legislative texts are often set in the past; sometimes they are passed too hurriedly, which detracts from their quality as laws. The gaps must be filled by other laws or amendments. The result is a plethora of provisions, sometimes internally contradictory, which can be as difficult to find one's way around today as used to be the case with the casuistry of judge-made law. There needs to be a comprehensive reworking of the texts so that the heap of normative sources can be brought together into some systematic order.

Another development has altered the traditional view of administrative law, namely the control over the constitutionality of statutes exercised by the *Conseil constitutionnel*. The existence of this control has had an indisputable influence on administrative law because fundamental rights are being protected by a constitutional court, the case law of the *Conseil d'Etat* being supplemented in the process. This aspect of recent French legal history is more closely examined in Chapter 5.

Despite the remarkable developments which have occurred in English administrative law in the last 30 years or so, England still has a long way to go before it matches the sophistication of the law in France. Not only is there no separate system of administrative courts in England, but the grounds for judicial review of administrative action are by no means as extensive as they are in France. Nor is there a discrete branch of contract law devoted only to administrative contracts. However, English judges seem to be going through a period of creativity at the moment, especially in the House of Lords, and many of them have had the opportunity to study the legal position in France. In due course this may prompt some borrowing of ideas.

It ought not to be forgotten, moreover, that French administrative law – like all other areas of law – has to co-exist with European Community law. The rules of EC law raise difficult questions concerning conflicts of laws. As noted in Chapter 1, until as late as 1989 the *Conseil d'Etat* showed itself reluctant to recognise the pre-eminence of EC law, the directly binding nature of Council Directives and the significance of referring disputes to the European Court of Justice under Article 177 of the Treaty of Rome. In a famous decision in 1968 the *Conseil d'Etat* refused to 'correct' Parliament whenever it ignored the existence of an older rule of EC law. Its attitude was based on the classic thesis that the *Conseil d'Etat* is competent only to control the validity of administrative acts; if it were to check statutory provisions it would be overstepping its competence. One solution, of course, would be expressly to confer upon the *Conseil d'Etat* the power to declare statutes inapplicable. It is also the case that the *Conseil d'Etat* used to reject the European Court of Justice's case law on the direct applicability of EC Directives, but in the *Compagnie Alitalia* decision in February 1989 the *Conseil* said that French authorities could not, after the period allowed for implementing a Directive had elapsed, allow regulations to subsist which were incompatible with the objectives set out in the Directive. By applying the *théorie de l'acte clair* (*in claris non fit interpraetatio*) the *Conseil d'Etat* has rebelled against the duty imposed on it by Article 177 of the Treaty of Rome as far as the interpretation of EC law is concerned.

Nevertheless, there are also signs of development and flexibility in the case law on this point. The *Conseil d'Etat*'s decision of 23 March 1984 is worth mentioning: the *Conseil* there confirmed the liability of the state because damage had been caused to the claimant due to the non-observance of EC law. In *Nicolo*, a decision handed down in October 1989, the plaintiff was contesting the validity of the 1989 elections to the European Parliament on the ground that French citizens from French overseas departments had been allowed to participate. For the first time the *Conseil d'Etat* assessed whether a law passed after 1957 (when France entered the EEC), in this case the law of 7 July 1977 on European elections, was compatible with the Treaty of Rome; it held that it was.

SERVICE PUBLIC AND *PUISSANCE PUBLIQUE*

French administrative law is dominated by two concepts: *service public* and *puissance publique*. They have produced a lively debate between the experts concerning the desirable criteria for allocating a dispute to administrative courts; the debate is affected by the changing nature of state responsibilities and the move from a state concerned with 'policing' functions to a welfare state.

One view has it that administrative law is built upon the notion of *puissance publique* (public authority) and that it is this alone which justifies having special rules for administrative activity and applying them to disputes. The underlying idea is that the administration has powers at its disposal which private individuals do not enjoy. These privileges were the hallmarks of the administration in the liberal period of the 19th century, when private initiatives were the rule and private law was judge-made, while the administration confined itself to guaranteeing private initiatives through upholding public order. To fulfil this task the administration conferred upon itself the authority to take unilaterally binding administrative action in the public interest (*intérêt général*). It was the recognition of this special nature of the administration's role which led to the development of the notion of *puissance publique*.

It is hardly surprising that since the development of state interventionism this notion has begun to be doubted and has been increasingly suppressed by that of *service public*. By the end of the 19th century the state was no longer just the guarantor of the liberal social and economic order; it was also taking on tasks which were not satisfactorily performed by individuals or which were viewed as being too important to be left to private initiatives. The idea of *service public* describes this expansion in the administration's sphere of operations. The state has become less a regulatory agency than a performer of tasks. Indeed, the continuing growth in the range of the administration's tasks raises the question whether *service public* is still able to serve as the key concept in this context.

Today it looks as if *puissance publique* and *service public* are not concepts in opposition to each other but rather internally connected. *Service public* is a functional concept: it indicates the aim of the administration's dealings. *Puissance publique* indicates the means: it is an organisational concept, the power being an instrument applied to a particular end. The administration pursues goals of the *service public* by means of the *puissance publique*. However, not all public services are performed by means of the *puissance publique*, just as, conversely, not all the means of the *puissance publique* serve the *service public*. Public services are also performed through private law bodies, and the *puissance publique* also indicates police power, which is not to be seen as part of the *service public*. In spite of the considerable lack of clarity here, both concepts remain key to the definition of administrative law and to the separation between ordinary and administrative courts. They form two axes along which the whole of French administrative law is orientated.

THE ORGANISATION OF THE ADMINISTRATION

Aware that knowing the legal rules does not suffice for an understanding of how the administration works, a science of public administration has developed in France as in other countries. Although the subject is still a fairly new one, there is already a comprehensive literature.

Two types of organisation can be distinguished in the structure of France's administration. There are regional bodies (*collectivités territoriales*) and public law bodies with special responsibilities such as *établissements publics* (*administratifs* or *industriels et commerciaux*) or *entreprises publiques* (some of these are *établissements publics*, others are corporations with public capital). First of all we must explore the principles upon which France's administration is organised. Two characteristics remain crucial for the structure of today's administration: centralisation and the uniformity of legal provisions.

The tendency towards centralisation has been increasingly criticised. Yet it reflects a socio-political reality: it has developed in tandem with the notion of the French nation state. The phenomenon did not begin with the French Revolution but with the pre-existing *ancien régime*. The Revolution and Napoleon I simply consolidated the tendency. The age and permanence of centralisation explain the hold which it still has today, even though attempts have been made by the post-1981 socialist governments to break it down and to bring the administration closer to the people being administered. Today decisions are no longer always taken in Parisian offices. The task of administration is by and large given to an official who functions at the local level and not as part of a central authority. Nevertheless, he or she remains a representative of the central power and acts not in a personal capacity but on behalf of the government, as a representative of the state's will. As has been well said: 'The same hammer is delivering the blows but the arm which is wielding it is shorter.'

But the process of decentralisation also has more far-reaching goals. It starts from the realisation that there are local interests which it would be useless or even dangerous to leave to a central government to consider and which are therefore entrusted to locally elected organs. This presupposes that the right to self-administration should be conceded to communities at a level lower than the state. Looked at in this way decentralisation is above all a reaction against the omnipotence of the capital city, Paris. The hallmarks are elected bodies which carry the responsibility for administering local areas.

However, a higher authority needs to have supervisory responsibilities in order to ensure that everything hangs together properly. There are therefore the *pouvoir hiérarchique* and the *contrôle de tutelle*. The former is exercised by the office further up the chain of command and embraces the power to initiate action (*pouvoir d'instruction*), the authority to introduce reforms and to annul lower decisions (*pouvoir de réformation et d'annulation*), and the authority to take or substitute measures (*pouvoir d'évocation et de substitution*). As the body supervising the subject-matter in question the *pouvoir hiérarchique* can operate on the basis of legal control or merits control, even if there is no express statutory basis for doing so. The *contrôle de tutelle* has the same goal, but the means it employs are more limited. It cannot interfere with initiatives, reforms or the taking of measures, while the annulment of decisions and substitution of new measures are possible only if strict preconditions are satisfied. It is restricted in the main to a simple legality check invoked by the local prefect (*préfet*) in the administrative court.

The second characteristic feature of French administration is the uniform nature of the way in which it is organised. Communities, *départements* and regions are built upon the same juristic model without any regard for the number of inhabitants, the urban or rural character of the locality or its economic structure. As this has led to considerable inequalities since the Second World War, Parliament has sought to provide remedies through various measures. The only constitutional provision relevant at this point is Article 72, which stipulates that the territorial units of the Republic are *communes, départements* and *territoires d'outre-mer*. This goes on to say that *'toute autre collectivité territoriale est créée par la loi'* (every other territorial grouping is created by statute) and that *'ces collectivités s'administrent librement par des conseils élus et dans les conditions prévus par la loi'* (these groupings are administered independently by elected councils under conditions laid down by statute). Today the administration of France is organised territorially into *communes* (or associations of communities), *départements*, regions, and the centre. Until 1982 the organisation resembled a neatly structured pyramid but, with the aim of introducing more local democracy, a statute of 2 March 1982 – together with other statutes and regulations – began the process of decentralisation. The measures dealt not only with the distribution of powers between local administrative offices and the state, but also with the state supervision of local activities. Following this reform, communities, *départements* and regions are all recognised as equal. Each has an elected council (*conseil municipal, général* or *régional*), chaired by a *président du conseil* or (in the case of *communes*) by a mayor (*maire*). Each *département* and region has a prefect (*préfet*); this person is an officer of the central state who is meant to oversee the functioning of the decentralised administration.

Communes

There are 36,400 communities or *communes* in France. This large number (by far the highest of all the EC states) is a problem that has troubled the government for years, although more than the actual number it is the disparity in size that causes concern: 90 per cent have fewer than 2,000 inhabitants and 60 per cent have fewer than 500, whereas numerous suburban communities have grown up around large cities (the Ballung area in Lyons has about two million inhabitants, while the city centre itself has only about half a million). The move of population away from the rural areas and the growth in cities have caused a splintering of administrative and financial functions which has put some communities into an unbearable position.

A *commune* consists of the community council, the mayor and the community's administration. The council is the decision-making body and deals with the most important affairs of the community. It is a representative body directly elected by the people for a period of six years. The mayor is elected from the council membership by a two-stage majority voting system and during tenure of the office he or she is the chairperson of the council. At the same time the mayor is the representative of the state administration at the community level and the executive arm of the regional corporation. However, within this distribution of functions (*dédoublement fonctionnel*) the self-governing responsibilities at the local level are the most important. The community's administration is the executive arm of the community council and is responsible for local administrative tasks. It is simply a group of people which by statute and through the mayor has the right to initiate actions and take decisions.

Formerly local communities dealt with all local business (*affaires locales*), though their powers were restricted by numerous statutes. These powers were significantly increased by the reform of 1982, particularly in the realm of town planning (*urbanisme*). Associations of communities (see below) have the right to draw up land development plans; today communities can plan buildings not only for their own use but also for others (*plan d'occupation des sols*). General state oversight concerning these measures is undertaken by the government's representative (*le préfet*). As the supervisory authority the *préfet* has the right to go to the administrative court, which is the body which actually carries out the necessary checks.

Associations of communities

Because of the way in which France is territorially divided, smaller communities have to work together to carry out their tasks. There are today three main varieties of associations of communities: *syndicats inter-communaux, districts urbains* and *communautés urbaines*.

The *syndicats de communes* are led by an indirectly elected council, each community being represented by one member of its own council. Despite the uniformity in the way communities are organised, this type of association is usually elected, since this is the best way of taking into account the independence of the small communities. There are about 10,000 *syndicats* to carry out single tasks (*syndicats intercommunaux à vocation unique*: SIVU) and 20,000 to carry out several tasks (*syndicats intercommunaux à vocation multiple*: SIVOM). They have been particularly active in ensuring proper water and electricity supplies. The *districts urbains* and *communautés urbaines* are comparatively new creations, first set up during the current Fifth Republic. The way in which they are organised depends on the size of individual communities. The means at their disposal come from contributions made by communities and from tax revenue. In 1980 there were 147 *districts* with a total of 5.5 million inhabitants and nine *communautés urbaines* with 4 million inhabitants. The two forms of association (governed by statutes of 31 December 1970 and 31 December 1966 respectively) were supposed to help solve the problems connected with the efficient provision of public services in outlying areas of cities, assisted by other newly formed organisations such as *établissements publics* which brought together several communities to perform common tasks. Still to be addressed was the problem of the high number of small, predominantly rural communities. The statute of 16 July 1971 provided for a process resulting in administrative reform through the voluntary or compulsory merger of communities.

Départements

Originally – in 1790 – *départements* were purely artifical entities. When, during the French Revolution, thought was being given to how the country should be divided – in a manner that would ensure the prevention of all federalist tendencies such as the *ancien régime*'s provinces had produced – the simple criterion used was the distance which a person could travel by coach in a day. Despite being frequently criticised, this unscientific method of dividing the country into *départements* has survived.

Like a community, a *département* is both a territorial unit of the central administration and a self-governing body; unlike a community, however, it operates for the most part as a unit of the central administration's authority. *Départements* are thus responsible for, amongst other things, social security, health, education (for children aged 11 to 15) and roads. By virtue of a statute of 7 January 1983, *départements* are expressly empowered to draw up plans for the financing of construction work and the protection of the countryside. At present France has 96 *départements* (not counting those overseas), each of which is administered by the president of the department's council (*le président du conseil général*); the *conseil général* is elected every three years and the president has the same functions as the mayor in a community.

The official called a 'prefect' (*préfet*) was known from 1982 to 1988 as the *commissaire de la République*. His or her former powers have been considerably restricted in favour of the president of the department's council. Besides having the authority to invoke the jurisdiction of the administrative court, the *préfet* has opportunities to influence the drafting process for building and planning schemes, and in certain circumstances he or she can personally issue building licences.

Regions

The large number of *départements*, their limited size and the changes occurring in their economic and demographic features have resulted in the creation of a new variety of administrative unit sitting between *départements* and the central authorities. Established only in 1972 as a public law entity, these regions were made into local corporations as a consequence of the move towards decentralisation. Chief responsibility for the administration of the region rests with the president of the regional council (*président du conseil régional*). The regional council itself is directly elected by the people of the region every six years. There are today 22 regions in mainland France, each consisting of between two and seven *départements* (e.g. the Ile de France has seven, Brittany has four, Corsica has two). They are responsible for such matters as professional education, research, secondary schools, planning, river navigation and the development of the local economy. To fulfil these tasks they have the advice of the so-called *comité économique et social*, which is made up of representatives from different organisations, including the trades unions. The regions also play a large part in co-ordinating and planning state investments in the local economy.

The *préfet* exercises legal control over the regional bodies by being able to invoke the jurisdiction of the administrative courts, as with *communes* and *départements*. He or she can also influence the economic development of the region through chairing the regional administrative conference (*conférence administrative régionale*). This comprises the senior officials in the region who are experts in economics.

State supervision

According to Article 72 of the 1958 French Constitution, local corporations are to be supervised in their administrative tasks by representatives of the government: *le délégué du Gouvernement a la charge des intérêts nationaux, du contrôle administratif et du respect des lois.* This state supervision takes the form of general control (*tutelle administrative*), financial control (*tutelle financière*) and technical control (*tutelle technique*).

As far as general control is concerned, prefects used to have the power, before 1982, to overrule decisions taken by local corporations. Now the *préfet* can simply invoke the jurisdiction of the administrative courts, within two months of the decision which it is sought to challenge. The judgment of the local administrative court can be appealed against to the *Conseil d'Etat*.

Financial supervision is the responsibility of a regional audit commission (*chambre régionale des comptes*), from which there can be an appeal to the *Cour des comptes*. The *préfet* can consult this commission if the region's budget is not agreed upon in time or if it does not balance income against expenditure. The commission can also be involved whenever the previous year's budget has produced a deficit.

Technical supervision means ensuring that statutes and regulations stipulate the conditions which must exist if the state wants to invest in the area.

Central administrative authorities

The central administrative authority consists of the state President and the Prime Minister, together with the offices and departments under the latter's control and the control of other specialist ministers. The way it is organised does not present as many problems for administrative law as it does for the science of public administration in general. One example of this is the need for co-ordination between ministries: the supremacy of the Prime Minister is not always sufficient to ensure homogeneity. One solution is to create inter-ministry committees and central offices in the Prime Minister's department. This explains the economic committee (*commissariat général au*

Plan) and the planning committee (*délégation à l'aménagement du territoire*). The government's secretariat-general (*secrétariat général du gouvernement*) is supposed to ensure general co-ordination of activities.

Public bodies

Public bodies (*établissements publics*) can be defined in a rather circular fashion as every entity recognised by public law besides the state and local corporations. They embody the decentralisation process based on a division of functions rather than on a division of territory. They have their own resources and financial autonomy, and they are subject to the principle of exclusivity, whereby a body with a particular function is forbidden from doing something outside its legally defined mandate. *Etablissements publics* are also subject to legal controls which are often more wide-ranging than in the case of local corporations.

This status has been elastic enough to serve as the legal foundation for a large number of organisations – universities, chambers of commerce, the state savings banks (*Caisse des depôts et des consignations*), national research centres (e.g. *Centre national de la recherche scientifique*), amongst others. Of particular significance are the *établissements publics à caractère industriel et commercial* (EPICs), which have proliferated greatly since 1945 and which can be contrasted with the classic *établissements publics administratifs*. Many of them are the result of nationalisation. The status of an EPIC is very similar to that of a *service public industriel et commercial* (SPIC). One can say quite generally that these diverse organisms differ significantly from one another as regards the independence they enjoy, the position of their staff and the nature of their particular remit.

THE ADMINISTRATION'S TASKS

French administrative law traditionally differentiates *services publics* from 'policing' activities and subsumes individual administrative tasks under these two heads. However, although these were for a long time viewed as separate poles, today many consider them to be not only compatible but sometimes even identical: one school of thought views the police force as itself a *service public*. It should be noted that in France the term *police* is used as a description not just of the force itself but also of the enforcement functions which are carried out by a variety of public bodies.

The 'policing' function and civil liberties

A major problem for any enforcement function is the way in which it must have regard to the upholding of public order on the one hand and the respecting of civil liberties on the other. However, the case law of the

Conseil d'Etat has by and large succeeded in arriving at satisfactory compromises. Naturally the solutions depend on the way in which civil liberties are protected by the law at any particular time. Whichever 'policing' measure is under consideration it must not go so far as to undermine completely the exercise of freedoms, for the *Conseil d'Etat* rejects general and absolute prohibitions. The room for policing discretion varies in accordance with the rights concerned. It is at its minimum whenever the policing measure interferes with private property. For freedoms which are guaranteed by statute, as is the case with freedom of assembly, the *Conseil d'Etat* views the freedom as the rule and any prohibition as an exception thereto. So a demonstration against an assembly cannot be enough to justify forbidding the assembly; the authorities must instead use all available means to ensure that the assembly can proceed, and only if this is impossible can the assembly be banned.

The policing function, moreover, is in general limited by the principle of necessity. Case law has imposed a series of restrictions upon policing based on this idea. Authorities must have regard for the official and legal relationships involved; they cannot generally forbid lawful activities and freedoms; the principle of proportionality means that measures taken must be confined to those which are absolutely essential; and the principle of equality must be observed. Yet, despite the balance which the *Conseil d'Etat* has struck between public order and individuals' freedoms, many of the latter seem to be poorly protected. This matter is further explored in Chapter 5, but one example relates to the showing of films. Despite the fact that films which have satisfied the standards of the state's controlling commission can be shown throughout France, mayors and others have sometimes banned their screening in local cinemas. In these cases the *Conseil d'Etat* has limited itself to asking the question whether there would be a danger of local unrest if the film were to be shown and has thereby implicitly allowed local policing authorities to be arbiters of public morality. Obviously the freedom to 'perform' does not enjoy the same degree of constitutional protection in France as the freedom to assemble.

The legal principles governing *services publics*

Services publics carry out administrative tasks in the broader sense, though increasingly tasks belonging to a *service public* are being entrusted even to private individuals, which naturally leads to demarcation disputes (e.g. as regards money-lending on homes). The special requirement for advance payment in public law contracts and the inalienability of public property are rules designed to ensure continuity of public services. It can be said that four principles govern the organisation of the *services publics*. They flow from the significance of and the public interest in this type of administrative activity:

(a) **The principle of continuity.** First of all, as already mentioned, there is the principle of continuity. Official actions have to be carried out properly and punctually. If the administration is itself the body responsible (*la régie*), every interruption in the service is unlawful unless it is as a result of some higher authority. If the task is being performed by a body which has the concession to carry it out, that body must ensure its continuity at all costs, even if this means suffering a deficit.

(b) **The principle of equality.** The general principle of equality also applies to people who use a *service public*. It entails equality of access to the service, as well as equality in the way one is treated by the service; the service has to be in all respects unbiased.

(c) **The principle of adjustment.** The principle of adjustment applies too, though it is sometimes viewed merely as a consequence of the continuity principle. It allows the *service public*, in the public interest, unilaterally to alter contractual terms or, in certain circumstances, to re-determine the contractual obligations owed. As we shall see in the chapter on contract law, in French administrative law, unlike in French civil law, a version of the doctrine of frustration is recognised (*théorie de l'imprévision*); this enables the administrative body in appropriate circumstances to claim extra renumeration from the other party to the transaction. Until quite recently the staff who worked in administrative bodies were not permitted to go on strike, again in the interests of continuing the public service.

(d) **The principle of priority.** The principle of priority means that if a conflict arises between the public interest underlying a *service public* and private interests, the latter must give way to the former. This raises the problem as to how far a local community can go in creating economic undertakings (*services publics industriels et commerciaux*: SPICs) in order to satisfy the needs of its citizens. Can these undertakings be set up without any statutory basis to them? The case law on this point is illustrative of the changing functions of the administration in the past 50 years. Originally the *Conseil d'Etat* would allow a local community to intervene only if every private initiative had failed: in the liberal economic climate that prevailed preference was given to private initiatives. Subsequently case law increasingly came to distinguish between different sectors: for some services (such as health, theatre entertainment, etc.) public bodies are now the norm, for other sectors the former principle remains valid but the exceptions to it have become more numerous: a local community can take the initiative if to do so is in the local public interest and if the services will not be competing unfairly with those provided by private undertakings.

Enterprises publiques

Enterprises publiques are organised in the form of either *établissements publics* or *sociétés anonymes*. Either they act as public utilities, like Air France, EDF (the electricity service), GDF (the gas service) or SNCF (the railway service), or they operate as classic profit-orientated undertakings, like the *Régie Nationale des Usines Renault* (the *Renault* concern). This is a result of a specific conception of the relationship between the state and the economy, according to which the economy is not to be left the exclusive playground of individual citizens. Despite the variety of enterprises in existence, state supervision of *entreprises publiques* is regulated by public law. The relationships with users and customers are governed by private law.

ADMINISTRATIVE ACTS

A characteristic feature of the administration in France is that it can unilaterally take binding decisions relating to an individual even without his or her co-operation or agreement (*un acte administratif unilatéral*). This power to act unilaterally is the special privilege of public authorities. According to some other European legal systems only administrative measures aimed at individuals can be administrative acts, but in French law the category also embraces general regulations. This means that in France judicial review proceedings (*recours pour excès de pouvoir*) can be taken even with respect to legislative measures (*règlements*).

On the other hand, not all administrative activities in France qualify as administrative acts. Those that do not, and which therefore escape the clutches of judicial review proceedings, fall mainly into two groups: the important category of government actions (*actes de gouvernement*) and the not so practically important category of administrative activities which have no executive character. *Actes de gouvernement* occur in the area where government and administration overlap and where judicial control is consequently dispensed with. They cover a host of different matters, making systematisation difficult. Examples from case law include acts which have to do with the relationship between government and Parliament, with the concluding, application or interpretation of international treaties, or with decisions to grant pardons to criminals. Originally the special status of these acts was attributed to the political intentions behind such acts and to the separation of powers doctrine; today the preferred view is that it is due to the legal rather than political nature of administrative disputes. Certain acts are felt not to be susceptible to judicial control because they have to do not principally with administration but with the relationships between public institutions or between states. It is as a result of the very nature of these acts that they are not subject to legal control. As Vedel has put it, 'the administrative judge must avoid boundary disputes with the state President, the Prime Minister and organs of foreign policy'.

Administrative measures with no executory character do not really bind persons to whom they are addressed. Examples would be simple instructions (administrative information) or measures preparatory to the real decision-making, and administrative circulars, orders and internal memoranda. These last do raise a few difficulties. Circulars are internal administrative documents by means of which an official interprets certain provisions as binding. The *Conseil d'Etat*, however, sees them as documents which can be judicially reviewed, at least to the extent that they add something of substance to the original legal provision. In-service directives are themselves enforceable: they provide detailed regulations for the inner workings of an organisation. The fact that they cannot be judicially reviewed is usually supported by the principle *de minimis non curat praetor* (judges should not deal with trivial matters), but they are nevertheless meant to ensure that public offices carry out their functions conscientiously.

French administrative law is strongly influenced by procedural considerations, with many of the concepts employed being the product of case law. The notion of *acte administratif* is just one of these concepts and, in the absence of a statutory definition, it will continue to be interpreted by judges in decisions which in turn can be changed on appeal.

COMPLIANCE WITH LEGALITY (*LÉGALITÉ*)

The administration has to comply with statutes and other written laws, such self-restrictions reflecting the very *raison d'être* of administrative law in France, and the fact that this phenomenon was established in the early days following the Revolution meant that the French way of doing things was able to affect the methods subsequently used in other civil law European countries. Today the subordination of French administrative law to higher legal rules (the Constitution, statutes, regulations and general legal principles – these are known as the sources of *légalité*) is, despite the enlarged regulatory power of the executive bodies, adhered to without exception.

In France, judicial review of administrative action is termed *contentieux administratif* or *recours pour excès de pouvoir* and the grounds upon which administrative acts can be challenged (*les cas d'ouverture*) are much wider than in England. The two most prominent grounds are *détournement de pouvoir* and *violation de la loi*. The former embraces but goes beyond the English doctrine of *ultra vires*, which is confined to the control of administrative action on the basis that it contravenes a statute. *Violation de la loi* is a catch-all ground for review which most commentators break down under headings such as *erreur manifeste d'appréciation des faits* (substantial mistake in fact characterisation), *erreur de droit* (mistake of law) and *proportionalité* or *le bilan* (proportionality or drawing up the balance sheet).

Collectively these heads of review far exceed the scope of *Wednesbury* unreasonableness in English law, and it is in this context that the *Conseil d'Etat* has been particularly inventive in its use of *principes généraux du droit*, even if, as in England, the pretence is maintained that the review in question is merely procedural and not an attack on the merits (*l'opportunité*) of the action in question. An example of review on the basis of *erreur manifeste d'appréciation des faits* occurs in the *Institut Technique Privé de Dunkerque* case (1980), where the *Conseil d'Etat* overturned both the prefect's and the Ministry of Education's interpretation of the concept of *besoin scolaire reconnu*: in deciding that this concept required a balance to be maintained between the provision of public and private colleges the administrative officials were held to have mistakenly evaluated the situation. An example of the use of *le bilan* is the case of *Ville Nouvelle Est de Lille* (1971). Here the *Conseil d'Etat* showed itself willing to re-examine the government's opinion that the compulsory acquisition of some land was in the public interest (*d'utilité publique*): although it held in favour of the government it did so only after expressly weighing up the pros and cons of that point of view.

Other grounds for review include *l'inexistence*, where the action in question is so obviously outside the jurisdiction of the administrative body that it can be said not even to exist, *l'incompétence*, where a mistake as to the scope of the body's powers has been made, and *les vices de forme et de procédure*, where there has been some formal irregularity. It is difficult neatly to relate these grounds to the grounds for judicial review available in English law, but the rules of natural justice may be said to be close to a *vice de forme*, while error on the face of the record is an example of *incompétence*.

It is noteworthy, however, that as yet, as in English administrative law, there is no general compulsion to supply reasons for administrative actions in France, though the *Conseil d'Etat* has in many cases judicially reviewed the reasons in fact given.

ANNULMENT OF ADMINISTRATIVE ACTIONS

In most cases the role of the administrative court is to decide whether to annul the challenged administrative action and to remit the matter to be reconsidered by the appropriate administrative authority (*le contentieux de l'annulation*). Occasionally the administrative court can substitute its own decision for that of the administrative body (*le contentieux de pleine juridiction*).

The rules applicable to the annulment of administrative actions are a classic topic for discussion in French administrative law. Originally the terminology used varied, but today the key concept of *rapport* has become established, and a distinction is drawn depending upon the effects in time of the annulment. If it relates to the future the French speak of *abrogation* (rescission *ex nunc*), whereas if it relates to the past they call it *retrait* (rescission *ex tunc*). *Abrogation* is generally viewed as creating no problems, even when administrative actions have suppposedly created legal rights, for the administration must always be in a position to adjust the legal position in line with changes to the facts of a case. But *retrait* does create difficulties when administrative actions have mistakenly created rights (*actes irréguliers créateurs de droits*). *Retrait* is not allowed in respect of lawful administrative acts: they can be rescinded only for the future. If the act was lawful but did not create any legal rights it *can*, however, be retrospectively rescinded; if it was unlawful as well as creating no legal rights it *must* be retrospectively rescinded.

For unlawful administrative actions which have created rights, French law starts from the principle that they can be retrospectively rescinded only for the period during which they could have been challenged by legal proceedings, provided they have not yet acquired the force of law. After that only rescission *ex nunc* is available. This reinforces the unqualified reliance citizens can place on rights which have already been given the force of law and does not require a weighing-up of competing interests. Yet case law has restricted this basic principle. Unlawful administrative acts which have created rights, even if those rights have acquired full legal recognition, *can* be retrospectively rescinded if they were issued as a result of malice or if they are so defective that they should be viewed as non-existent. The *Conseil d'Etat*, moreover, has limited the very notion of an *acte créateur de droit*. This means that administrative acts which establish or which recognise rights, as well as decisions or acts which are made conditional upon something else occurring, can all be rescinded. The absoluteness of the basic principle has thus been noticeably qualified, even though in the interim its clarity has to a certain extent persuaded the European Court of Justice to adopt a similar rule.

CONTRACTS INVOLVING ADMINISTRATIVE AUTHORITIES

In place of unilateral administrative acts the administration can also fulfil its functions by entering into contracts. French law is peculiar in that it allows the administration to choose between two types of contract – a private law contract or a public law contract. For French legal scholars the main controversy therefore relates not to whether such contracts are permissible or whether the administration's actions can be divided into two groups (*théorie des actes détachables*), but to how private law contracts, which are governed by the rules of the *Code civil* and subject to the jurisdiction of the ordinary courts, can be demarcated from public law contracts, which are governed by special rules and subject to the jurisdiction of administrative courts. The concept of an administrative contract (*contrat administratif*) is therefore not identical to that of a contract of the administration (*contrat de l'administration*). The latter is a general term for all the contracts entered into by the administration. A *contrat administratif* is one category of such contracts, one for which rules other than those of private law are applicable and with which administrative courts have jurisdiction to deal. The following are the main types of administrative contract recognised by the law:

(a) concessions (*concessions de service public*): here the administration transfers a public service to a private legal person, who is paid for performing the service by the users of the service (an example would be private concerns who run city transport systems);
(b) contracts for the supply of essential services: an example would be the delivery of office equipment (*marché de fournitures*);
(c) contracts for public works (*marchés de travaux publics*): technically these include all works connected with land, such as the construction and maintenance of roads;
(d) employment contracts for people who are in the civil service but who are not civil servants properly so called.

Before looking more closely at the special rules, it is first necessary to explain the distinguishing features of a *contrat administratif*. For certain contracts categorisation presents no difficulties since they are already categorised by statute. Thus *contrats administratifs* include all contracts concerning public procurement (*marchés de travaux publics*) or the occupation of public land (*contrats comportant occupation du domaine public*). Difficulties arise whenever there is no statutory categorisation. Case law requires two preconditions to be fulfilled for an administrative contract to exist: at least one of the contracting parties must be a legal person in the eyes of public law, and the contract must either contain a provision which goes beyond the rules of private law (*clause exorbitante du droit commun*) or have as its object the carrying out of a *service public*. The first precondition means that we can exclude contracts between private law companies, even when the state owns the majority capital interest. In one decision, however, the *Tribunal des Conflits* characterised as administrative a contract between a private concern and a *société d'économie mixte*, which is also subject to private law rules. What may have been the determining factor in that case was the fact that the *société* was really acting on behalf of the state and was under its direct control. The second precondition still fully applies. The notion of a *clause exorbitante du droit commun* represents the early attempt of case law to develop a criterion for distinguishing administrative contracts. It refers to contractual clauses which grant rights to the parties, or impose duties on them, which by their nature are different from those which are voluntarily taken on board in the spheres of civil or commercial law. They are clauses which are not impermissible in private law but nevertheless unusual. They include provisions imposing a contractual penalty or conferring on the administration a unilateral right of rescission. It is this formal feature, and not the actual content of the contract, which puts the contract into the administrative category.

The notion that one party must be a participant in the performance of a public service is a more recently developed criterion. Quite apart from whether there is a *clause exorbitante*, a contract is administrative in character whenever one party is fulfilling a public service. This applies, for instance, to franchise agreements and to money-lending arrangements. Considerable difficulties arise from the need to establish whether the contracting party is himself or herself directly performing the public service or is merely the contractually bound collaborator of the administration. Demarcation disputes also result from the category of *services publics à caractère industriel et commercial* (SPICs). These public concerns undertake the sorts of activities which could also be performed by private commercial companies; their contracts are therefore taken as private until the contrary is proved. As regards contracts between consumers and a SPIC, the presumption in favour of the private law character of the arrangement is irrebuttable. On the other hand, many contracts are viewed as public law contracts because of their overall character. For instance, contracts between the EDF and private producers for the supply of electricity are categorised as public because statute says they are not subject to private law. The decision of the *Conseil d'Etat* in this case exemplifies the consequences which can now flow from the administration's activities.

Traditionally French administrative law has always viewed *contrats administratifs* and private contracts as fundamentally different. Private contracts are the expression of the free will of two private contracting parties who stand on an equal footing and exchange promises. In public law the private individual is opposed by the state, the representative of the public interest. As a result the administration is recognised to be in a special legal position and is granted special rights in order to fulfil its public functions. Other countries would not recognise this kind of private–public relationship as contractual at all, and even in France the classification of it as a contract with special features is sometimes disputed. In a common law system many would see the need for administrative contracts to be governed by special rules ensuring the protection of the private party rather than of the administration.

The peculiarities of administrative contracts are apparent at all stages. Even when the administration is choosing its contractual partners it is limited by the rules on inviting tenders (*cahiers des clauses administratives*) and on accepting the lowest or most competent offer. The special features become even more apparent as the contract unfolds. Contrary to Article 1134 of the *Code civil*, the administration has unilateral privileges which are balanced by the contracting partner's right to claim monetary compensation if the administration exercises the privileges. If the privileges are not expressly mentioned in the contract they are nevertheless taken to exist by implication: they flow automatically from the public nature of the transaction to which the parties have submitted themselves.

More particularly, the administration has the authority to control the performance of the contract, including the right unilaterally to take measures, if it is not fully performed, which will alter or rescind the agreement. The right to make changes to the contract is probably the most characteristic feature, as it is irreconcilable both with civil law thinking on ordinary contracts and with common law thinking on all contracts (though the Consumer Credit Act 1974 makes an exception *vis-à-vis* regulated credit agreements). A necessary corollary of these rights is the other party's right to financial compensation. This restores the balance between the parties, even though not as would be done in private law cases. The doctrinal basis for this system is the theory of unforeseeability (*théorie de l'imprévision*), something which is not recognised in French private law (*see* Chapter 8).

Another special situation is that covered by the *théorie du fait du prince*. This deals with cases where the administration imposes additional burdens as a result of dealings outside the contract to do with the general implementation of statutes. Administrative courts will in these circumstances approve an award of compensation to the other contracting party provided that party has suffered some special disadvantage. The legal justification for this is difficult to accept, because, in the absence of fault, there is no question of official liability for losses. The compensation can perhaps best be explained by recourse to the principle of equal treatment in the contractual sphere.

There is a school of thought in French legal scholarship which views as a mistake the idea that administrative contracts are special because of the privileges inherent in the state. It sees the reasoning as based on a false interpretation of case law and not corresponding with the real world, and it points to the fact that a large number of administrative contracts do not display any special features in comparison with private law contracts. This applies in particular to transactions concerning the necessities of life, which are contracts for the sale of goods. Other rules uncommon in private law flow directly from the parties' own free will and from the contracts themselves, so they do not need to be explained as due to the privileges of the administration. In any event, the right to supervise and control the performance of a contract is nothing out of the ordinary: such rights also accrue to the employer or client in a contract for services, and a private client in a construction contract can alter the plans provided he or she undertakes to pay the additional costs. The classic theory lays store by the argument that the administration can turn to a second contract partner if the first is not in a position to take responsibility for physical conditions or to carry out required technical alterations. The newer view is that this right is based not on the administration's privileges but on its general authority to organise public services.

At the centre of the traditional view is the idea that the administration has the right unilaterally to change the contract, and it gains support for this in the famous *Tramways* case (1910). A prefect had made a franchise arrangement with a transport company which ran the public transport system in Marseilles. He later insisted upon timetable alterations, which resulted in greater expenditure, his reason being public order considerations. When the company took legal action the *Conseil d'Etat* upheld the decision to change the contract but required the public authority to compensate the company for the extra expenditure it was incurring. This decision, which some authors view as the cornerstone of the law on administrative contracts, is interpreted by the new school of thought as merely an application of the *théorie du fait du prince*. The administration had not in fact relied upon the contract when altering matters but upon its 'policing' authority. It was, moreover, obliged to compensate the other contracting party. Even with regard to the unilateral right of alteration, the special position of administrative contracts is therefore not without uncertainty, and according to the more recent thinking does not exist at all.

THE *MÉDIATEUR*

The gaps in protection for fundamental freedoms led to the appointment, under a statute of 3 January 1973, of an ombudsman (*médiateur*). The Presidents of the National Assembly and the Senate, and the highest officials in the justice and administrative sectors, suggest the names of three candidates, one of whom is appointed for a six-year period by a decree of the Cabinet. If there are complaints against the administration, public bodies or the judiciary, one of the six standing Parliamentary Commissions applies to the *députés* in the Assembly or to the senators with a request that the powers of the *médiateur* be invoked. This independent person can then turn to the relevant office to request its assistance. He or she makes suggestions for compromise solutions to disputes and is kept informed of how these suggestions are being implemented. The *Conseil d'Etat* can itself adjudicate upon the *médiateur*'s decisions because of his or her status as an administrative authority, but it does not attribute the justiciable character of an administrative decision to his or her suggestions for compromises.

An annual report has to be submitted by the *médiateur* to the President of the Republic. The report of Jacques Pelletier for 1992 shows that more than 35,000 cases were dealt with by his office that year, an increase of 17 per cent over the 1991 figure. Of the cases notified nearly one-third related to health, social security or employment, but nearly 37 per cent were inadmissible because the complaint fell outside the *médiateur*'s jurisdiction. In almost one-half of the admissible cases the complaint was found to be at least partially justified. In addition, in 1992 the *médiateur* made numerous suggestions for the reform of laws or administrative practices; if past experience is anything to go by some two-thirds of these can expect to be accepted by the government. By all accounts the office of the *médiateur* has been a great success in France; its impact on the administrative authorities has probably been more noticeable than the impact of the Parliamentary Commissioner for Administration in England.

FURTHER READING

There is an excellent book in English on this subject: *French Administrative Law*, by Neville Brown and John Bell (4th edn, 1993). A summary account appears in R. David, *English Law and French law* (1980), Chapter 7. Useful journal articles include the following: Weil, 'The Strength and Weakness of French Administrative Law' [1965] Camb LJ 252; J. Bell, 'The Expansion of Judicial Review over Discretionary Powers in France' [1986] *Public Law* 99; N. Brown and J. Bell, 'Recent Reforms of French Administrative Law' (1989) 8 *Civil Justice Quarterly* 71.

Important decisions of the French administrative courts, especially the *Conseil d'Etat*, are regularly noted in the journal *Public Law*. For a slightly dated survey of legal provisions on ombudsmen, see Stacey, *Ombudsmen Compared* (1978), Chapter 6, which deals with the French *médiateur*.

The types of literature available for students and practitioners in France correspond to those on *droit civil*. The textbooks worth singling out are the following: G. Dupuis and M.-J. Guédon, *Droit administratif* (4th edn, 1993); Laubadère, Venezia and Gaudemet, *Traité de droit administratif* (4 vols; 1990–92); C. Leclercq and A. Chaminade, *Droit administratif* (1992); G. Vedel and P. Delvolvé, *Droit administratif* (12th edn, 1992, 2 vols); J.-M. de Forges, *Droit administratif* (2nd edn, 1993); J. Rivéro and J. Waline, *Droit administratif* (14th edn, 1992). There are separate books on how the various administrative authorities in France are organised: Olivier Gohin, *Institutions Administratives* (1992); J.-M. Auby and J.-B. Auby, *Institutions Administratives* (6th edn, 1991); J.-M. Becet, *Les Institutions Administratives* (3rd edn, 1992); and C. Debbasch, *Institutions et droits administratifs* (4th edn, 1991, vol. 1). In the *Que Sais-Je?* series there are P. Weil, *Le droit administratif* (15th edn, 1992), and M. Gentot and H. Oberdorff, *Les cours administratives d'appel* (1991). Specialist books on particular topics include Stirn, *Le Conseil d'Etat* (1991); Mogenet, *Les marchés de l'Etat et de collectivités locales* (2 vols; 1986); J.-P. Costa, *Le Conseil d'Etat dans la société contemporaine* (1993), and Dominique Pouyaud, *La nullité des contrats administratifs* (1991).

The major looseleaf encyclopaedias (*répertoires*) devoted to this area (and designed mainly for practitioners) are *Jurisclasseur administratif* (6 vols; cited as JCA), and Dalloz, *Répertoire de contentieux administratif*. As well as the *Code administratif* published by Dalloz there is a *Code des procédures administratives* issued by Litec.

Administrative law continues to be based more on case law than on legislation. Administrative law cases are reported in the general collections of case law (*Dalloz, Gazette du Palais*, etc.), but also in a special collection – the *Recueil Lebon*, abbreviated to *Rec.* – which contains nearly all the case law emanating from the *Conseil d'Etat* since the start of the 19th century, that of the *Tribunal des Conflits* since 1872, that of the *tribunaux administratifs* since 1953, and that of the *cours administratives d'appel* since 1989. The decisions are published in chronological order and there are subject-matter and party name indexes at the end of each year's volumes. The method of citation is as follows: the level of the court (*Conseil d'Etat, Tribunal des Conflits*, etc.), then the date of the decision, then the name of the party (who is usually claiming against the administration), and finally the page number where the decision is reported. An example would be: *C.E. 2 juillet 1915, Durand, Rec. 473*. Litec also publishes an annual *Recueil de jurisprudence des tribunaux administratifs et des cours administratives d'appel*, and every year La Documentation Française (France's equivalent to HMSO) publishes a thin collection of the most important decisions of the *Conseil d'Etat* for that period. Most of the leading cases are also extracted in M. Long, P. Weil, G. Braibant, P. Delvolvé and B. Genevois, *Les grands arrêts de la jurisprudence administrative* (10th edn, 1993), or in J.-F. Lachaume, *Droit administratif: Les grandes décisions de la jurisprudence* (7th edn, 1993); they are also recorded in the public law journals.

The relevant journals include the *Revue du droit public et de la science politique* (RDP), *Etudes et documents du Conseil d'Etat* (EDCE), *Actualité juridique/Droit administratif* (AJDA), *Cahiers juridiques de l'électricité et du gaz* (CJEG), *Revue internationale de sciences administratives* (RISA), *Droit administratif* (DA), *Revue administrative* (Rev. adm.), and *Revue française de droit administratif* (RFDA). The most important of these journals are the RDP, which contains learned articles, surveys of case law and case notes, the AJDA, which publishes decisions and comments thereon shortly after they have been issued, and the RFDA, even though this was first published only in 1985.

Besides the *Journal Officiel* there is the unofficial *Code administratif* (reissued every few years by Dalloz); this is not a proper codification but rather a collection of public law statutes and regulations. For the codified material regard should be had to the output of the *Journal Officiel*'s own imprint – the *Code rural et code forestier*, the *Code de mines*, the *Code d'urbanisme*, etc.

CHAPTER 5

Civil liberties

THE FRENCH CONCEPT OF FUNDAMENTAL FREEDOMS

Two chief characteristics of the French notion of *libertés publiques* stand out. On the one hand they have an indisputable antiquity: they were developed during revolutionary times and as a result may appear a little anachronistic today. On the other hand there is a lack of uniformity in the rules by which they are governed: though they are increasingly being studied as a separate subject in their own right, they have traditionally been examined as adjuncts to one or more of four other popular legal fields – constitutional law, administrative law, criminal law and civil law. Specialist books on the subject are increasingly common but still a discussion of personal rights is relegated to the textbooks on *droit civil* at the point where they deal with *les personnes*. Under this heading it is common to find material on topics such as abortion, the right to recognition of one's personality, the right to privacy, the right to protection of one's image, and even the intellectual property rights of authors and artists.

The overview provided in this chapter reveals the incompleteness of the protection afforded to fundamental rights in France. As it is divided among several institutions, the process of control, in so far as it is available at all, is not easy to set in motion or to develop. The system is flawed in that there is a variety of 'remedial channels' for violations of fundamental rights. The actual result of a challenge is not always satisfactory either. A decision that a right has been violated may be announced, but frequently an act contrary to statute (such as a ban on a meeting) has already produced its effects, so a judicial decision on the point comes too late as the administration, in the absence of the court action having any suspensory effects, will have already implemented its measure. In these cases only interlocutory injunctions (*sursis à l'exécution*) are effective.

However, the first piece of positive law in this area dates back to the French Revolution. The Declaration of the Rights of Man and of the Citizen (*Déclaration des droits de l'homme et du citoyen*) of 1789 was designed to encompass all individual rights and to guarantee them *vis-à-vis* the state. This was also the aim of the revolutionary human rights declarations of 1793 and 1795, Chapter II of the Republican Constitution of 1848 and the Preambles to the Constitutions of 1946 and 1958. These documents bear witness not only to political fluctuations but also to a broadening of the concept of fundamental freedoms to embrace social and economic rights as well as civil and political rights.

The Preamble to the 1958 Constitution expressly cross-refers to the 1789 and 1946 documents. It solemnly proclaims the attachment of the French people to 'the Rights of Man and the principles of national sovereignty as defined in the Declaration of 1789, confirmed and completed by the Preamble to the Constitution of 1946'. The 1958 Preamble therefore accords the same legal efficacy to the 1789 and 1946 principles as it does to itself and the 1789 Declaration is still part of French law today. The *Déclaration* of 26 August 1789 mentions in its own Preamble that it is based on the consideration that 'ignorance, forgetfulness or contempt of the rights of man are the sole causes of public misfortune and governmental depravity'. It then proceeds to list its tenets in 17 separate articles, not all of them conferring rights. Article 2 asserts that the natural and imprescriptible rights of man are those of liberty, property, security and resistance to oppression; the right to liberty is further expounded in Article 7, while Article 11 states that the free communication of thoughts and opinions is one of the most precious rights of man. Article 12 recognises that the purpose of a police force is to guarantee the rights of man, and Article 13 acknowledges that the upkeep of the police force requires taxation which must be borne by all citizens equally, according to their means. Article 15 is a particularly far-seeing provision: 'Society has the right to demand from every public servant an account of his administration.' The 'inviolable and sacred' right to property is asserted by Article 17.

The chief features of the Declaration are universality and individualism. It was influenced by the enlightened views of Voltaire and Montesquieu, and to that extent it is an expression of the rational conception of mankind and of natural law. That explains its universality: all persons, however different they might appear to be, enjoy the same rights. But the Declaration's focus on individualism comes out here too: the rights and freedoms are acknowledged as belonging to individual persons, the rights of groups of people being largely ignored. The Declaration's wording is as a result very abstract; it does not deal with concrete conflictual situations but rather with impersonal, general problems. This is also partly due to the ambitions and idealistic character of the philosophy of the Age of Enlightenment in the 18th century. According to this way of looking at things, all that was required to guarantee rights and freedoms was to proclaim them solemnly. The declaring of human rights was viewed as more important than guaranteeing them through workable procedures. This French attitude is different from the English one, which for centuries has concentrated on ensuring effective trial procedures (e.g. through granting writs of *habeas corpus*). The criticism has often been made that the French are fond of using grandiloquent phraseology but do not in practice provide effective civil libertarian protection.

The rather theoretical concept of *libertés publiques* as embodied in the *Déclaration* was first questioned during the *travaux préparatories* for the Constitution of 27 October 1946. More effective protection and the need to recognise economic and social rights became significant, the latter finding a place in the Preamble to that Constitution, still in force today because of its mention in 1958. Besides cross-referring to the 1789 Declaration, the 1946 Preamble contained the following 'novelties':

- equality between men and women;
- the right to political asylum;
- the right to work and to join a trade union, to freedom from discrimination, to associate and to strike;
- the right of workers to have a say in their conditions of work and in the running of their place of employment;
- recognition of nationalised industries;
- the right of everyone, but notably children, mothers and elderly workers, to health care, material security, rest and leisure; and
- the right of adults and children to equal access to education, professional training and culture.

Such a development meant that rights were henceforth viewed in a positive light and as part and parcel of the character of a welfare state, made necessary by economic and social 'progress'. At the same time as 'abstract individualism' faded into the background the concept of *libertés publiques* became relativised because it was seen as linked to economic and social development.

MECHANISMS FOR PROTECTING CIVIL LIBERTIES

In France as in other countries two questions are of overriding importance when evaluating *libertés publiques*: who has the power to make rules concerning those liberties, and who ensures that these rules are respected? According to the 1958 Constitution the former task falls chiefly to the National Assembly and Senate as the representatives of the people's will. But administrative authorities have a role to play as well. Unlike in some other European countries, in France fundamental freedoms are not formally laid down in the Constitution itself: to that extent the position is the same as in the United Kingdom.

Article 34 of the Constitution provides that among the matters to be regulated by statutes (*lois*) are the following:

les droits civiques et les garanties fondamentales accordées aux citoyens pour l'exercice des libertés publiques . . . la détermination des crimes et délits ainsi que les peines qui leur sont applicables; la procédure pénale . . .

(the civic rights and fundamental guarantees which are necessary for citizens to exercise their civil liberties; . . . the definition of serious and less serious offences (*crimes* and *délits*) and punishments for those offences; criminal trial procedures . . .)

In these areas one or more statutes lay down the details of the relevant rights and freedoms. By way of contrast, Article 34 goes on to say that Parliament can enact statutes only on the general principles (*principes généraux*) concerning employment law, social welfare, education and training, and private property; more detailed regulations on these topics are a matter for the government. However, some statutes which pre-date the 1958 Constitution and which affect particular freedoms are still in force, examples being the law of 30 June 1881 on the right of assembly and the law of 1 July 1901 on the right of association. The main disadvantage of this system is an acute proliferation of particular rules. As there are often amendments to take account of, it can be difficult to get a precise picture of the legal position affecting a particular right at any set time. Nor is it easy to detect any common theoretical foundation underpinning the various rights and enabling the prediction of new ones.

As mentioned in Chapter 3, at times of crisis the powers of Parliament and the fundamental freedoms themselves can be restricted. This can occur, first, if the Cabinet declares a state of siege (*état de siège*) or a state of emergency (*état d'urgence*), as during the Algerian civil war. During the continuance of these states the government can limit the exercise of rights and freedoms by, for example, regulating people's movements, prohibiting residence or meetings in certain places, or deporting people, but the declarations require Parliamentary approval if they are to endure for longer than 12 days. Secondly, rights can be suspended if there is a state of crisis, something expressly provided for by Article 16 of the 1958 Constitution. The people must be informed of the President's actions during such a crisis and Parliament must meet immediately, even though, during the period in which Article 16 is operative, it is deprived of all its powers to make laws, including those regarding *libertés publiques*.

When exercising their 'policing' functions, administrative authorities can issue regulations. In France one must distinguish between the general policing function, which ensures public security and order (*see* Article 88 of the Code of Local Administration, *Code de l'administration communale*), and special policing functions, which apply in particular sectors (e.g. the railway police). The body issuing regulations has the difficult task, at the level of *départements* and local districts, of giving real substance to rights and freedoms in a way which does not violate the rights protected by the Constitution or by relevant statutes. The local authorities must, for example, limit people's freedom of movement or right of assembly if particular circumstances prevail. The administrative authorities are therefore closely involved in making rights and freedoms a practical reality. If illegal actions are taken they can be challenged in front of the administrative courts. However, the *Conseil d'Etat* has developed the notion of 'exceptional circumstances' (*circonstances exceptionnelles*), which allows mistaken administrative actions to be regarded as legal if they have been committed in an extraordinary situation. This also applies in the context of *libertés publiques*. 'Exceptional circumstances' can therefore enlarge the powers of administrative authorities: they can restrict the exercise of freedoms in a way which would normally be illegal. Over and above this, *libertés publiques* must always take second place to public policy (*ordre public*), a doctrine which is sometimes also invoked in the United Kingdom in order to limit a claimed freedom.

On account of the fact that fundamental rights and freedoms are not referred to in the body of the French Constitution itself, but only in the Preamble, some commentators conclude that *libertés publiques* are not legally binding norms: they view the Preamble as merely explaining the intent behind the Constitution, as more of a programme than a set of legal rules. Today this position seems untenable. The preferred view amongst academics as well as judges is that the Preamble does have constitutional status, and several consequences flow from this. The rights contained in the Preamble are for the most part positively worded and can therefore be seen as directly applicable provisions which have to be observed by all state bodies. The phrases which refer to objectives, and which require further Parliamentary elaboration, are an exception to this: individuals then have rights, but these are not actionable. In practice the lack of a separate constitutional court allows Parliament to ignore the Constitution's provisions and to limit or leave unregulated the fundamental freedoms. This raises the question of how exactly to control and implement civil liberties. The problems associated with giving legal protection against violations of fundamental freedoms are complex and difficult, as different methods are used without creating any guarantee of comprehensive control. However, in the two Constitutions since the Second World War there have been impulses leading to a direct – albeit limited – degree of constitutional control, first through the *Comité constitutionnel* (1946) and then through the *Conseil constitutionnel* (1958). The roles of the *Conseil d'Etat* and of the ordinary courts also need to be mentioned.

The *Conseil constitutionnel*

The creation and powers of the *Conseil constitutionnel* have already been dealt with in Chapter 3. Here it is only necessary to add that the *Conseil* consists of nine members, three being appointed for a nine-year period by each of the State President, the President of the National Assembly and the President of the Senate. The appointees are not usually career judges who have already served in other courts; instead they tend to be retired politicians who have gained a reputation for wisdom and impartiality. For present purposes the most important of the Council's many tasks (which include the oversight of elections) is the control *a priori* (i.e. before they are officially proclaimed) of the constitutionality of statutes specifically referred to it. Unlike in the United States or Germany, there is no procedure before the *Conseil constitutionnel* whereby a *citizen* can challenge the constitutionality of a statute, whether before or after it has been promulgated. The *Conseil's* jurisdiction can be invoked only by the State President, the Prime Minister, the Presidents of the National Assembly and of the Senate, or (since 1974) by 60 members of either of the chambers of Parliament. When they sit to consider a draft law submitted for their comments the *conseillers* do not listen to or read arguments put to them by advocates for the opposing points of view: they decide the matter for themselves, referring if they wish to the *travaux préparatoires* preceding the law in question. Some of the *Conseil's* most influential decisions (as can also be said of the *Conseil d'Etat*) have been in cases where the application has in fact been rejected. Unlike the judgments of other courts in France, and those in United Kingdom courts, the rulings of the *Conseil constitutionnel* are given *in abstracto*, not depending on the facts of a particular case; although in recent years they have become more detailed, at times they can be no less cryptic than the notoriously brief judgments of, say, the *Cour de Cassation*.

Nevertheless, the recent achievements of the *Conseil constitutionnel* in protecting civil liberties have been quite considerable. After a period of apparent quiescence from 1958, the breakthrough came in a momentous decision on 16 July 1971. In May 1970 the Cabinet had ordered the dissolution of a small left-wing political party, *La Gauche Prolétarienne*. Activists such as Jean-Paul Sartre and Simone de Beauvoir were so incensed by this that they set up another group calling itself the *Association des Amis de la Cause du Peuple* (named after the title of the banned party's newspaper). The government ordered the local prefect not to accept the group's registration papers (which it needed to deposit in order to obtain a legal personality). A local administrative court, however, was brave enough to annul the prefect's refusal on the basis that he had exceeded his powers. The government thereupon introduced a Bill in Parliament to widen the prefect's powers. Although this Bill passed through Parliament it was then referred to the *Conseil constitutionnel* by the President of the Senate, under Article 61 of the Constitution. That the *Conseil constitutionnel* held the Bill to be unconstitutional was surprising enough, but the really startling thing was the basis it chose for its decision: it relied upon the 1946 Preamble's solemn reaffirmation of 'the fundamental principles recognised by the statutes of the Republic' and it declared that one of those principles was freedom of association:

> By virtue of this principle associations may be formed freely and they can be made public on condition of no more than the deposit of a declaration; and therefore . . . the formation of associations, even if they appear to be

vitiated by nullity or to have an illicit objective, cannot be subjected to the prior intervention of administrative authority, or even of judicial authority.

One of the strange aspects of this decision is that the 1946 Constitution had itself expressly provided that its Preamble was not to have constitutional force (although Article 81 appeared to contradict this by providing that all French citizens were entitled to enjoy the rights and freedoms set out in the Preamble, and in 1956 the *Conseil d'Etat* held that those rights and freedoms could not therefore be diminished by government action). The 1958 Constitution was silent as to the effect of its Preamble, but one might have assumed that the same principle would have prevailed. That it did not is an indication of how important a role the *Conseil constitutionnel* was taking upon itself. Unfortunately, as is its wont, the *Conseil* did not elaborate upon the reasons for its decision and there are no accompanying submissions or reports which might provide clues to the line of thought adopted by the *conseillers*, as there might be in the report of an ordinary civil or administrative case.

Since 1971 the *Conseil constitutionnel* has consolidated its position as France's final line of protection for civil liberties. In 1973 it announced that only Parliament, and not the government, could pass laws imposing a deprivation of liberty on persons found guilty of minor crimes (*contraventions*). In doing so it relied expressly upon Article 66 of the Constitution: 'No one may be arbitrarily detained. The judicial authority, guardian of individual liberty, ensures respect for this principle in the conditions laid down by *loi*.' By implication it also employed Article 7 of the 1789 Declaration: 'No man may be accused, arrested or detained except in cases laid down by *loi* and according to the forms prescribed by *loi*.' For a while it looked as if imprisonments based on regulations were all invalid, but the two other 'supreme' courts in France soon stepped in to redress the balance: the *Conseil d'Etat* in a decision on 17 January 1974, and the *Cour de Cassation* in a decision on 26 February 1974. Both pointed out that Article 464 of the Criminal Code did in fact provide statutory backing for the imposition of imprisonment by regulations. On this occasion, then, the sting of the *Conseil constitutionnel* was pulled. It is perhaps fortunate for future developments that before this could happen, just a month after its own decision in the case dealing with *contraventions*, the *Conseil constitutionnel* issued another pronouncement which subjected the validity of a *loi* to a principle contained in the 1789 Declaration. This was in a case where the *Conseil* declared unconstitutional a proposed legislative provision which said that a taxpayer who expended more than a certain amount of money each year could not argue that he or she was attempting to evade payment of normal taxes. This was said to be contrary to 'the principle of equality before the law contained in the Declaration of 1789'.

After getting its fingers burnt in the early part of 1974 it was well over a year before the *Conseil constitutionnel* had both the opportunity and the courage to return to its task of ensuring protection for fundamental civil liberties. In January 1975 it refused to strike down any part of a proposed statute on abortion, even though the Bill gave a virtually absolute right to abortion if the mother demanded it during the first 10 weeks of pregnancy. The *Conseil* could find nothing in the constitutional texts or in the 'fundamental principles recognised by the statutes of the Republic' which was contravened by the proposed Bill. The reasoning of the decision is even less transparent than usual, perhaps because the *Conseil* did not want to become embroiled in what is for most individuals a very personal and controversial issue. The case also involved consideration of the European Convention on Human Rights, an aspect which is further examined below.

In July 1975 the *Conseil constitutionnel* struck down another proposed law, this time one which extended the discretion of the President of the *tribunal de police* to order that a person charged with a *délit* (the second of the three categories of offences into which French criminal law is divided) should be tried by a court consisting of only one judge. The first ground for the decision was the same as that used in the decision in 1973, *égalité devant la justice* (derived from the 1789 Declaration), but to this was added the ground that Article 34 of the Constitution reserves to Parliament the making of rules concerning criminal procedure and Parliament could not delegate this power to another official, even a senior judge. This preparedness to control the application of all rules 'of a constitutional character' which regulate the passage of *lois* derives from Article 61 of the Constitution and the *Conseil constitutionnel* has taken its role very seriously in this respect.

The principle of *égalité devant la justice* was again invoked in a decision of 15 July 1976, where the *Conseil* upheld a proposed *loi* allowing the files of candidates for admission to the civil service to be examined by the selection panel: the *loi* was acceptable because it provided that if one candidate's file was to be looked at then all the other candidates' files were to be looked at too. The *Conseil* in this case also relied upon Article 6 of the 1789 Declaration, part of which reads, 'all citizens, being equal in the eyes of the law are equally admissible to all . . . public employment, according to their capacity and without other distinction than that of their virtues and their talents'.

Perhaps the second most important decision of the *Conseil*, after the groundbreaking one of 1971, is that of 12 January 1977, when it struck down a proposed *loi* which gave power to police officers to search any vehicle on the public highway. It was not the power itself which the *Conseil* found objectionable but rather the lack of restrictions on its use: it did not require the police to have any kind of suspicion, or to give any reason for the search; all that had to be ensured was that the owner or driver of the vehicle was present at the time. Not the least remarkable feature of this decision is that at the time it was taken the President of the *Conseil*, Roger Frey, was himself a former right-wing Minister of the Interior.

In November 1977 the *Conseil* considered a proposed statute (the *loi Guermeur*) regarding private (i.e. mainly Catholic) schools in France. This statute imposed on teachers an obligation to respect 'the proper character of the establishment' in which they taught. Asked to rule that this was a breach of the teachers' right to freedom of conscience, the *Conseil* held that it was not: it was 'a legitimate measure to maintain the character and nature of the educational establishments involved, and therefore a constitutionally permissible manner of implementing freedom of education'. Six months later the *Cour de Cassation* clearly had this decision in mind when it held that a Catholic school could legitimately dismiss a divorced Catholic teacher who had remarried.

During the 1980s the *Conseil constitutionnel* continued to develop its stance on civil liberties, most of its decisions elaborating the notion of equality, perhaps no coincidence in a decade dominated by socialist politicians. It applied the notion in contexts as diverse as those of voting rights, access to jobs and offices, taxation procedures, judge and jury issues, and penalties for criminal offences. In a 1984 case it refused to condemn a law which allowed high-ranking civil servants to retire at a higher age than others: the *Conseil* was prepared to tolerate differential treatment between groups of people provided a rational and objective justification for the difference could be presented. In 1986 approval was given to a statute which removed juries from the *cours d'assises* when suspected terrorists were being tried (replacing them with a further six professional judges), but the statute was declared *pro tanto* unconstitutional in so far as it also applied to non-terrorist trials. In 1989, in a decision dealing with the penal provisions in a taxation law, the *Conseil* emphasised that as well as upholding the 1789 *Déclaration* its task was to apply the *principes fondamentaux reconnus par les lois de la République,* and these were taken to include the principle against retroactivity of penal laws and the rights of defendants to challenge the arguments of the prosecution. In a subsequent decision the *Conseil* pointed out that penalties must be proportionate to the offence committed (*le principe de proportionalité*).

During the first 16 years of its existence there were only nine references to the *Conseil constitutionnel* under Articles 54 or 61; during the next 12 years there were 113. Since 1986 there have been about 15 per year. In addition there is a handful of cases each year on whether a proposed legislative text is within the competence of the government (Article 37) or Parliament (Article 41) to make. There is now widespread agreement that the role of the *Conseil constitutionnel* in protecting civil liberties in France is central and indispensable. In its elaboration of the 1789 rights, its determination to resurrect the political, economic and social principles enunciated in the 1946 Preamble, and its repeated reliance on fundamental principles recognised by the statutes of the Republic, it has quickly obtained for itself a high reputation for innovative and trenchant judgments.

The role of the *Conseil d'Etat*

The *Conseil d'Etat* controls the making of regulations through judicial review actions (*recours pour excès de pouvoir*). Administrative acts are annulled if they are contrary to *légalité*, that is, the complete body of laws which bind the administration (see Chapter 4). This includes, of course, the Constitution, as well as its Preamble. As far as the Constitution is concerned, the *Conseil d'Etat* annuls administrative acts which directly contravene it only if they do not rest upon some statutory foundation. If the administrative act or regulation does rest upon a statutory foundation then the responsibility for the flaw is not that of the administration but of Parliament, which is not subject to any retrospective constitutional control. Nor can the constitutionality of a statute be questioned incidentally during other proceedings. On the other hand, the control by the *Conseil d'Etat* over the constitutionality of the administration is all the more meaningful in the area of civil liberties precisely because an individual's civil liberties *are* usually protected by statutes: the action for judicial review enables the *Conseil d'Etat* to annul regulations or administrative acts which contravene a statute governing a particular civil liberty. The *Conseil d'Etat* can also examine the way in which an administrative decision is being enforced, provided the alleged illegality is considerable and the enforcement of the decision would lead to a disadvantage which would be difficult to remedy.

Not the least important of the achievements of the *Conseil d'Etat* has been the development of *principes généraux du droit*, already mentioned in Chapter 1. To some extent these have acted as a substitute for constitutional review and many of them coincide with the *principes fondamentaux* recognised by the *Conseil constitutionnel*, thereby acquiring a constitutional status, even if the *Conseil d'Etat* does not expressly concede this. Examples are the principle of equality, the right of accused persons to defend themselves and the need for impartiality on the part of judges and other adjudicators. Given the similarity of some of the complaints being lodged in the two areas, and the developed state of administrative law in France, cross-fertilisation of ideas between administrative law and civil liberties law is, of course, an understandable and healthy phenomenon.

Principes généraux du droit seem to have been first referred to in the *Trompier-Gravier* decision in 1944, and in the 1959 case involving the *Syndicat Général des Ingénieurs-Conseils* the *Conseil d'Etat* confirmed that the general principles are applicable even to post-1958 government legislation. *Trompier-Gravier* was a case where a local prefect's revocation of a concession to run a newspaper kiosk in the Boulevard Saint Denis in Paris was quashed because the concessionaire had not been given the opportunity to put her arguments for its continuation (a breach of the *audi alteram partem* rule). Similarly, in *Davin* (1966) the expulsion of a pupil from a school was quashed because the headmistress had not given reasons for her action, and in 1989, after being asked for its opinion (*avis*), the

Conseil d'Etat ruled that pupils at schools could wear religious symbols (e.g. a headscarf worn by Muslim girls) provided these were not, for instance, provocative or dangerous. In *Joudoux* (1957) the court refused to overturn a decision by the Minister of the Interior to ban sales of the Jehovah Witnesses' magazine *The Watchtower*, and in *Lebon* (1978) it upheld the dismissal of a school-teacher because he had allegedly committed sex offences; in both instances the *Conseil d'Etat* said that the measure taken was not out of proportion to the 'offence' in question. On the other hand, in *Vicini* (1965) a prefect's decision concerning a camp for gypsies was overturned because it violated the basic principle of personal freedom of movement.

The *Conseil d'Etat* has also been involved in decisions regarding the powers of the police. In *Lecomte et Daramy* (1949) it placed a strict liability on the police for the shooting of innocent bystanders, while in *Bernard* (1954) and *Marabout* (1972) the police were held liable for, respectively, the discharge by an officer of his gun while he was on duty and the failure to keep a cul-de-sac clear of traffic. As regards 'policing' measures taken by public bodies and municipalities, the *Conseil d'Etat* has struck down a ban preventing a photographer from entering Chartres Cathedral (*Carlier*, 1949) but upheld a prefect's ban on certain photographers at Mont St Michel (*Leroy*, 1968).

The civil liberties of immigrants have also been much influenced by the jurisprudence of the *Conseil d'Etat*, as well of course by conflicting legislation passed by successive French governments in the past 15 years or so. In *Pardov* (1975) the *Conseil d'Etat* held that violating the immigration laws on entry into, and residence in, the country did not of itself constitute a threat to public order (*ordre public*) such as would justify removal (*refoulement*) or deportation (*expulsion*). Two years later, in *Dridi*, the *Conseil* went one logical step further by holding that no violation of any criminal law was an automatic threat to *ordre public* in this context. Subsequent protections have resulted more from the supervision exercised by the *Conseil constitutionnel vis-à-vis* draft statutes: in 1980 that Council struck down a provision in a proposed Immigration Law which permitted the detention of allegedly illegal immigrants for up to seven days without prior judicial approval; when the government replaced the provision with one which allowed judicial detention for up to six days, and then, in 1986, sought to allow three-day extensions of this period, the *Conseil constitutionnel* again intervened to uphold individual liberty. In 1992 the Council once more prevented the government from authorising any period of non-judicial detention of an illegal immigrant prior to his or her deportation.

The role of ordinary courts

Lastly, the ordinary courts have also been involved in defending civil liberties in France. Criminal law and, even more so, criminal procedure are areas which can have a great significance for individual freedoms. Civil liberties are particularly important in the context of arrests, powers of search and *in camera* judicial interrogations. They can be said to exist only if they are anchored in statutory provisions and observed in everyday practice. Civil courts can deal with certain 'acts of state' (*voies de fait*) committed by the administration. These are clearly unlawful administrative actions which obviously infringe basic civil liberties such as freedom of movement, privacy or rights over private property. Traditionally, as explained in Chapter 4, such outrages are not categorised as administrative acts but as matters to be dealt with by the civil courts. In addition, these courts are involved in cases of unlawful expropriation of land (*l'emprise irrégulière*): they establish the degree of damage caused by the expropriation but administrative courts retain jurisdiction over the lawfulness of the expropriation in the first place. The area which has been most affected by the criminal and civil courts is probably that of privacy; the courts have certainly been more activist in this area in France than they have in the United Kingdom.

As long ago as 1858 a court in the *département* of Seine held that the family of a famous actress, Rachel, could sue for damages in respect of the unauthorised publication of portraits of the actress as she lay on her deathbed (*Felix* v *O'Connell*). Ever since then the French have believed that their law guarantees to each individual the right over his or her own likeness, further exemplified in a well-known 1890s law-suit involving the artist Whistler, where the Court of Appeal for Paris decided that a portraitist could make no use of a portrait which the subject had commissioned but which the artist did not wish to hand over (*Eden* v *Whistler*). Many other famous people have succeeded in obtaining damages from the French courts for the unauthorised use of their photographs; they range from Brigitte Bardot and Ursula Andress to Prince Rainier of Monaco and Britain's Duchess of York. The law has been limited, however, by a decision of the Paris Court of Appeal to the effect that if an individual appears in public he or she gives implied consent to being photographed.

Some would classify this right to one's likeness as separate from the right to one's privacy, but in practice they overlap. The courts have long held that the general tortious right of action conferred by Article 1382 of the *Code civil* (*see* Chapter 9) is available for the protection of a person's private life. Moreover, the statute of 29 July 1881 on freedom of the press provides that statements, even if true, cannot be published if they relate to an individual's private life. A statute of 17 July 1970 inserted a new paragraph into Article 9 of the *Code civil*. This now states quite simply: '*Chacun a droit au respect de sa vie privée*' (Everyone has the right to respect for his or her private life). Four years later France ratified the European Convention on Human Rights, Article 8 of which reads very similarly: '*Toute personne a droit au respect de sa vie privée et familiale, de son domicile et de sa correspondance.*' Even the descendants of someone who is dead can now sue if the deceased's family's privacy has been improperly invaded, although recent decisions have tended not to support such claims because of the restrictions they would place on historical publications or doumentary features. The 1970 statute also inserted new articles into the *Code pénal*; these made it a criminal offence to bug a person's private conversation or to photograph a person in a private place (unless of course the person consents). English law, of course, as the Prince and Princess of Wales know to their cost, has no law preventing this kind of behaviour. On the other hand, the French and English law on protection of computerised data is similar because both systems have had to comply with a Council of Europe Convention on the topic. In France there is a *Commission nationale de l'informatique et des libertés*; this oversees the operation of the law and deals with individual complaints. Its 1992 Annual Report indicates that over 26,000 queries were raised with the Commission, more than double the number for the previous year.

As regards physical integrity, freedom of movement is first protected in France via the criminal law, which penalises false imprisonment (*séquestration*) whenever it occurs without proper authority. A person also has the right not to have his or her home invaded: not only is this a crime, it is also a principle recognised by the *Conseil constitutionnel*. But civil law also plays a part here by striking down any clauses in an agreement which have the effect of restricting an individual's movements; an example would be a condition attached to a gift whereby the donee agrees to live in a certain town. Clauses of this nature are acceptable only if the restriction is justified because of a legitimate interest of the other party, such as where an employee or franchisee agrees not to undertake work which puts him or her in a conflict of interest with the employer or franchisor (*clauses de non-concurrence*). In a case in 1980 a firm called Cyna, which held a franchise from another firm called Natalys, failed to persuade a court to strike down a clause in the franchise agreement whereby Cyna had agreed, after termination of the contract, not to compete with Natalys, nor to affiliate to another firm competing with Natalys, for a period of two years; the *cour d'appel* held that the clause was valid because it did not impose a restriction on *liberté de commerce* which was unlimited in time or space. The courts have also relied upon the right to physical integrity in order to prevent people from, in effect, 'selling' their bodies. In 1973 four young strip-tease artists (the Ladybirds) were not allowed to enforce a contract with a nightclub owner. It is illegal for a man to sell his sperm or for a woman to sell her eggs, and contracts of surrogate motherhood (*les conventions de mères porteuses*) are struck down because of Article 1128 of the *Code civil*: '*il n'y a que les choses qui sont dans le commerce qui puissent être l'objet des conventions*' (only things which can be bought and sold can form the subject-matter of agreements). However, French law does recognise that organs of the body *can* be transferred provided the transfer is voluntary, anonymous and not for any consideration (*volontaire, anonyme et gratuit*): a 1952 statute permits blood donations, a 1976 statute (*loi Caillavet*) allows organ transplants, a 1988 statute (*loi Huriet*) regulates biomedical research on human beings, and a 1991 statute facilitates the establishment of sperm banks. A draft bill has been prepared on embryo research. French law also goes further than English law in protecting bodies which are no longer alive. In one recent case the *Cour de Cassation* awarded damages to the family of a person whose body had been negligently allowed to decompose in the defendants' hospital.

FRANCE AND THE EUROPEAN CONVENTION ON HUMAN RIGHTS

As mentioned earlier, France did not ratify the European Convention on Human Rights until 1974 and did not allow the right of individual petition until 1981. The delay in ratifying (the Convention having been signed in 1950) may be attributable to France's wish not to subject its constitutional provision on emergency powers (Article 16) to international scrutiny, especially in view of the Algerian crisis in the 1960s; alternatively it may be due to the fear that Protocol One, which guarantees education rights, would tilt the balance in favour of private (i.e. church-based) schools. There was also a suspicion, since vindicated, that France's rules of criminal procedure might not be consistent with the Convention's standards.

By ratifying the Convention, due to Article 55 of the Constitution, France incorporated the Convention into its domestic law and accorded it *priorité*. As a result, judges in France have been able to rely upon the Convention when deciding cases, and several have done so. Others, though, have sought to place obstacles in the way of the Convention's direct application, by relying, for example, on the principle that an international treaty must take second place to a domestic statute enacted after the treaty has been ratified. The *Cour de Cassation* has now settled down to giving the Convention priority in all instances and the *Conseil d'Etat* looks like following suit (*Nicolo*, 1989). Most of the cases where a French judge has applied the Convention have involved questions of procedure or of criminal law, many of them requiring consideration of Articles 5(3) and 6(1) of the Convention, which say, respectively, that an arrested person must be brought promptly (*aussitôt*) before a judge and that every person has a right to have his or her case dealt with by a court within a reasonable time (*dans un délai raisonnable*). In a significant case decided by the *cour d'appel de Versailles* in 1989, a delay of 16 months between the date of a person's committal for trial by the *cour d'assises* and his actual appearance there was held to be unreasonable. In 1984 the *Cour de Cassation* held that an administrative authority, which had refused to renew the passport of someone who owed money to the Exchequer, was in violation of Article 2(2) of Protocol Four of the Convention, which guarantees the right to leave a country unless such exit is denied by law on specified serious grounds such as national security.

France has also been in the dock many times at Strasbourg. In recent years more cases by far have been lodged against France under the Convention than against any other state: 400 in 1991 and 353 in 1992. By early 1993 there had been 27 cases brought against France in the European Court of Human Rights since the right of individual petition was recognised in 1981; countless more had been considered by the European Commission of Human Rights. Of the 27 cases before the Court, 19 have to some extent been lost by the French government. Probably the most memorable of these defeats have been in *Kruslin* (1990), where the Court held that France's imprecise law permitting a *juge d'instruction* to order the tapping of a suspect's telephone lines was a breach of Article 8 on the right to a private life because the interference was not sufficiently 'prescribed by law' as required by Article 8(2); in *Pham Hoang* (1992), where a presumption of guilt raised by France's tax code – and denial of the right to a lawyer in the *Cour de Cassation* – were held to be a breach of Article 6(2) and (3); in *Funke* (1992), where the tax code's tendency to draw conclusions of guilt from a taxpayer's silence in response to queries was held to be a breach of Article 6(1); and in *X v France* (1993), where the Court decided that an Algerian's expulsion from France on the ground that he was a threat to public order was again a breach of Article 8 because it interfered with the right to a family life.

CONTROL OF THE BROADCASTING MEDIA

Freedom of expression, and political freedom within a state, are heavily dependent upon how the state is structured, the degree to which it is pluralistic and the extent of state influence on information services. In France there has often been criticism in this context. The press is, as it has always been, mainly centred on Paris. In the provinces the daily newspapers carry mainly local news stories. The quality press is losing ground to the sensational press, even though the latter does not have the size of readership enjoyed by the tabloids in Britain. Nearly all the daily papers are in financial difficulties which cannot be solved merely by advertising revenue. One significant reason for this is the development of audio-visual media.

The law concerning audio-visual media (radio and television) has in recent years been radically reformed on three occasions. Formerly subject to a state monopoly or to executive control, the state radio service (and the private channels which the government permitted to broadcast from abroad, such as Radio and TV Luxembourg, Europe I and Radio Monte Carlo) competed with private broadcasting stations (*radios libres*). A statute in 1981 enabled the monopoly to be changed so that radio stations could broadcast on different frequency modulations, and a further statute in 1982 created a whole new legislative foundation for radio and television services, based upon the principle that there was freedom of the air-waves.

This law was very significant. In effect it constituted the first example of a French government divesting itself of its supervisory powers and transferring them to a new body charged with maintaining the independence of an important public service. Legally speaking, a public broadcasting monopoly remained in place in the shape of a public body administered by state or quasi-state officials but accessible to private concerns. The body concerned was entitled the *Haute Autorité de la Communication Audio-visuelle* and its composition was comparable to that of the *Conseil constitutionnel* – nine members elected for nine years, three chosen by each of the Presidents of the Republic, the National Assembly and the Senate. It was charged with ensuring freedom and variety of expression, as well as the impartiality and independence of the public broadcasting service, and it was to achieve its goals by making recommendations, issuing decisions and exercising controls. The Authority was complemented by a *Conseil national de la communication audio-visuelle*, which consisted of 56 persons appointed for a three-year period and representing groups such as cultural organisations, consumer associations and workers in the broadcasting industry; this *Conseil* could be consulted on broadcasting issues both by the *Haute Autorité* and by the government.

In 1986 the socialists lost power and the new conservative government wasted little time in amending its predecessor's laws on broadcasting. It considered the 1982 law to be ineffective in securing *liberté de la communication* because it permitted too much power to be retained by the state or state-controlled bodies. A new balance between public and private sector involvement in broadcasting services was called for. The resulting proposed statute was submitted to the *Conseil constitutionnel* for an assessment of its constitutionality. The Council gave the draft a clean bill of health but took the opportunity to assert categorically that plurality of socio-cultural viewpoints is a valuable constitutional objective and one of the preconditions for a democratic society. The main consequence of the 1986 statute (*loi Léotard*) was the abolition of the *Haute Autorité* and its replacement by a *Commission nationale de la communication et des libertés* (CNCL). This was given 13 members, only six of whom were overtly political appointees, and it was allocated the tasks of authorising the use of telecommunication services in the private sector and of monitoring the programmes and advertisements broadcast by such users to ensure their plurality. It also had to publish an annual report on its activities.

Once more, however, this new structure for broadcasting services was not destined to endure. President Mitterrand and the socialist party did not conceal their dislike for it, mainly because it seemed to be giving too much ground to the private sector (it had effectively privatised one of the existing television channels – TF1). When the reins of power changed hands again in 1988 yet another statute was prepared and enacted (in January 1989). The

CNCL was replaced by the *Conseil supérieur de l'audio-visuel* (CSA). Like the 1982 *Haute Autorité*, the CSA has nine members, the three Presidents (of the Republic, the National Assembly and the Senate) each nominating three individuals for a six-year term. Amongst the powers given to the new body are the right to deprive a broadcasting licensee of its licence and the authority to impose a monetary sanction. Again the law was submitted in draft to the *Conseil constitutionnel*, but the *Conseil* could see nothing unconstitutional in it, even though sanctions are supposedly the preserve of judicial and not administrative authorities.

FURTHER READING

There is an account in English of selected aspects of civil liberties in France in Kramer, *Comparative Civil Rights and Liberties* (1982); he deals with freedom of speech, freedom of association, the relationship between church and state, race and ethnic relations and criminal proceedings. John Bell, in *French Constitutional Law* (1992), devotes one long chapter to fundamental freedoms; it covers freedom of the person (as regards the police, the criminal law, one's privacy and one's right to health), freedom of association, freedom of education, freedom in employment, freedom of communication and information, freedom of property and freedom of enterprise.

For good accounts in French see C. Leclercq, *Libertés publiques* (1991); J. Robert and J. Duffar, *Droits de l'homme et libertés fondamentales* (5th edn, 1993); J. Rivero, *Les libertés publiques* (4th edn, 1989; 2 vols); Colliard, *Libertés publiques* (7th edn, 1989); Langlois, *Le guide du citoyen face à la police* (1989); Tiberghien, *La protection des réfugiés en France* (2nd edn, 1988); C. Debbasch, *Droit de l'audio-visuel* (3rd edn, 1993); Derieux, *Droit de la communication* (1991). In the *Que Sais-Je?* series, see J. Morange, *Les libertés publiques* (5th edn, 1993), J.-C. Masclet, *Textes sur les libertés publiques* (1988) and P. Bilger and B. Prévost, *Le droit de la presse* (2nd edn, 1990). A useful work of reference is L. Favoreu and L. Philip, *Les grandes décisions du Conseil constitutionnel* (7th edn, 1993), and a good study of the contribution made by ordinary courts in this area is Stavros Tsiklitiras, *La protection effective des libertés publiques par le juge judiciaire en droit français* (1991).

CHAPTER 6

Criminal law and criminal procedure

INTRODUCTION

As is the case in so many legal fields, the differences between French and English criminal law and procedure are often exaggerated. Whatever the discrepancies in theory, in practice the outcome in individual cases is likely to be the same. Increasingly the ethos of fairness, of defendants' rights and of consideration for the victim is pervading both systems. While the European Convention on Human Rights has not been directly responsible for any harmonisation of practice in this context, its brooding presence must nevertheless serve as a reminder to policy-makers and decision-takers that there are certain basic standards which must not be ignored.

Reform of criminal law (*droit pénal*) was one of the main aims of the Revolutionaries at the end of the 18th century. Prior to then the criminal justice system had operated very unfairly, being heavily weighted against the workers and peasants and in favour of the aristocracy. In 1791 a new draft criminal code was published, but it was not until 1810 that a final version was agreed and entered into force. Although this *Code pénal* appeared to operate satisfactorily in the early part of the 19th century, it became increasingly outmoded. In 1892 an attempt was made to prepare a new code but came to nothing; further efforts initiated in 1934 and 1974 also proved fruitless, despite the publication of proposed amendments in 1976 and 1981. It was only when the socialists came to power in 1981 that a really meaningful revision got under way. The Minister for Justice at the time, Robert Badinter (now President of the *Conseil constitutionnel*) was appointed President of a Commission to prepare a code which would reflect the spirit of the age, in particular the need to recognise and protect human rights. Badinter's Commission completed the first three books of its draft legislation in 1986 but no action was taken during the next two years when the Gaullists were back in government. Only at the end of 1988 did the Commission renew its efforts to achieve change by issuing Book 4 of the intended code, and Parliament began debating the recommendations in April 1989.

In all, four different proposed laws had to be considered. The first general law, constituting Book 1 of the new code, was debated at irregular intervals until April 1991. Later that summer Parliament looked at Book 2 (offences against the person) and Book 4 (offences against the state and public order). Book 3, on offences against property, was discussed by the Senate in the autumn of 1991 and by the National Assembly in the following spring. A joint Parliamentary committee (*commission mixte paritaire*) then prepared a final agreed draft of all four books and the complete package was approved by Parliament in April 1992. In October 1992 one final statute was enacted to make consequential amendments to the code of criminal procedure and other codes (*loi d'adaptation*); it also made provision for the creation of Book 5 in the new code.

The original intention was to bring the new *Code pénal* into force on 1 March 1993. Later the commencement date had to be postponed to 1 September 1993, and then to 1 March 1994. As from that date the code of 1810 has been entirely replaced. Even though a fair number of the pre-existing provisions remain unchanged, the paragraph numbering system in the new code has been modernised: rather than using a straightforward continuous sequence the new code employs a decimal system familiar to lawyers in the USA. Article 431–6 thus refers to the sixth subsection of the first section of the third title of Book 4. This system makes it easier to see at a glance what kind of provision is being referred to. In all, the first four books are divided into 11 titles which in turn comprise 39 sections. Book 5 has at present only one article, on cruelty to animals, but eventually it will contain measures on offences relating to the environment, the economy, employment, public finances, etc.

As is generally the case, therefore, the sources of the relevant law in this area are much much accessible and manageable in France than in England. All the relevant provisions on the substantive criminal law, as well as those on criminal procedure, are conveniently set out in two pocket-sized books. What makes matters even better is that private publishing firms issue updated annotated versions of the codes every year and they are on sale for prices which even impecunious law students can afford.

A translation of the 1810 French Criminal Code was published in 1960 as the first book in *The American Series of Foreign Penal Codes*, translated by Jean Moreau and Gerhard Mueller. Even before the Code's replacement this translation was quite out of date, retaining some archaic English expressions such as felonies and misdemeanours, but the introduction, by Marc Ancel, is still well worth reading. He draws attention, in particular, to the influence on French criminal justice of the Declaration of the Rights of Man and of the Citizen, proclaimed on 26 August 1789. This led almost immediately to the Criminal Code of 1791 (the predecessor of the Criminal Code of 1810) and to a comprehensive law on procedure, dated 1795, which formed the basis for the Code of Criminal Procedure of 1808. In the same American series there is a translation of the 1958 Code of Criminal Procedure, by Gerald Kock (1963). Again, the introduction provides a useful comparative survey, though mostly in relation to the United States rather than England. As yet there do not appear to be any full-scale English translations of the two new 1992 Codes on *droit pénal* and *procédure pénale*.

TYPES OF CRIMINAL OFFENCE

In a country such as France, where in theory at least law is always laid down by Parliament or by the government and never by judges, the principle of *nullum crimen nulla poena sine lege* is supposedly an absolute guarantee of liberty. As is explicitly stated in Article 111–3 of the new *Code pénal*, no one can be convicted of a crime, or given a punishment, unless there is a written law to support such an action. This amounts to a prohibition against applying laws retrospectively and a ban on drawing analogies to the detriment of the suspect. All judgments in criminal (as in civil) cases must cite the particular legislative provisions on which they are based. As a general rule French judges cannot rely on less specific 'principles of common law', unlike in England, although in recent times both *principes fondamentaux* and *principes généraux* have been increasingly referred to by the very highest courts. Nor is there any question of French judges creating new criminal offences, as their English counterparts are still wont to do (e.g. the House of Lords' invention of the offence of conspiracy to corrupt public morals in *Shaw* v *DPP*, 1962).

Nevertheless, the limitations on Parliament's statute-making power imposed by Article 34 of the 1958 French Constitution must be noted. These provide that Parliament can enact statutes only in the realms of 'crimes' and 'delicts' (*crimes* and *délits*), the two most important categories of offences in France. It cannot legislate for *contraventions*, the third and least important category, itself sub-divided into five classes with the first being the least serious and the fifth the most serious. To a certain extent the difference between *crimes* and *délits* on the one hand and *contraventions* on the other corresponds to the distinction in English law between indictable offences and summary offences, but of course the dividing lines do not fall at the same points. To reflect the threefold categorisation of offences, the *Code pénal* of 1810 (as it looked prior to March 1994) was divided into the following four books (after five preliminary articles):

1   Liability for *crimes* and *délits*, and the effects thereof (Articles 6–58).
2   Persons who may be held criminally liable (Articles 59–69).
3   Conduct punishable as *crimes* and *délits* (Articles 70–463).
4   Minor offences (*contraventions*) (Articles 464–477).

Clearly the meat of the 1810 Code was in Book 3. The material in Book 4 referred to government-created regulations not in the original code. The *Code pénal* of 1992 preserves the distinction between *crimes*, *délits* and *contraventions* (Article 111–1) as well as the constitutional division of labour between Parliament and government (Article 111–2), but it does not contain provisions on *contraventions* except in Articles 131–12 to 131–18, which deal with the kinds of punishment available for persons convicted of these minor offences (*contravenants*). This omission from the criminal code of regulatory offences may seem extraordinary, given that the formal statute-making power of Parliament has always been seen in France as a bulwark against excesses by the executive. But such a practice is hardly novel: English law has issued secondary legislation in the area of criminal law for some time. It is true, however, that the French Constitution has gone a significant step further than England by completely dispensing with the need for primary statutory provisions to enable the making of subsidiary regulations. A generic French word covering all three types of criminal offence is *infraction*.

Most published editions of the *Code pénal* usually include at the end the main provisions of the European Convention on Human Rights and Fundamental Freedoms, which France incorporated into its domestic law by a decree published on 4 May 1974 (although the right of individual petition was not recognised until after the socialists were elected to government in 1981). As explained in Chapter 5, in recent years France has lost several cases before the European Court of Human Rights in Strasbourg because its rules on criminal procedure were regarded as out of step with European standards. The 1992 Code has rectified the worst excesses. The Dalloz version of the *Code pénal* also contains a very useful Appendix (longer than the Code itself), which sets out the legislative provisions affecting a range of specific topics, organised alphabetically. The topics vary from alcoholism to road traffic and from the position of foreigners to the duties of the press. The book's extensive indexes facilitate reference to the multitude of laws set out within its covers.

The division of offences into *crimes*, *délits* and *contraventions* also has consequences for the prosecution process. An attempt to commit a *crime*, for example, is always punishable, but an attempt to commit a *délit* is punishable only if this is expressly provided for (*dans les cas prévus par la loi*) (Article 121–4). Attempts to commit minor offences, and aiding and abetting such offences, are not normally punishable. The limitation period for bringing prosecutions is 10 years for *crimes*, three years for *délits*, and one year for minor offences (Articles 7–9 of the new *Code de procédure pénale*). France also has limitation periods for the enforcement of punishments: those for a *crime* are considered to be time-barred after 20 years, those for a *délit* after five years, and those for a *contravention* after two years (Articles 763–767). As explained in Chapter 2, the courts' jurisdiction and the type of trial also depend on the kind of offence in question. *Crimes* are dealt with by the *cour d'assises* and a pre-trial judicial investigation is compulsory. For *délits* the involvement of a *juge d'instruction* before the judgment of the *tribunal correctionnel* is discretionary. In the interests of expediting matters, in many cases a process of *correctionalisation* occurs, whereby *crimes* are dealt with as if they were *délits*. The process of *contraventionalisation* is one whereby *délits* are dealt with as if they were *contraventions*. Such minor offences are processed in a *tribunal de police*.

In the early-1980s France dispensed with its special courts concerned with political and military offences. Until then the *Cour de Sûreté de l'Etat* had dealt with political offences, but this was abolished by statute in 1981. Its jurisdiction was taken over by a special chamber of the *cour d'assises*. The military tribunals, which were abolished by statute in 1982, have had their jurisdiction transferred to a division of the *tribunal de grande instance*. There is a *Haute Cour de Justice* which can try the President of the Republic for treason and, since 1993, a newly created *Cour de Justice de la République* which can try members of the government for *crimes* and *délits* allegedly committed in the exercise of their official functions.

THE GENERAL PART OF FRENCH CRIMINAL LAW

In French legal thinking an offence consists of three elements: the substantive (*élément matériel*), the legal, and the moral. These are roughly comparable to the concepts of causation, unlawfulness and *mens rea* in English law. What English lawyers refer to as the 'general' part of criminal law is essentially the subject-matter of Book 1 of the new French *Code pénal*; the 'special' part is the subject-matter of Books 2 to 5.

The substantive element

L'élément matériel embraces not just the English doctrine of *actus reus* but also its notion of causation. It refers mainly to the actualisation of an intention, i.e. to the requirement that there be a positive, objectively recognisable piece of behaviour. In the case of an attempt, there must be at least the beginnings of this actualisation, but a piece of behaviour is punishable even if it cannot be successfully completed, as in the case of an impossible attempt (e.g. trying to pick an empty pocket). This is now also the position in English law, after the House of Lords decision in *R v Shivpuri* (1987). A voluntary withdrawal during the course of an attempt will nevertheless exonerate a person in French law. Again, as in English law, an omission to do something is not enough to establish liability unless this is expressly provided for by statute, as in Article 434–11 of the new *Code pénal*, which criminalises a failure to give evidence if this would exonerate a person from a criminal offence – the maximum sentence for this is three years' imprisonment and a 300,000 franc fine (about £36,000).

French legal doctrine also categorises the various ways of participating in offences under the heading of *élément matériel*. An objective classification prevails, the actual state of mind of the person in question being largely irrelevant. A *co-auteur* is someone who directly performs a misdeed. Persons found guilty of *complicité* (aiding and abetting) or of *provocation* (incitement) are regarded in much the same light as the main miscreant, provided that the main deed has been fully performed, or at least been attempted, and that it constitutes punishable misconduct.

The element of unlawfulness

L'élément légal refers to two requirements. One is that of *nullum crimen sine lege*, already touched upon (*see* page 100). The other is a need for non-compliance with a law. The modern view in France is that pleas of justification are to be considered at this juncture, while defences properly so called are more appropriately dealt with in the context of *l'élément moral*, described below. The second title of Book 1 of the new *Code pénal* contains the provisions dealing with absence of liability or reduced liability.

There is, first of all, the case where at the time of the act in question a person was not in control of his or her senses (*atteinte d'un trouble psychique ou neuropsychique*: Article 122–1). If the lack of control was total then no punishment can be applied; if it was only partial then this must be taken into account when deciding the appropriate punishment. English law adopts a broadly similar position. Secondly, however, in Article 122–2 French law permits a defence of duress (*contrainte*), while in English law this is not allowed in cases where the charge is murder. In France it is enough if the person acted *sous l'empire d'une force ou d'une contrainte à laquelle elle n'a pu résister* (under the influence of a compulsion which he or she could not resist). Thirdly, France even allows an accused to plead the defence of mistake of law, despite the general maxim that *nul n'est censé ignorer la loi* (ignorance of the law is no excuse):

> *N'est pas pénalement responsable la personne qui justifie avoir cru, par une erreur sur le droit qu'elle n'était pas en mesure d'éviter, pouvoir légitimement accomplir l'acte.*

> (A person is not criminally liable if he or she can show that he or she believed, through a mistake of law which he or she was not in a position to avoid, that it was lawful to perform the act in question.)

Mistakes of fact can also play a defensive role, unless they are mistakes as to a person's identity or as to the intended target of the action; in these situations case law considers the criminal act to be nevertheless intended. Fourthly, the case where the defendant argues that a binding legal rule (whether a *loi* or a *règlement*) required him or her to carry out the conduct in question. This justification is referred to in Article 122–4 of the new Code, which replaces Article 327; the latter allowed the defence only in relation to homicide and assault, but despite the rule that they should not argue by analogy French judges had extended it to all other offences. The second paragraph of Article 122–4 makes it clear that performing an act in compliance with lawful orders is a defence to a criminal charge, but qualifies this by adding '*sauf si cet acte est manifestement illégal*' (except when the act is obviously unlawful).

Articles 122–5 to 122–7 contain the rules on when it is lawful to use force in self-defence or for some other purpose. They exonerate a person who in immediate reaction to an unjustified attack on him- or herself, or on a third party, takes action '*commandé par la nécessité de la légitime défense d'elle-même ou d'autrui*' (Article 122–5, para. 1) as well as a person who, when confronted with an actual or imminent *threat* to him- or herself, to a third party or a piece of property, takes action '*nécessaire à la sauvegarde de la personne ou du bien*' (Article 122–7). Likewise they excuse a person who, in order to stop a *crime* or a *délit* in relation to a piece of property, takes defensive action '*stictement nécessaire au but poursuivi* (Article 122–5, para. 2); this measure was not included in the old criminal code but had been developed by the judges prior to the drafting of the 1992 Code. In all three instances, however, the Code expressly provides that the action taken must be proportionate to the seriousness of the attack, threat or offence (as the case may be). It adds that in situations where an offence is being committed in relation to a piece of property a voluntary homicide is deemed never to be proportionate, but goes on to say that a defendant is to be presumed to have acted legitimately if he or she repulses a night-time intruder in a place of residence or defends him- or herself against thieves or looters who are using violence. In recent years there have been a few famous instances of French juries acquitting landowners who have killed intruders while supposedly protecting their property.

Generally speaking French *droit pénal*, like English criminal law, does not acknowledge a person's consent to be a justification for an accused's otherwise criminal act. In French legal jargon criminal law is *d'ordre public*, a matter of public policy, and cannot vary according to the will of individuals, an approach confirmed by the English House of Lords in a recent case involving sado-masochists (*R v Brown*, 1993). In both countries a person's consent may affect the kind of charge laid against the suspect, but it is legal or customary permission (*l'autorisation de la loi*) which, for instance, prevents criminal charges arising out of medical operations or sporting injuries.

The 'fault' element

L'élément moral refers to 'fault', in the sense of blameworthiness. It embraces first of all the idea of culpability; by Article 121–3 every offence requires a *mens rea*: '*il n'y a point de crime ou de délit sans intention de le commettre*'. Persons who are mentally ill (Article 122–1) and children under the age of 13 (Article 122–8, drawing on an ordonnance first issued in 1945) cannot be found guilty of any offence. But young persons aged 13 to

17, if found to have committed a *crime* or a *délit*, must be subjected to educational and supervisory measures issued by the juvenile court. In English law, of course, a child under 10 is regarded as incapable of committing a criminal offence (Children and Young Persons Act 1933, s. 50, as amended) and a child aged 10 to 13 is presumed incapable of being criminally liable unless it is proved that he or she knew that what was done was wrong.

In France, anyone who is partially non-culpable will receive a reduced punishment, and there are special rules for persons whose free will has been affected by alcohol or drugs. Such persons can be found guilty not just for acting of their own free will, but also for being aware of the possible consequences of behaviour induced by the intake of alcohol or drugs. Quite apart from this, Article 1 of the Road Traffic Code (*Code de la route*) penalises drunk driving in the same way as England's road traffic law makes a special offence out of such behaviour. As mentioned earlier, statute law can prescribe that a *délit* (but not a *crime*) may be committed '*en cas d'imprudence, de négligence ou de mise en danger délibérée de la personne d'autrui*' (in situations of imprudence, carelessness or deliberate endangering of a third party). Carelessness is applied slightly differently in the context of *contraventions*, where it is enough if it appears that there has been a breach of the regulations, even though no specific evidence of negligence is tendered.

Criminal sanctions

There are basically three types of criminal sanctions recognised by French law: primary punishment (loss of liberty), secondary punishment (loss of some other rights), and security measures (prohibitions to protect the public). The strong influence of modern criminological thought is unmistakable in the way sanctions have been developed. Marc Ancel's notion of a 'new social defence' (*défense sociale nouvelle*), and that of rehabilitation, have become increasingly prominent. Even the reforms introduced by the *Code de procédure pénale* of 1992 do not seem to depart significantly from the Ancelist school of thought, despite many people's growing disillusionment (in France no less than in England) with apparently 'soft' criminological theories.

The severest penalty known to French law is now life imprisonment (*emprisonnement à perpétuité*), the death penalty having been abolished by a law of 9 October 1981. By that time the number of executions was in any event small, because frequent use was made of the power to commute sentences. Besides life, serious offences (*crimes*) carry a sentence of up to 30 years' imprisonment (*réclusion criminelle*), though political offences such as spying or disclosure of national defence secrets, interestingly, lead instead to *détention criminelle* (Article 131–1). The period served for a *crime* must be at least 10 years. The former *Code pénal* provided also for punishments such as expulsion from the country for periods of 5 to 10 years (*bannissement*) and civil 'humiliation' (*dégradation civique*), but the new Code has abolished these. Less serious offences (*délits*) are punishable with *peines correctionnelles*, the most important of which are imprisonment, lasting up to 10 years, and limitless fines (*amendes*), of at least 25,000 francs (about £3,000). The sentence imposed may well be increased if the court decides that the offence was committed in one or more of a fixed set of aggravating circumstances; these include involvement of *une bande organisée* (an organised group), premeditation, *effraction* (breaking and entering), *escalade* (climbing a barrier) and use of arms (Articles 132–71 to 132–75). When imposing a fine as well as a prison sentence French judges now tend to ask for 100,000 francs (about £12,000) for every year to be spent in prison. The system also allows for daily fines (*une peine de jours-amende*), a useful punishment for situations where a person who has been sent to prison has committed an on-going offence and where no other fine is imposed. This fine can be up to 2,000 francs (about £250) per day and can endure for up to 360 days (Article 131–5); for every two days of fines not paid the convicted person must serve one extra day in prison (Article 131–25). In place of imprisonment or a fine (not in addition thereto or to any other punishment) the courts can sentence an accused to community work (*travail d'intérêt général*) and can disqualify him or her from driving, possessing a firearm or other piece of equipment, hunting, issuing cheques, holding public office, or practising a profession or social activity (Article 131–6). The accused can also be denied the right to vote or to stand for election, but only for a maxium period of 10 years in the case of conviction of a *crime* and five years in the case of a *délit*.

The commonest penalty for minor offences (*contraventions*) is a fine; since the new *Code pénal* came into force it has not been possible to send defendants to prison for these offences. In a system reminiscent of the more wide-ranging scale fines in English criminal law, the fine imposable depends on the classification of the *contravention*: up to 250 francs (about £30) for an offence in the first category, 1,000 francs (£120) for the second, 3,000 francs (£360) for the third, 5,000 francs (£600) for the fourth, and up to 10,000 francs (£1,200) for the fifth. The maximum under the old *Code pénal* was 6,000 francs and the new maximum can be doubled if the convicted person is a recidivist. As is possible in Britain, French judges can convert unpaid fines into days of imprisonment.

If a person is sentenced for several *crimes* or *délits* the basic rule is that the most severe penalty is the only one which counts. The new *Code pénal* repealed all references to *minimum* prison sentences, a reform which will simplify the sentencing process for judges by allowing them to take full account of extenuating circumstances in each individual case. But in Article 132–23 the Code does provide for what is known as *la période de sûreté*, which is the period during which a person who has been sent to prison is not allowed to benefit from any provisions concerning parole, home leave, conditional release, etc. This is comparable to the recommended minimum sentence sometimes mentioned by English judges when sentencing persons to life imprisonment. For life sentence prisoners in France the period is now set at 18 years (rather than the previous 15), while for persons sentenced to 10 years or more in prison the period is one half of the sentence. In individual cases, though, the judges can increase (to, respectively, 22 years or two-thirds of the sentence) or decrease these periods, and the period can be extended to 30 years in cases where a person has premeditatively and barbarously murdered a child under 16 years of age. The French Code permits most punishments to be suspended (*assorti du sursis simple*) and sometimes the suspension can be made subject to some conditions (*mise à l'épreuve*), including the duty to carry out community work (Articles 132–54 to 132–56). Just as English law uses the sentences of absolute or conditional discharge (where there is a finding of guilt but no immediate punishment), France uses *la dispense de peine* and *l'ajournement de la peine* (Articles 132–58 to 132–70). Convicted persons can also be granted mercy (*grâce*), even an amnesty (*amnistie*): the former cancels any punishment but leaves the person's conviction intact, whereas an amnesty not only cancels the conviction but also forbids any official from referring to the conviction in future. In any event convicted criminals in France, as in England, are considered to be automatically 'rehabilitated' if a certain period has elapsed after their punishment has been served without their being convicted of a further offence: the periods are three years in the case of a fine, five years in the case of a prison sentence up to one year, and 10 years if the sentence itself was up to 10 years (Articles 133–12 to 133–17: *De la réhabilitation*). In English law no prison sentence longer than 30 months can ever be considered 'spent' in this sense.

For the first time the new *Code pénal* includes provisions on the punishment of legal persons (*personnes morales*), i.e. corporations. The fines to which they can be subjected are five times what would be imposed on an individual (Article 131–38), or ten times in situations of recidivism. In addition, on some occasions further punishments can be imposed such as dissolution of the corporation, restriction of its activities, the placing of it under judicial supervision for up to five years (*le contrôle d'un mandataire de justice*), closure of a branch, exclusion from public procurement contracts, etc.

It is the administrative authorities who are responsible for the needs of offenders who are mentally ill, alcoholic or drug-addicted. Education is the most important part of 'punishment' for young offenders, but the aim is also to make adult offenders fit persons to rejoin society. Most prisoners are under a duty to work while in prison, with a part of their remuneration going towards the cost of their upkeep and to the reduction of any fines they may have been ordered to pay. They can spend the remaining amount as they see fit, though a portion is set to one side for use on their release. Prisoners who still have more than one year of their sentence to endure are first of all assessed at the *Centre national d'orientation* in Fresnes. They are then sent to specialised units throughout France. Articles 132–25 and 132–26 attempt to facilitate a prisoner's reintegration into society by creating a scheme of 'semi-freedom' (*semi-liberté*), which involves work and school attendance outside the prison.

THE SPECIAL PART OF FRENCH CRIMINAL LAW

The rules concerning specific *crimes* and *délits* are contained in Books 2 to 5 of the *Code pénal*, and often they are very detailed. Among the offences are some which even in other civil law countries are dealt with in special statutes. It is instructive to see at a glance the layout of these Books:

Arts 211–213	Genocide and other crimes against humanity
Art. 221	Intentional and unintentional assaults on a person's life
Art. 222	Intentional and unintentional assaults on a person's health and well-being, sexual assaults, drug-trafficking
Art. 223	Causing risk to others, abandoning a person unable to protect him- or herself, obstructing the provision of assistance to persons in need, experiments on human beings, illegal interruptions of pregnancy, incitement to suicide
Art. 224	Kidnapping (*l'enlèvement*) and false imprisonment (*la séquestration*), hijacking means of transport
Art. 225	Discrimination, living off immoral earnings (*le proxénétisme*), providing unfit working conditions or shelter, showing disrespect to the dead
Art. 226	Invasions of privacy, abusing a person's image, malicious prosecution (*la dénonciation calomnieuse*), breach of confidentiality (*l'atteinte au secret*), abuse of data collection
Art. 227	Deserting a child (*le délaissement*) and abandoning a family, challenging parental authority or legitimacy, putting children in danger
Art. 311	Theft and aggravated theft
Art. 312	Extortion (*l'extorsion*), blackmail (*le chantage*)
Art. 313	Fraud (*l'escroquerie*) and related offences
Art. 314	Abuse of trust (*l'abus de confiance*) or of a guarantee (*détournement de gage*), fraudulent preferences (*l'organisation frauduleuse de l'insolvabilité*)
Art. 321	Receiving stolen goods (*le recel*) and related offences
Art. 322	Criminal damage, threats of damage, hoax alerts
Art. 323	Computer hacking (*atteintes aux systèmes de traitement automatisé de données*)
Arts 410–411	Treason, spying and sabotage
Arts 412–414	Other attacks on national institutions
Arts 421–422	Terrorist acts

Art. 431	Obstructing basic freedoms, participating in an unlawful assembly (*l'attroupement*), unlawful demonstrations and meetings, paramilitary groups
Art. 432	Abuse of authority, absence of probity
Art. 433	Corruption and intimidation of, and outrages against, officials, and related offences
Art. 434	Obstructing the operation of justice
Art. 441	Forgery
Arts 442–444	Counterfeiting coinage and falsifying documents or marks
Art. 450	Unlawful associations (*les associations des malfaiteurs*)
Art. 511	Cruelty to animals (*les sévices graves et actes de cruauté*)

Some additional words need to be said about offences against private individuals and those against public order. As in England, the French *Code pénal* distinguishes between offences against the person and offences against property.

Offences against the person

One of the main ideas underpinning the recasting of the *Code pénal* was the need to protect people against violent attacks. The priority given to this goal is symbolised by promoting offences against the person to the top of the list of substantive offences, whereas offences against the state are relegated from that position to the end of the Code. The first title of Book 2 is devoted to *crimes contre l'humanité*. (England too has recently taken legislative action in this context, in the shape of the War Crimes Act 1991, even though it had to do so contrary to the wishes of the House of Lords.) Previously French criminal law had recognised such crimes only to the extent of saying that the offences qualifying as such (murder, rape, etc.) could be prosecuted no matter how much time had elapsed since their commission. Now the new Code specifically creates new offences.

Génocide is defined in Article 211-1 in exactly the same terms as in Article 2 of the United Nations Convention Against Genocide (1948); it embraces any act which is part of the planned destruction of a group of people defined by some arbitrary criterion such as race or religion. Article 212 goes on to criminalise comparable behaviour, including the planned deportation, enslavement or systematic execution, kidnapping or torture of members of a group for reasons of politics, philosophy, race or religion. The penalty for all these offences is life imprisonment. In no case is a defendant allowed to rely on the excuse of lawful orders.

Intentional killing is murder (*meurtre*) or assassination (*assassinat*). The former is defined in Article 221-1 as '*le fait de donner volontairement la mort à autrui*'; it is punishable with up to 30 years' imprisonment. The latter is *meurtre commis avec préméditation*; together with other forms of *meurtre aggravé* it is punishable with life imprisonment. The former code used to say that killing someone after lying in wait (*guet-apens*) was also *assassinat*, but this detail has been dropped in the new Code. Other aggravating factors besides premeditation include killing a child under 16, killing one's own parent or grandparent, killing a particularly vulnerable person such as someone who is disabled, elderly or pregnant, and killing someone who is involved in the administration of justice. Poisoning (*empoisonnement*) is also punished with life imprisonment if any of these aggravating factors is present in the circumstances, otherwise the penalty is 30 years' imprisonment; it is enough if the poisoning occurred with the intention of killing the victim, even though the cause of death was something else (Article 221–5).

Articles 222–1 to 222–18 deal in detail with the intentional causing of bodily harm. The punishment imposed is made to depend not just on the way in which the harm was caused, and on the consequences flowing from it, but also on the relationship between the offender and the victim. Torture and barbarity are specifically criminalised by Article 222–1 and made punishable with 15 years' imprisonment. Rather surprisingly, negligent killing (*homicide volontaire*) is punishable with only three years in prison and a fine of up to 300,000 francs (£36,000) (Article 221–6); negligently causing injury can, if the victim is not capable of working for at least three months, lead to up to two years in prison and a fine of up to 200,000 francs (£24,000) (Article 222–19).

The criminal law relating to the aborting of a foetus is now contained in Articles 223–10 to 223–12 of the *Code pénal*. The first of these provisions criminalises an abortion without the consent of the mother with a maximum punishment of five years' imprisonment and a 500,000 franc (£60,000) fine. If an abortion is carried out elsewhere than in a hospital, or by someone other than a doctor, or at a stage of the pregnancy when the law does not permit abortions (i.e. after the tenth week of the pregnancy, unless it is for reasons of health – *sauf si elle est pratiquée pour un motif thérapeutique*) a lesser penalty is imposable (two years' imprisonment and a 200,000 franc fine – £24,000); the higher maximum applies if the person found guilty practises this kind of abortion habitually. The 1992 *Code pénal* also criminalised the action of a woman who commits an abortion on herself, the penalty being up to two months' imprisonment and a 25,000 franc fine (£3,000), although the court could waive the penalty on account of the woman's distress or personality. But in January 1993 this provision of the new Code was repealed even before it was brought into force; what remains a crime is providing a woman with the means to carry out an abortion on herself, the penalty being three months' imprisonment and a 300,000 franc fine (or five years and 500,000 francs if the offender is habitual).

In the wake of a general liberalising of sexual mores in the 1960s and 1970s, the criminalisation of adultery was abolished in France in 1977. The pre-1992 code spoke of the crime of *outrage public à la pudeur*, but Article 222–32 now speaks instead of '*l'exhibition sexuelle imposée à la vue d'autrui dans un lieu accessible aux regards du public'* (exposing one's sex to others in a public place); the maximum penalty is one year in prison and a 100,000 franc fine (£12,000). Rape (*viol*) is defined as any act of sexual penetration of any person, of whatever nature it might be, committed by force, duress, threat or surprise (Article 222–23). The basic penalty is 15 years' imprisonment, though this can be increased to 20 years if there are aggravating factors such as mutilation or a relationship of authority between defendant and victim. In English law rape is still a crime which can be committed only against women and only if a penis penetrates the woman's vagina. In both countries a husband can now be guilty of raping his wife. The French Criminal Code goes on to deal in detail with procuring, pimping and living off immoral earnings (*proxénétisme*), and in Article 222–33 it specifically criminalises certain forms of sexual harassment:

> *Le fait de harceler autrui en usant d'ordres, de menaces ou de contraintes, dans le but d'obtenir des faveurs de nature sexuelle, par une personne abusant de l'autorité que lui confèrent ses fonctions, est puni d'un an d'emprisonnement et de 100,000 F d'amende.*

> (A person who abuses his or her authority by harassing another through the use of orders, threats or duress in order to obtain sexual favours can be punished with one year in prison and a fine of up to 100,000 francs (£12,000).)

This provision is complemented by Article 123–1 of the *Code du travail*, which protects employees or applicants for jobs against being victimised for their attitude towards harassment (see Chapter 11).

Other crimes worthy of note under the heading of offences against the person are discrimination, showing disrespect to the dead, invasion of privacy and misrepresenting a personal image. None of these are crimes according to English law, which relies instead upon civil law remedies to rectify grievances. Discrimination is very broadly defined in Article 225:

> *Constitue une discrimination toute distinction opérée entre les personnes physiques à raison de leur origine, de leur sexe, de leur situation de famille, de leur état de santé, de leur handicap, de leurs moeurs, de leurs opinions politiques, de leurs activités syndicales, de leur appartenance ou de leur non-appartenance, vraie ou supposée, à une ethnie, une nation, une race ou une religion déterminée.*

> (Discrimination is any distinction drawn between human beings on the basis of their origin, their gender, their family situation, their health, their disability, their traditions, their political opinions, their trade union activities, or their belonging or not belonging, real or supposed, to a particular ethnic group, nation, race or religion.)

Such discrimination can be punished with up to two years' imprisonment and a 200,000 franc fine (£24,000) if it takes the form of refusing to provide goods or services, obstructing the normal exercise of an economic activity, or refusing to recruit or grant a licence or authorisation to a person. Making the provision of goods or services or the offer of employment subject to a discriminatory condition (what English law would call indirect discrimination) is also outlawed. Article 225–3 creates certain exceptions for discrimination based on health or disability grounds, and for sex discrimination there is a variant of English law's genuine occupational qualification: *'lorsque l'appartenance à l'un ou l'autre sexe constitue . . . la condition déterminante de l'exercice d'un emploi ou d'une activité professionnelle'* (when being of one or other gender constitutes the determining condition for the exercise of an employment or a professional activity). Later in the *Code pénal* there is a special provision dealing with discrimination by persons holding public office: if they discriminate against someone by refusing to extend to him or her a right accorded by the law, or by obstructing the normal exercise by him or her of an economic activity, a sentence of one year's imprisonment and a 300,000 franc fine can be imposed (Article 432–7).

Any assault on a corpse and any violation of a burial site is an offence punishable with a year's imprisonment and a 100,000 franc fine (Article 225–17), and if the offence in question has been committed because of the nationality, race or religion of the deceased person the penalty can rise to five years' imprisonment and a fine of 500,000 francs (Article 225–18). These special provisions should help to curb anti-semitic attacks on Jewish graveyards, of which there has been a spate in recent years. They are a logical corollary to the provisions in Articles 226–1 to 226–12, which deal with *atteintes à la vie privée, atteintes à la représentation de la personne,* and *la dénonciation calomnieuse.* Breach of privacy consists of recording or transmitting, without the speaker's or subject's consent, words uttered privately or the image of a person when he or she is not in a public place. Misrepresenting a person's image can occur if a *montage* is published using a person's picture or words without that person's consent and without it being made clear that it is a *montage.* The penalty for these crimes can reach a year's imprisonment and a 300,000 franc fine. Also criminalised is the entry into a person's home as a result of a trick, threat or force (one year's imprisonment and a 100,000 franc fine – £12,000).

Offences against property

Theft (*vol*) is defined in Article 311–2 as *'la soustraction frauduleuse de la chose d'autrui'* (the fraudulent misappropriation of another's property). This is very similar to the definition in the Theft Act 1968, s. 1, whereby a person is guilty of theft if he or she 'dishonestly appropriates property belonging to another with the intention of permanently depriving the other of it'. *Soustraction* is basically the same as misappropriation in English law and can be committed even by someone who was originally given lawful possession of the item in question or by someone taking 'lost' property. In France, however, there is no requirement that the defendant should have intended permanently to deprive another of the property. Theft tends to be given an expansive interpretation in French law because the *Code pénal* deals with the separate crime of deception in only a few specific instances. The very concept of 'thing' (*chose*) is given a wide-ranging meaning, so that, for example, the redirection of energy is theft (Article 311–2). The unjustified use of a third party's computer program is dealt with in a separate part of the Code, Article 323. In English law electricity is not regarded as 'property' and its dishonest use or diversion has to be specially provided for (s. 13 of the 1968 Act).

As in other civil law countries, the French *Code pénal* contains exemptions from the law of theft for persons in a close family relationship (Article 311–12). It also differentiates between various types of theft, the punishment varying accordingly. For *vol simple* the maximum penalty is three years' imprisonment and a 200,000 franc fine, but Article 311–4 specifies eight sets of circumstances where the penalty can be increased to five years' imprisonment and a 500,000 franc fine (£60,000); these aggravating factors include the use of force, targeting a particularly vulnerable person and thefts committed by two or more persons acting in consort. The old *Code pénal* used to cite theft at night-time as an aggravating factor, but this has now been repealed. Article 311–10 says that a life sentence and a 1 million franc fine can be imposed on a thief who in the course of the crime uses lethal violence or commits acts of torture or barbarity. The Theft Act 1968 in England talks of robbery (theft accompanied by the use of force: s. 8) and of burglary (theft while trespassing: s. 9), but the only offence for which a higher maximum penalty is provided when the offence is committed in aggravating circumstances is burglary (s. 10).

Just as French law's conception of theft is relatively broad, so its conception of fraud (*escroquerie*) is correspondingly narrow (Article 313–1), though the new Code has extended it to cover the fraudulent obtaining of services as well as goods. There are no exact equivalents to the English law offences of obtaining property by deception (s. 15 of the Theft Act 1968) or obtaining a pecuniary advantage by deception (s. 16). *Escroquerie* requires the use of a false name or of a false attribute, or the misuse of a true attribute, or the use of fraudulent behaviour (*manoeuvres frauduleuses*) amounting to actual deception. The maximum penalty is five years' imprisonment and a 2.5 million franc fine (about £300,000).

In accordance with the general principle against criminalising mere omissions, fraud cannot be constituted by silence or by failure to rectify a mistake. It has therefore been necessary to create an extra category of offences akin to fraud (*infractions voisines à l'escroquerie*: Articles 313–4 to 313–6). These include the following types of misconduct: fraudulently taking advantage of a person's known ignorance or weakness so as to cause this person to perform an act which is severely harmful (*gravement préjudiciable*); being served drinks, food, petrol or oil, or taking accommodation or a ride in a taxi, knowing that one is not going to pay for the service provided (*la filouterie*); seeking to fix an auction (*les enchères*).

Offences against public order

Book 4 of the new *Code pénal* is the one which contains the most changes compared with the pre-existing Code. Various old offences have been discarded (such as vagrancy, *le vagabondage*) and new ones have been devised in their place (such as undermining the fundamental interests of the nation, *atteintes aux intérêts fondamentaux de la nation*). But probably the most topical of the new provisions, certainly those most likely to be invoked at the present time, are those dealing with terrorism. Terrorist offences (*infractions terroristes*) were first recognised as a category in French criminal law by a statute passed in 1986. But that statute simply altered certain rules relating to criminal procedure (e.g. abolishing jury trial) or to the treatment of offenders (e.g. providing a system for 'repenters', *les repentis*). The 1992 *Code pénal* goes further in actually criminalising certain terrorist acts. These are of two types. First, there are acts which are already crimes, such as murder, theft, possession of explosives etc., but which are connected with an individual or collective plan to severely disrupt public order through the use of intimidation or terror (*sont en relation avec une entreprise individuelle ou collective ayant pour but de troubler gravement l'ordre public par l'intimidation ou la terreur*) (Article 421–1). The maximum penalties for these offences are higher than they would be if no terrorist element were involved. Secondly, there are acts which have now been made into offences if connected with a plan of the kind just mentioned; these acts are the release into the atmosphere, ground or water of any substance which will endanger the health of humans, animals or the environment (*une substance de nature à mettre en péril la santé de l'homme ou des animaux ou le milieu naturel*) (Article 421–2). This type of terrorism is punishable with 15 years' imprisonment and a 1.5 million franc fine (or, if it causes death, life imprisonment and a 5 million franc fine). The Code seeks to encourage repentance on the part of terrorists by providing in Article 422–1 that anyone who has attempted to commit a terrorist act is exempt from punishment if, having warned the authorities, he or she has prevented the act and identified the other persons responsible. This is supplemented by Article 422–2, which cuts in half a convicted terrorist's prison sentence if he or she provides information which puts a stop to the acts in question (*les agissements incriminés*), or prevents loss of life or permanent injury or (if this is relevant) identifies his or her co-offenders. Foreigners convicted of terrorist acts can be banned from France for life (Article 422–4) and corporations can be convicted in the same way as individuals (Article 422–5).

CRIMINAL PROCEDURE: INVESTIGATIONS AND PROSECUTIONS

There are three distinct stages in a criminal prosecution in France: the investigation stage, the pre-trial judicial stage (*l'instruction*), and the main trial. As in the area of substantive criminal law, France has recently gone through a period of intense reform of its rules on criminal procedure and the variations from English criminal procedure remain numerous and stark. The reforms were initiated in 1988 by the then Minister for Justice, Pierre Arpaillange, who set up a Commission on justice and human rights with Professor Mireille Delmas-Marty in the chair. The Commission reported in 1990 and recommended fundamental changes to the then current *Code de procédure pénale*, which dated from 1958; this was a new version of the original code of 1808, itself a redraft of a 1795 prototype. The Commission was in favour of drawing a distinct line between the investigative and judicial functions involved in processing an alleged criminal: the application of provisions dealing with basic rights should, it said, be entrusted to a new breed of *juges des libertés*, while the public prosecutor's office (*le ministère public*) should take over responsibility for all aspects of the investigation of criminal offences.

Even the socialist government at this time was not prepared to be quite as radical as the Delmas-Marty Commission proposed, partly because of the opposition to the Commission's proposals emanating from the existing *juges d'instruction*, who saw their position as being completely undermined. In 1992 the government announced that it was proposing to remove only some of the detention powers of the *juges d'instruction* (replacing *l'inculpation* with *la mise en examen*) and to improve the rights of suspects (*les droits de la défense*); this was enough to gain the support of socialist and communist members of Parliament, but all the conservative members voted against the draft Bill when it was narrowly approved by Parliament in December 1992. Some of the new Code's provisions came into force on 1 March 1993 (also the original intended commencement date for the new *Code pénal*) but the application of others was delayed until 1 January 1994. The new system does not greatly affect the position of juvenile offenders in France; the specific procedures relating to delinquency prevention and child protection remain virtually unchanged.

The investigation stage

Under the new system investigations into crimes remain the primary responsibility of the 'judicial police' (*officiers de police judiciaire*), who are recruited from the ranks of the administrative police but, unlike them, are under the supervision and direction of the public prosecutor's office (*le ministère public*). The officers in the *police judiciaire* may be members either of the national police, who operate under the auspices of the Ministry of the

Interior, or of the local paramilitary *gendarmerie*, who operate under the Ministry of Defence; altogether there are about 20,000 throughout the country. The other police forces are *les renseignements généraux*, roughly the equivalent to MI5 in Britain, *la surveillance du territoire*, comparable to MI6, and the *Compagnie Républicaine de Sécurité* (the CRS), who serve as riot police. In 1992 recorded crime (*crimes et délits constatés*) was 2.3 per cent higher in France than in 1991. There were 2.75 million offences detected by the *police nationale* and a further 1.08 million detected by the *gendarmerie*.

The *enquête préliminaire* which the police conduct is expressly regulated by Articles 75 *et seq.* of the *Code de procédure pénale*. The Code distinguishes between investigations into offences which have just been committed (*flagrants délits*) and those into offences uncovered at a later stage, but in both situations it is possible for the police, under certain circumstances, to detain in custody the person who is the subject of the investigation. This detention is called *garde à vue*; it can generally last for up to 24 hours, but can be extended to 48 hours if the public prosecutor or an examining magistrate (*juge d'instruction*) agrees. Prior to the recent reforms even a witness to the commission of an offence could be held in *garde à vue*, but this is no longer possible except in cases of *flagrants délits*. In 1992 there were approximately 370,000 *gardes à vue*; 47 per cent related to theft or cognate offences, 37 per cent to drugs, 10 per cent to offences against the person, and 8 per cent to financial matters.

Any searches or seizures carried out during this stage require the consent of the person affected (Article 76). The 1992 Code introduced several new safeguards for the detainee (*le gardé à vue*). First, the detainee has the right to have his or her family informed about the detention, unless the police investigation makes it necessary to deny this. Secondly, the detainee has the right to consult privately for 30 minutes with a lawyer; initially this right was to be accorded only after the detention had lasted for 20 hours but from 1 January 1994 it has been made available immediately, except in cases where the offence being investigated is a terrorist or drug-trafficking offence, in which event access to a lawyer is denied for a 48-hour period. Previously there had been no right of access at all to a lawyer during the *garde à vue*. *Avocats* are entitled to little remuneration under the legal aid scheme for providing this kind of assistance, and during the course of their interview with the detained person they are not permitted access to the police's file (*dossier*). Thirdly, the detainee has the right to be medically examined by a doctor whose name appears on a list drawn up by the public prosecutor's office. Fourthly, the detainee has the right to be informed in understandable language about the legal rights he or she possesses while in custody. These safeguards are very significant, affecting as they do nearly 500,000 detainees each year, especially the 100,000 or so who are detained for longer than 20 hours.

It has taken the police, the legal profession and the judges quite a few months to come to terms with the new procedures, much as it did the equivalent bodies in England after the passage of the Police and Criminal Evidence Act 1984. There was considerable opposition not just from the conservative political parties, but also from the *Association française des magistrats instructeurs*, which in reaction issued a 27-page document entitled *Propositions pour une instruction rénovée*. Several *juges d'instruction* asked to be relieved of their duties by way of protest against the government's proposed reforms. The left-wing *Syndicat de la magistrature* felt on the other hand that the reform did not go far enough in ensuring rights to suspects. Nevertheless, it is clear that the reforms do counteract the trend towards undermining the presumption of innocence in French criminal law. They should make it less likely that France will be on the losing side of applications taken to Strasbourg under the European Convention on Human Rights (*see* Chapter 5).

After the police investigations have been completed the prosecutor (*procureur*) may discontinue the prosecution (*classer sans suite*) if he or she believes it would not be appropriate to carry on. Unlike in some countries, such as Germany, there is no obligation to pursue a prosecution whenever there is good evidence of a crime having been committed: the French prosecuting authorities, like the English, have a discretion in this respect (*principe de l'opportunité des poursuites*), though so long as the limitation period has not expired the prosecution can still be pursued at any point in the future.

The public prosecutor does not have a monopoly over the bringing of prosecutions, for the victim of an offence is also able to set a prosecution in motion (Article 1 of the *Code de procédure pénale*). This power is exercised quite frequently, as is the victim's related power to pursue a civil claim during the course of a criminal trial (*action civile*), although that also carries risks both as regards costs if the defendant is found not guilty and as regards the running of limitation periods. The 1992 reform has increased the maximum 'civil fine' which can be imposed if a person abuses the right to bring an *action civile*: it is now 100,000 francs (about £12,000). English law does permit private prosecutions but will not countenance the mixing of a civil claim with a criminal prosecution; the nearest it comes to this is allowing a judge in a criminal trial to make a restitution or compensation order in favour of the victim of a crime. French experience indicates that the presence of a civil party in a criminal trial can considerably poison the atmosphere and delay the conclusion of the trial. Nevertheless, in 1993 the law was altered so as to permit campaigners against road traffic offences to assist victims of these offences when claiming compensation in *actions civiles*. The same law, incidentally, abolished the rule (*les privilèges de juridiction*) whereby cases involving suspects who were police officers or elected officials, such as mayors, could not be dealt with by *juges d'instruction* but had to be referred immediately to the criminal division of the *Cour de Cassation*. It also said that handcuffs no longer needed to be used on arrested persons unless those persons were dangerous or likely to flee.

The pre-trial judicial stage

As soon as there are strong indications (*indices graves et concordants*) that a person, whether already in detention or not, has participated in the offence being investigated, he or she is placed under inquiry (*mise en examen*), either by the prosecutor or by the *juge d'instruction*. This has three immediate consequences: the person is informed that he or she is to be prosecuted, he or she acquires the right to a defence lawyer (*le droit à la défense*), and the case which he or she has to answer is explained. A pre-trial judicial stage (*instruction*) is mandatory in cases involving *crimes*, but for other offences it is discretionary.

Juges d'instruction have been central to the operation of French criminal procedure for the past 200 years, and still are. They have much greater powers than either the police or the prosecutors but these have been curtailed somewhat by the 1992 reforms. The *juge d'instruction* continues the investigations already begun by the police and can extend them to cover other persons. To this end he or she can have persons arrested and brought before the *juge* for questioning. The person being questioned by the *juge d'instruction* now has the right to be accompanied by a lawyer, who is granted access to the relevant *dossier*. Any party involved in the case can ask the *juge d'instruction* to follow up a particular line of inquiry and the judge must reply to this, giving reasons for his or her decision, within a month. If the party is dissatisfied the matter can be taken on appeal to the *chambre d'accusation*, a branch of the *cour d'assises*. Any person officially placed under investigation by the *mise en examen* procedure who has not been questioned for a period of three months can demand to be interviewed by a judge within the following fortnight. Similarly, if the judge has taken more than a year over the investigation a party involved can ask for the case to be dismissed (*ordonnance de non-lieu*) and the judge must supply a reasoned response within a month. In cases which are particularly serious or complex the president of the local court can appoint one or even two additional *juges d'instruction* to assist the original appointee.

Most important of all, until the new Code the examining magistrate could hold accused persons in preventive custody (*détention préventive*). Before 1960 this preventive custody sometimes lasted a very long time and was employed rather too readily; the institution was therefore heavily criticised. Lawyers had been allowed since 1897 to sit in on the interviews between a *juge d'instruction* and the suspect (*l'inculpé*) as well as to have access to the case file (*dossier*), but the *juge* was nevertheless regarded as a very powerful figure. In 1960, Article 105 of the *Code de procédure pénale* was altered so as to strengthen the defendant's rights, especially the right to remain silent and to have a lawyer present. To prevent there being any delay to the charging process in order to have the suspect re-examined as a witness, Article 105 obliged the examining magistrate to charge the suspect as soon as there were compelling grounds for suspecting him or her of the offence. A statute of 1970 set out the grounds for detention one by one, strengthened the protection afforded by the law to the accused and provided for compensation to be paid to persons who are subjected to preventive custody but later found to be innocent. The 1992 reform has abolished the power of the *juge d'instruction* to order a suspect's detention; instead this role is given to the president of the local court (*tribunal correctionnel*), or to a judge to whom the president has delegated the power (*un juge délégué*), assisted by two 'assessors': the *juge d'instruction* requests the authority of this *chambre* to detain the suspect and the decision is taken only after an adversarial debate (*un débat contradictoire*) attended by the suspect's lawyer and a representative of the public prosecutor's office. However, if the *juge délégué* is not available to deal with the case the *juge d'instruction* can 'provisionally' order the accused's detention for up to two days or, if the accused wants more time to prepare a defence, four days. It is hoped that one of the consequences of this reallocation of responsibility for detaining suspects prior to trial will be a reduction in the number of persons held on remand in French prisons; at a time when there is gross overcrowding in these prisons it is alarming that nearly one half of all prisoners are there not because they have been convicted and sentenced but because they are awaiting trial.

At the end of the *mise en examen* the *juge d'instruction* explains to the detainee the charges being laid against him or her and takes a note of any comments he or she may make on them. The *juge d'instruction* completes an official record of the proceedings (*le procès-verbal*) and – a novelty introduced by the 1992 reform – the accused and his or her lawyer then have 20 days within which to require further investigations to be conducted or to challenge procedures to date. After this period has elapsed the *dossier* is sent to the public prosecutor's office with a recommendation (accompanied by reasons) as to which charges should be prosecuted (*ordonnance de présomption de charges*). This replaces the former 'committal' order (*ordonnance de renvoi*) and does not have the appearance of finality which that order displayed. If the decision is taken not to prosecute this has only limited legal significance, because if new facts are discovered the *mise en examen* can be re-opened. If a prosecution proceeds and the suspect is to be tried for a *crime*, the remand to the *cour d'assises* by the *juge d'instruction* must be confirmed by a majority of the three judges from the *cour d'appel* who sit as the so-called *chambre d'accusation*. By the time the suspect appears for trial, therefore, it is generally recognised that there is a strong likelihood that he or she is indeed guilty. The pre-trial stage in France leads to a higher presumption of guilt against the accused than does the committal stage in English criminal procedure. In both countries, though, the pre-trial stage is seen in some quarters as unnecessarily cumbersome: although there is not as strong a campaign in France for its abolition as there is in England *vis-à-vis* committal proceedings, there are nevertheless vocal critics of the system.

The main trial and judgment

The main trial (*l'audience publique*) is oral, public and supposedly adversarial in nature. Its orality is particularly noticeable in cases before the *cour d'assises*, where even the judges' deliberations are conducted in the absence of written documents. In the *tribunal correctionnel* and *tribunal de police*, however, the reading of documents is permissible. Indeed, by the time the case comes to trial there will already be a thick *dossier* of information for perusal.

In contrast to pre-trial examinations, the main trial must be held in public unless this is not feasible on account of a threat to public order or decency (the so-called *huis clos*). Press reports can be issued, though it is a crime to insult the court or to publish a report with the object of exerting pressure on witnesses or judges.

The 1992 code also improves the rights of suspects *vis-à-vis* the press. Previously the French press had been able with relative impunity to suggest that an accused person was in fact guilty. Now a paragraph has been added to Article 9 of the *Code civil* saying that if, before being convicted, a person is publicly presented as being guilty of an offence currently under official investigation, a court can order the publication of a retraction so as to restore the presumption of innocence and the person accused can within three months claim compensation. Likewise, after an accused person's acquittal a court can order the publication of this decision in one or more newspapers or broadcasting channels. Within three months of an acquittal the acquitted person is given the further opportunity to exercise a right of reply (*droit de réponse*) to allegations of guilt in the media. If a newspaper refuses to accord the right of reply it can be fined up to 15,000 francs (about £1,800) and the offence is now a *délit* rather than a mere *contravention*. These provisions are the French equivalent to England's law on contempt of court.

Conversely, the new code underscores the freedom of the press in some respects: it permits journalists not to reveal their sources, and any search (*perquisition*) of newspaper premises must be conducted by or under the supervision of a *juge d'instruction* and not just by the police; the *juge* is under a duty to ensure that the search does not undermine journalistic liberties or constitute an unjustifiable obstacle to the dissemination of information.

The adversarial nature of the trial supposedly follows from the fact that the accused is present throughout its duration, although in certain situations, contrary to the position in English law, it is possible for him to be tried *in absentia*. The accused, moreover, has the right to be legally represented

(Article 417). Such a representative *must* be appointed for cases in the *cour d'assises*; if necessary a duty-lawyer will be appointed. After the prosecution has tendered its evidence, the accused has the right to make a statement.

The kinds of evidence that can be adduced at a trial include confessions (viewed as particularly influential), witness testimony, documents, inspections and experts' reports. The value to be placed on technical recordings is still a matter of some controversy. The standard of proof required in all French criminal cases, at the pre-trial as well as the trial stage, is that of 'inner certainty' (*intime conviction*), which is as difficult a standard for the prosecution to satisfy as English law's 'belief beyond a reasonable doubt'. An important safeguard lies in the rule that if a person is charged with a *crime*, there must still be a trial even though he or she wishes to plead guilty. This concession is not made in England, where the possibility remains that a person may plead guilty to an offence even though the prosecution do not have evidence against the person which would satisfy a jury of guilt beyond a reasonable doubt.

What gives rise to the impression that convictions are easier to obtain in France – and to the popular misconception on the part of the English that in France an accused person is guilty until proven innocent – is the fact that, whatever the theory, criminal procedure there is basically inquisitorial or investigative in nature. It is not as much of a contest between opposing sides as in England, nor are there as many rules to exclude potentially prejudicial evidence. There is no examination-in-chief or cross-examination, all questions being addressed by or through the judges. The prosecutor, moreover, is a public servant, not an independent barrister. In Packer's famous terminology, the French system is orientated more towards 'crime control' than to 'due process'. In the opinion of most English commentators, the French system may be more effective at getting at the truth than the English but protections for defendants are probably weaker.

After the trial the judgment will be either an acquittal (*relaxe, acquittement*) or a conviction (*condamnation*). In certain circumstances French law recognises a special type of acquittal (*absolution*), for instance in cases of theft between members of the same family. The English notion of absolute discharge is comparable, except that in France the accused can still be ordered to pay compensation and to reimburse costs. For a judgment to be reached there has to be a majority of judges in favour of it; this presents no problems as far as the *tribunal de police* and the *tribunal correctionnel* are concerned, but for the *cour d'assises* a majority of at least 8:4 is required for decisions going against the accused. The three professional judges in such cases therefore need the support of five of the nine jurors if they wish to hold the accused guilty. What is especially remarkable to an English lawyer is that jurors are also involved in the sentencing process, which is decided on a straight majority vote of judges and jurors combined. Judgments are registered in the national sentencing registry (*casier judiciaire*), which has been centralised in Nantes since 1982.

Like the 1958 version, the current *Code de procédure pénale* grants considerable flexibility to the court when sentencing an accused. This is in contrast to the earlier version of the Code published in 1791, which had reacted to the frequent examples of judicial arbitrariness during the days of the *ancien régime* by fixing punishments in advance. The 1810 Code first allowed the judge a discretion to impose a sentence between a given maximum and minimum, and amendments later in the 19th century (especially 1832 and 1863) removed most of the minimum limits. The remainder were abolished in the 1992 revision. Sentences today are very much tailored to meeting the needs of the particular accused (*individualisation des peines*). This is also the general principle in English law, where there are few statutory minima and only approximate tariffs occasionally laid down by judges.

Challenging judgments

The normal method of challenging judgments of the *tribunal de police* and the *tribunal correctionnel* is by appeal (*appel*). Since 1958 these appeals are heard by the *cour d'appel*. The appeal must be lodged within 10 days with the judge whose decision is being appealed. As far as challenges to decisions by courts of final resort are concerned (e.g. the *cour d'assises*, the *cour d'appel*, and the *tribunal de police* in those cases where an appeal is not allowed), the method of proceeding is by way of review to the *Cour de Cassation* (*pourvoi en cassation*) for an order that there has been a breach of the law (Articles 591 *et seq.* of the *Code de procédure pénale*).

Even after cases have gone all the way through the courts they can be re-opened by taking review proceedings in the *Cour de Cassation* (*pourvoi en révision*). Originally only three grounds for allowing cases to be re-opened were recognised:

(a) in homicide cases, the presentation of documentary evidence suggesting that the person whom the accused has been convicted of killing is still alive;
(b) the conviction of someone else for the same offence; and
(c) the conviction of a witness for perjury.

As a result of the notorious *Dreyfus* affair in the 1890s a fourth, much more general, ground was added, namely the discovery of a new fact (*fait nouveau*) or the presentation of documents which show the accused person's innocence.

FURTHER READING

Although it has to some extent been overtaken by the 1992 reforms to the *Code pénal* and the *Code de procédure pénale*, one of the best accounts in English is

Richard Vogler's very practical *France: A Guide to the French Criminal Justice System*, published by Prisoners Abroad in 1989. There is also a good chapter on criminal procedure in West *et al.*, *The French Legal System: An Introduction* (1992), and useful straightforward accounts of the same area in C. Dadomo and S. Farran, *The French Legal System* (1993), pp. 181–209, and in *An English Reader's Guide to the French Legal System* by Martin Weston (1991), pp. 119–38. For an American perspective on the French system, see Wise (ed.), *French Criminal Procedure Revised* (1988).

As part of its commissioned research to help it with its own deliberations, the Royal Commission on Criminal Justice in England and Wales sponsored a report by Leonard Leigh and Lucia Zedner on the administration of criminal justice in the pre-trial phase in France and Germany (1992); this contains many pertinent insights into the characteristics of the two systems. The recent attempts to reform traditional parts of the law on criminal procedure are described by Helen Trouille, 'The *juge d'instruction*: a figure under threat or supremely untouchable', (1994) *Modern and Contemporary France*, vol. NS2, pp. 11–19. Further interesting journal articles include Tomlinson, 'Nonadversarial Justice: The French Experience' (1983) 42 *Maryland LR* 131, and McConnell, 'Reasonable murder' (1993) New LJ 1082.

As yet few of the standard textbooks in France have taken on board all the changes introduced by the 1992 Codes (especially as the *nouveau Code pénal* did not come into force until March 1994). But for useful coverage it is still worth consulting Vouin, *Droit pénal spécial* (6th edn, 1988); Pradel, *Procédure pénale* (5th edn, 1990); J.-H. Robert, *Droit pénal général* (2nd edn, 1992); Soyer, *Droit pénal et procédure pénale* (10th edn, 1993); Stefanie, Levasseur and Bouloc, *Droit pénal général et procédure pénale* (15th edn, 1994). The Delmas-Marty report is also an important background to the recent procedural reforms: *La mise en état des affaires pénales* (1990). The publishers known as Editions 10/18 have produced *Nouveau code pénal, mode d'emploi* (1993), a manual on the new criminal code comprising the code itself and a preliminary commentary. The criminal law affecting businesses is dealt with in Jeandidier, *Droit pénal des affaires* (2nd edn, 1994), one of several recent books on this topic, while good texts on criminological theories and practices are Picca, *La criminologie* (3rd edn, 1993); L. Négrier-Dormant, *Criminologie* (1992); and Gassin, *Criminologie* (2nd edn, 1990). For juvenile crime, see Chazal, *L'enfance et la jeunesse délinquantes* (12th edn, 1993). Each year the Prison Service issues to the Ministry of Justice a *Rapport général sur l'activité de l'Administration pénitentiaire* and the Ministry of the Interior issues an annual volume entitled *Aspects de la criminalité et de la délinquance constatées en France*.

CHAPTER 7

Civil procedure

INTRODUCTION

While there is much in common between English law and French law in the manner in which they handle civil claims, there is also much that divides them, and it is naturally upon the differences that attention tends to be focused. In both countries, however, there is great pressure on the legal system's resources in this context. The courts are having to handle more cases than ever before, delays are getting longer and costs higher. Increasingly attempts are being made to short-circuit judicial proceedings or even to avoid them altogether. Litigants are encouraged to settle their claims in advance of a full judicial hearing, mediation services and alternative dispute resolution mechanisms are being developed, and judges as well as court administrators are being reminded that the judicial system must provide good value for money. In the light of these larger concerns it may seem trivial, or irrelevant, to dwell on comparatively minor distinctions between the methods employed in the two legal systems when civil claims are being processed. Nevertheless, those distinctions do reflect more fundamental differences between the two legal cultures and allow us to appreciate more readily the way in which a French or an English lawyer acts and thinks.

In this chapter we cannot look in great detail at the multitude of issues which arise during the processing of civil claims. We can simply attempt to highlight the main features of the French system with a view to grasping its essential nature. Although French civil procedure has not been as closely examined in England as French criminal procedure, it is of course of great importance: while it may not often bring into play issues of civil liberties and human rights, or at least not directly, the civil procedure system nevertheless needs to be accessible and affordable to ordinary law-abiding people whom the law is supposedly intended to serve. The alternative is an elitist procedure which fails to ensure basic justice.

SOURCES OF THE LAW

The most significant influence on the early French laws dealing with civil procedure was canonist thinking. While efforts had been made to settle some basic principles as early as the reign of Louis IX (1226–1270), the effect was to superimpose rules derived from Roman law on the comparatively barbaric practices preferred by the Germanic tribes. There was still a need to infiltrate notions of impartiality and secrecy into civil proceedings; canon law supposedly exemplified these even if at the same time it tended to be excessively technical. In the 16th century at least two important royal *ordonnances* were issued, each serving to make civil procedure more uniform; one required the use of the French language in all proceedings, while another greatly reduced the reliance on oral testimony, preferring the relative indisputability of written documents. A century later another step forward was taken when the *ordonnance civile*, otherwise known as the *Code Louis*, was issued in 1667. This brought together in one law all the existing rules on civil procedure and directed that they should apply throughout France, without local variations. It was a very early example of the codification process at work in Europe and it was to stand the test of time admirably. Indeed, when Napoleon's codifiers set about creating a new *Code de procédure civile*, which appeared in 1806, they based themselves almost entirely on the 17th century precursor. In particular they resisted the temptation, not surprisingly given the international circumstances of the day, to follow the English practice of allowing civil claims to be dealt with almost exclusively through oral hearings.

It was not until 1935 that further radical reforms were enacted, these being supplemented in 1958 and 1965. The most innovative feature of the 1965 reform was the creation of a formal pre-trial stage for cases heard in France's main civil courts, the *tribunaux de grande instance*. This *procédure de la mise en état des causes* was entrusted to a cadre of judges labelled *juges de la mise en état*. The dual aim was to reduce costs and expedite trials by ensuring that parties to disputes clarified what was dividing them as definitely as possible; to achieve this civil procedure had to become less adversarial and more inquisitorial than previously. The reformers were able to look at inquisitorial aspects of French criminal procedure and deduce what could usefully be borrowed therefrom.

Still, however, there was considerable dissatisfaction with the way in which the system was operating in practice. The Minister for Justice of the day, Jean Foyer, consequently set up a Commission in 1969 to devise a whole new Code. To a large extent this Commission achieved its goal, but not totally. In 1975 a new *Code de procédure civile* was duly enacted by *décret* (the Constitution does not require procedural laws to be introduced in the guise of a *loi*, which means that they can be scrutinised by the *Conseil d'Etat*), but it did not completely replace all of the provisions in the 1806 Code. French lawyers therefore had to speak of the *nouveau Code* and the *ancien Code*, and this remains the case today.

The *nouveau Code* consists of five books. Book 1 (Articles 1–749) contains provisions which are relevant to all courts, from the initiation of court actions to the filing of appeals. Book 2 (Articles 750–1037) is divided into seven parts (*titres*), each devoted to a particular kind of court – *tribunaux de grande instance, tribunaux d'instance, tribunaux de commerce, conseils de prud'hommes* (these provisions are reproduced from the *Code du travail*), *tribunaux paritaires de baux ruraux, cours d'appel* and the *Cour de Cassation*. Book 3 (Articles 1038–1441) has specific provisions relevant to particular issues, such as who can sue or be sued. Book 4 (Articles 1442–1507) covers arbitrations. Book 5, however, like its counterpart in the new *Code pénal*, is an empty vessel: it is awaiting new measures dealing with enforcement of judgments (*voies d'exécution*). Published versions of the *nouveau Code* are usually accompanied by the articles of the *ancien Code* still in force, of which there are some 189. In addition, the same book often contains relevant provisions of the *Code de l'organisaton judiciaire*, first issued in 1978. The Dalloz version includes a 600 page appendix which sets out the relevant legislative provisions on a wide variety of topics connected with the handling of civil claims; these encompass *aide juridique* (legal aid), *avocats* (lawyers), *frais et dépens* (costs), etc. Thus, even if the process of codification in this area is not complete, the efforts of publishing houses make the work of the interested lawyer significantly easier.

INITIATING CIVIL PROCEEDINGS

As in England, civil proceedings in France are permissible only if there is a genuine dispute as to a person's legal entitlements. In the words of Article 1 of the *nouveau Code*: '*Seules les parties introduisent l'instance, hors les cas où la loi en dispose autrement*' (Actions can be begun only by the parties, unless a statute provides otherwise). It cannot be permissible to put a further strain on already over-stretched forensic resources by asking the courts to adjudicate upon hypothetical questions purely in order to satisfy curiosity as to the exact legal position on a moot point. This is expressly forbidden by Article 5 of the *Code civil*: '*Il est défendu aux juges de prononcer par voie de disposition générale et réglementaire sur les causes qui leur sont soumises*' (Judges are prohibited from issuing general regulatory pronouncements on claims submitted to them). But a person can seek what in England would be termed a declaration of his or her rights (*action déclaratoire*). Also it sometimes happens that the *ministère public* will instigate proceedings, perhaps because there is no other party to challenge a person's claim, or because it is necessary to protect a vulnerable person such as a child, or because it is deemed important to bring a case in the public interest. This last situation is reminiscent of a relator action in English law; the other situations are akin to wardship. As a corollary to the monopoly given to private litigants, judges must not decide matters which are not put to them by the parties concerned, nor can they decide of their own motion to deal with a dispute. Civil proceedings belong to the parties and they must be allowed to control the way in which those proceedings unfold. Article 5 of the *nouveau Code* encapsulates this neatly: '*le juge doit se prononcer sur tout de qui est demandé et seulement sur ce qui est demandé*' (the judge must deal with every issue raised and only with what is raised). However, a judge is not barred from indicating to a litigant what remedy he or she might have if the flawed claim currently under consideration were to be resubmitted in a different form.

It is not of course every individual who can bring a dispute before the courts: he or she must have *locus standi*, that is, some degree of interest in the outcome of the dispute. Article 31 of the *nouveau Code* requires every plaintiff (*demandeur*) or defendant (*défendeur*) to have *un intérêt légitime au succès ou au rejet d'une prétention* (a legitimate interest in the success or failure of a claim). In a few instances statute law itself bestows such an interest on a person, the best example being the 1988 *loi* permitting recognised groups of consumers to bring civil claims. Otherwise it is not possible to instigate a class action in France.

Under Article 101 a judge may desist from hearing a claim, transferring it instead to another judge, if it is so linked to another claim before that other judge that it would be in the interests of justice (*qu'il soit de l'intérêt d'une bonne justice*) for the two claims to be dealt with together. A common example of one judge deferring to another arises where the victim of a crime decides to make a civil claim at a time when a criminal prosecution against the alleged offender is still pending. As in England, preference is given in France to concluding the criminal proceedings first (Article 4 of the *Code de procédure pénale*). The reason for this is twofold: criminal proceedings are, potentially if not always in reality, more serious in their outcome, and the standard of proof required to be attained in criminal proceedings is more demanding – it makes sense to see if this standard can be satisfied first, thereby facilitating the processing of the civil claim. But French law mitigates this subservience of crime victims by permitting them to intervene directly in the criminal proceedings: as so-called *parties civiles* they can obtain civil redress in the same judgment which sentences the accused to a criminal punishment (*see* Chapter 6). In a similar vein, Article 367 permits a judge, whether on request or on his or her own initiative, to order several actions pending to be joined together if again this would be in the interests of justice. Of course such a joinder of actions does not presuppose that the two or more claims will from then on be dealt with exactly alike: the judge is still free to issue different interlocutory orders in relation to the claims and may even come to differing conclusions in respect of them.

Limitation periods

The rules concerning the time limits within which civil actions must be initiated are contained in Articles 2219 to 2283 of the *Code civil*. The basic rule is that civil actions can be brought at any time within a 30-year period following the accrual of the cause of action (Article 2262), but there are many exceptions to this. A person who acquires a piece of immovable property in good faith and by apparently good title (*de bonne foi et par juste titre*) cannot be sued by the true owner after 20 years have elapsed, and this period is reduced to 10 years if the owner lives within the area served by the same *cour d'appel* as the acquirer (Article 2265). Whereas in English law the limitation period is 12 years for contracts under seal (i.e. in a deed) and six years for other contracts, in French law all contractual claims must be brought within 10 years:

> *Les obligations nées à l'occasion de leur commerce entre commerçants ou entre commerçants et non-commerçants se prescrivent par dix ans si elles ne sont pas soumises à des prescriptions spéciales plus courtes.*

> (Obligations arising out of relations between traders or between traders and non-traders are statute-barred after 10 years unless they are made subject to shorter periods.) (Article 189 of the *Code de commerce*)

By a provision enacted in 1985, tort claims (*les actions en responsabilité civile extra-contractuelle*) are statute-barred 10 years after the damage in question becomes apparent (Article 2270–1 of the *Code civil*). Any limitation periods which had already begun to run at the time of the enactment of the 1985 law are to be taken as expiring in 1995. Again, it is to be noted that the 10-year period in France is significantly longer than the standard six-year period available in the English law of torts, and the English period is of course shortened to three years in cases where the plaintiff is claiming in respect of personal injury. France also applies a 10-year rule to claims brought in connection with the construction of a building (Article 2270); this covers the liability of builders, architects, surveyors, etc.

If the claim is for payment of money owed by way of periodically due wages, rent, maintenance or interest, the limitation period is reduced to five years (presumably because the amounts owed are more easily ascertained) (Article 2277). A person whose goods are stolen or lost has three years within which to reclaim them from the current possessor (*revendication*), despite the normal principle set out in Article 2279 that '*en fait de meubles, la possession vaut titre*' (as far as movable property is concerned, possession means ownership), but always provided the possession is '*continue et non interrompue, paisible, publique, non équivoque, et à titre de propriétaire*' (continuous and uninterrupted, peaceful, public, unequivocal, and by way of supposed ownership) (Article 2229). Against insurance companies claims must be lodged within two years. Likewise, doctors, surgeons, dentists, midwives, pharmacists and lawyers, as well as merchants (*marchands*) selling goods to private individuals, have to bring their action within just two years (Articles 2272–2273). France's lawyers are not in the same position as English barristers, who, while they may be immune from being sued for negligent handling of a court case, cannot in turn sue for their own fees. In most claims relating to transport the limitation period is one year, while suppliers of accommodation or of food have only six months within which to sue (Article 2271). As in English law, a limitation period is interrupted (and then starts afresh) if the debtor or possessor acknowledges the legal right of the creditor or owner (Article 2248). No limitation period runs as between spouses or against a minor (Articles 2252–2253).

How matters are proved

English law sharply distinguishes, in theory at least, between the standard of proof required in civil actions, and that in criminal proceedings: proof on the balance of probabilities for the former and proof beyond a reasonable doubt for the latter. In some instances, such as unfair dismissal suits, a hybrid standard seems to be applied. French law is not so categorical. While it requires adjudicators in criminal cases to have an *intime conviction* of an accused's guilt, in civil cases it simply says, on the one hand, that '*à l'appui de leurs prétentions, les parties ont la charge d'alléguer les faits propres à les fonder*' (to support their claims parties are under a duty to allege the appropriate facts on which to ground them) (Article 6 of the *nouveau Code*) and, on the other, that '*il incombe à chaque partie de preuver conformément à la loi les faits nécessaires au succès de sa prétention*' (it falls to each party to prove in conformity with statute law the facts which are necessary for his or her claim to succeed) (Article 9). This comparative imprecision in the law does not seem to cause French lawyers much concern. Litigants, moreover, are assisted in their legal actions by a number of statutory presumptions (*présomptions légales*); two legislative examples of these in the *Code civil* are Article 553, which says that all buildings on a piece of land are presumed to have been erected by the owner of the land, or at his or her expense, and to belong to the owner, and Article 1792, which presumes that an architect is liable for any damage resulting from a building which he or she has designed. A third example can be given from judge-made law: an unfaithful fiancé is presumed to be at fault if an engagement is broken off.

The fact that the first two examples just cited are taken from the *Code civil* rather than from the *Code de procédure civile* is reflective of the tendency for French law to subsume questions relating to evidence within the substantive legal rules. French law students do not study a subject called evidence and there are no textbooks in the area. Instead the issues are discussed in books on *obligations*. English law adopts this approach on some matters – the parol evidence rule is sometimes discussed in books on contract law, the *res ipsa loquitur* rule in books on tort, and the required form for land transfers in books on real property. But the French go much further. They happily live without technical rules of evidence such as the hearsay rule. Of course many of English law's rules on evidence were established at a time when civil as well as criminal proceedings took place in front of a jury: special care had to be taken to ensure that jurors did not too readily jump to conclusions about propositions made by litigants. French law has not been burdened by such historical legacies. In addition, the French preference, since at least the 17th century, for written as opposed to oral evidence has meant that particular rules have been developed for the proving of written documents. Whereas English law usually requires the maker of a document to testify in court that the document is genuine, in France it is enough if the writing is in a certain form. Thus, if the document has been drawn up by a *notaire* as an *acte authentique* its content is taken to be true unless there is positive proof that the document has been forged; a less formal document, say a contract which the parties have each signed (*un acte sous seing privé*), is indicative of the truth unless other written evidence can be adduced in rebuttal. All *actes juridiques* (such as contracts and wills) must in theory be proved by a written document, though contracts for goods valued at less than 5,000 francs and all contracts with traders (*commerçants*) are exempt (Article 1341 of the *Code civil* and Article 109 of the *Code de commerce*).

In this context a most important provision is Article 132 of the *nouveau Code*. This imposes a general duty on parties to civil proceedings to disclose to each other the documents in their possession on which they intend to rely in order to substantiate their claim: '*La partie qui fait état d'une pièce a la communiquer à toute autre partie à l'instance. La communication des pièces doit être spontanée.*' (The party relying on a document must disclose it to every other party in the case. The disclosure must occur voluntarily.) This provision is complemented by Article 10 of the *Code civil*: '*Chacun est tenu d'apporter son concours à la justice en vue de la manifestation de la vérité*' (Everyone is under a duty to co-operate with the justice system with a view to uncovering the truth). Article 11 of the *Code de procédure civile* is worded very similarly *vis-à-vis* pre-trial measures ordered by the judge (*mesures d'instruction*). But disclosure of documents in the possession of third persons is not required if there is a legal impediment thereto (*empêchement légitime*: Article 11); an example of this would be documents covered by what in English law is termed legal privilege (i.e. correspondence between a solicitor and client).

HOW THE CASE PROCEEDS

A typical civil action in France (*demande en justice*) is begun by the plaintiff issuing a writ (*une assignation*). This will have been drafted by a lawyer and is usually served on the defendant by a process-server (*un huissier*), but if personal service is not possible it is enough to leave a copy of the writ at the defendant's local town hall. The writ will contain a statement of claim (*l'objet de la demande*) and the grounds therefor (*l'exposé des moyens*), as well as the name of the plaintiff's lawyer. Within four months of the writ being served (*signification*) a further copy of it must be lodged at the clerk's office in the local court (*secrétariat-greffe*), and within a further 15 days the defendant must have indicated the name of his or her lawyer (Article 755). The defendant's lawyer must notify the plaintiiff's lawyer as well as the court clerk that he or she has been appointed to act (Article 756); this is tantamount to the English concept of 'entering an appearance'. By the time two more months have elapsed a preliminary hearing will have occurred in front of the president of the local court for a decision as to whether the case is so straightforward that it can be set down for trial without more ado (*l'audience de l'appel des causes*: Article 759). If it cannot be set down a pre-trial procedure (*l'instruction*) is set in motion.

If a defendant does not enter an appearance to contest the plaintiff's claim the judge can decide the case in his or her absence, although the judge must still be satisfied that the claim is '*régulière, recevable et bien fondée*' (proper, admissible and well founded) (Article 472). These default judgments (*jugements rendus par défaut*) must be served on the judgment debtor within six months; they can be set aside, by a procedure called *opposition* (Articles 571–578), provided the debtor can show that he or she was not properly served with the writ, but otherwise the judgment is deemed to have been delivered after full argument (*réputé contradictoire*) and can then only be appealed, unless even this is expressly forbidden by a particular piece of legislation (Article 476). If a defendant does enter an appearance to a writ the plaintiff does not have the option, as he or she would have in England, of applying for a summary judgment (Order 14 of the Rules of the Supreme Court).

Pre-trial procedure is now almost fully under the control of the *juge de la mise en état*, the civil equivalent to the *juge d'instruction* in criminal cases. It is this judge who can dictate the pace of the pre-trial proceedings by setting time limits within which the parties must take further procedural steps, the first of which is the exchange of written pleadings (*conclusions*). In these pleadings the defendant can make a counterclaim (*demande recon-ventionnelle*), and the plaintiff can make additional claims, provided in both cases that these are sufficiently linked to the original claim (*par un lien suffisant*). The plaintiff's additional claim must not simply be a counterclaim to the defendant's own counterclaim. If the *juge de la mise en état* or any other judge is asked to make an interlocutory order he or she is said to act as the *juge des référés* and the orders issued are known as *ordonnances de référé* (Article 484). Naturally they do not make anything res judicata (*chose jugée*) and they can be appealed to the same court within 15 days, but otherwise they are enforceable immediately and to ensure compliance with them the judge can pronounce an *astreinte* (Article 491). This is, in effect, a fine imposed by a court in a civil case, usually at so much per day. It serves as an incentive to the defaulting party to comply with the court's decision in the case. In English law the nearest equivalent is a fine for contempt of court, except that that money goes to the court whereas in France the money paid under an *astreinte* goes to the plaintiff in the action. It was judges who first devised the *astreinte*, as early as 1834, but a statute of 5 July 1972 put it on a legislative footing. An *astreinte définitive* is one that cannot later be altered, while an *astreinte provisoire* is one which can be altered, and often is.

The outstanding feature of an English civil case is its orality: judges like to hear witnesses rather than read documents. In France civil proceedings in the *tribunaux d'instance* are also mainly oral in character, but in the more important *tribunaux de grande instance* the opposite is the case. The French do not take as seriously as the English the notion that every litigant is entitled to his or her day in court: instead there is often a whole series of mini-hearings, often involving written documents only, and a rather perfunctory final trial. But while most French civil proceedings are predominantly documentary in nature, it nevertheless remains necessary on occasion to resort to oral testimony even in the higher courts. Three separate types of procedure need to be mentioned in this regard. The first is personal appearance by the parties themselves (*comparution personnelle*: Articles 184–198 of the *Code de procédure civile*). While this is of course the norm in English civil procedure, it is relatively uncommon in France: whether a party can appear in person is entirely a matter for the judge's discretion and the judge decides where and when it is to occur (and whether in open court or in chambers – *chambre du conseil*). The judge asks the questions, both on his or her own behalf and on behalf of the other party to the dispute if he or she is present, and can draw whatever legal inferences seem appropriate (*toute conséquence de droit*) not just from the replies given to questions but also from the refusal to answer questions (Article 198). When answering questions the party is not allowed to read an *aide mémoire* but a signed transcript (*procès-verbal*) is kept of the proceedings.

When the judge decides to hear oral evidence not from the parties but from another witness the procedure used is called *une enquête* (Articles 204–231). The initiative can come from the judge or from one of the parties, but in the latter case the party must make it clear to the judge which facts he or she hopes to have clarified through the *enquête*. The persons eligible to be heard are all those whose appearance the judge thinks would be *utile à la manifestation de la vérité* (helpful in uncovering the truth) and any person refusing to attend such a hearing is liable to a civil fine of between 100 and 10,000 francs (Article 207). At the hearing he or she must take an oath to tell the truth (*serment de dire la vérité*). As in *comparution personnelle*, the judge is the one who poses the questions, but he or she can also serve as the channel through which questions from the parties may be put: the parties and their lawyers will usually be present during the hearing. Again a transcript is retained and the judge is permitted to include his or her own observations on the conduct of the witnesses during the hearing (Article 220). Once the witness has given evidence he or she may be asked to wait until the other witnesses have been heard and may then be recalled to add to or alter what he or she has already said.

The third oral procedure takes place when expert testimony is heard. This is supplied by what the *Code de procédure civile* refers to as *un technicien* and comes in three varieties. A *constatation* is a process whereby a person is charged with confirming a certain fact; a *consultation* is where a person investigates a purely technical and non-complex question; an *expertise* is used in other situations where clarification is still required. The persons appointed to supply these expert testimonies can be anyone of the judge's choosing (*toute personne de son choix*), though either party can challenge the appointment by what is called *une demande de récusation* and the judge can later replace the expert if he or she has failed to perform the duties associated with the position. Article 237 obliges the expert to carry out his or her investigation *avec conscience, objectivité et impartialité* but the expert must confine his or her attention to the points raised in the terms of reference; as in English law, the expert must not venture an opinion on the legal points in the case (*'il ne doit jamais porter d'appréciation d'ordre juridique'*: Article 238) and the judge is not bound to accept the findings of the expert (Article 246). The expert has the right to ask the parties as well as others for access to all documents and in cases where this right is disputed a judge can adjudicate upon the matter. At all times the expert is allowed to consult with the judge, who may, in turn, ask the expert to explain more fully his or her conclusions on an investigation. In cases where an *expertise* is conducted, but not in cases of *constatations* or *consultations*, the parties are entitled to be present when the investigation is being carried out and to comment on it (Article 276): this is in furtherance of the *principe du contradictoire*, whereby each party must be allowed to contest evidence submitted against him or her. Also in cases of *expertise*, the parties are allowed to appeal against decisions of the judge (e.g. on the expert's terms of reference) and the expert is permitted to seek the views of other experts while conducting the investigation.

In addition to these procedures whereby oral testimony may be elicited, the *juge de la mise en état* may receive written testimony from persons other than the parties (*attestations*: Articles 200–203), or may personally conduct investigations into the disputed facts (*vérifications*: Articles 179–183). The latter usually means an on-site examination of a relevant location but Article 179 allows much more than this:

Le juge peut, afin de les vérifier lui-même, prendre en toute matière une connaissance personnelle des faits litigieux . . . Il procède aux constatations, évaluations, appréciations ou reconstitutions qu'il estime nécessaires . . .

(The judge can, in order to verify them himself (or herself), undertake in every case a personal investigation of disputed facts . . . He (or she) can carry out whatever confirmation, evaluation, assessment or reconstruction he (or she) deems necessary . . .)

THE TRIAL AND APPEAL

Once the pre-trial judge is satisfied that the pre-trial proceedings are complete (*dès que l'état de l'instruction le permet*), he or she closes the pre-trial stage (*clôture de l'instruction*) and transmits the case to the trial court (Article 779). It is the trial court which will set it down for trial on a particular day. Unlike in criminal cases the pre-trial judge does not have to prepare a report for the benefit of the trial judges, though the president of the court may ask for this '*s'il estime que l'affaire le requiert*' (if he (or she) thinks that the case requires it) (Article 785).

At the final trial (*l'audience publique*) the pre-trial judge will present his or her report (if there is one), the lawyers for the parties will present their oral arguments (*plaidoiries*) based on the *dossiers* collected at the pre-trial stage (these oral arguments are known collectively as *les débats*), the judges will consider whether it is necessary to order *comparution personnelle des parties* or an *enquête*, and then they will retire to deliberate upon their decision (*le délibéré*). This deliberation takes place of course in private (Article 448) and the decision is reached by majority vote (Article 449). The judgment may be issued immediately (*sur le champ*) or be reserved (*renvoyé*), but when it eventually appears it must succinctly set out the parties' respective claims and arguments and then provide a reasoned decision (*un dispositif motivé*) (Article 455). If one or more judges have dissented they do not publish a dissenting judgment. Compared with English judgments the French versions are remarkably short; it is often difficult to deduce the exact line of reasoning which has led the judges to a particular conclusion, or at any rate to know what implications the decision may have for other similar but not identical cases. There is virtually no scope for *obiter dicta* in French law.

The appeal system in civil cases has been outlined in Chapter 2. The aggrieved party can lodge an appeal (*appel*) with the *cour d'appel*, usually within one month. Until the time for appealing has expired, and contrary to the position in English law, the judgment of the first instance court in France is considered to be unenforceable in the absence of a special court order: the possibility of an appeal is said to have a suspensive effect on the judgment or, as Article 500 puts it, '*a force de chose jugée le jugement qui n'est susceptible d'aucun recours suspensif d'exécution*' (a judgment renders an issue *res judicata* if the judgment is no longer subject to an appeal suspending its enforcement). The appeal means that the case 'devolves' to the *cour d'appel* for a consideration of the parts of the judgment under attack (*les chefs du jugement*) (Articles 561–567: *l'effet dévolutif*).

The procedures adopted in the *cour d'appel* are similar to those used in the *tribunal de grande instance*, with the pre-trial stage being kept separate from the trial stage. For the former it is still necessary to employ an *avoué*, a special kind of lawyer largely specialising in appeal cases, but at the final appeal hearing itself an *avocat* can again be used. There are interesting provisions in Articles 559 and 560 of the *Code de procédure civile* which say, respectively, that if an appeal is dilatory or an abuse of process (*dilatoire ou abusif*) the appellant can be subjected to a civil fine of between 100 and 10,000 francs (even if the appeal is successful), and that if an appeal is lodged by an appellant who for no good reason (*sans motif légitime*) did not appear at the first instance court the appeal court can require him or her to pay damages.

There are some decisions, such as those concerning claims below 13,000 francs (about £1,500), against which no appeal can be lodged; however, in cases where an appeal is possible but the time limit for lodging an appeal has elapsed, a party to the case can still seek to have the decision re-opened (*recours en révision*) within two months of becoming aware of new factual information suggesting that the earlier decision was wrong (Articles 595–596). The decision of a court of last instance can also, of course, be subjected to *un pourvoi en cassation*, which allows the *Cour de Cassation* to review the law applied by the lower court but not the findings of facts. Unlike an *appel*, an application for *cassation* does not normally suspend the effects of the judgment in question; the application is dealt with almost entirely through documents rather than oral argumentation, the documents (*mémoires*) being drafted by another special branch of the legal profession (of which there are only about 60 members), *les avocats au Conseil d'Etat et à la Cour de Cassation* (Article 973).

Once it is no longer possible to challenge a judgment on appeal it can be executed by serving a copy of the judgment on the unsuccessful party, but if this party refuses to comply with the judgment the successful party must obtain a further court order. Articles 545–749 of the *ancien Code de procédure civile* provide for remedies such as distraint of property (*saisie*).

CASES WITH A FOREIGN ELEMENT

If the defendant in a civil case is based outside France then any documents which must be served on him or her will be sent via the *ministère public* and the Ministry of Justice (Articles 684–685 of the *nouveau Code de procédure civile*), though the *huissier* must send a copy by registered mail directly to the addressee abroad. The defendant is given a two-month extension on time limits applying to matters such as registering an appearance, submitting a defence or lodging an appeal (Article 643).

The 1968 Brussels Convention on Jurisdiction and Enforcement of Judgments in Civil and Commercial Matters has been part of domestic French law since it was ratified by France and brought into force across Europe in 1973; in England this was achieved by the Civil Jurisdiction and Judgments Act 1982. The *nouveau Code de procédure civile* reproduces the Convention in an annex. France has also incorporated the 1970 Hague Convention on the Obtaining of Evidence Abroad in Civil and Commercial

Matters. For countries not party to this Convention, Article 733 of the Civil Procedure Code provides more generally that a French judge can issue letters rogatory (*une commission rogatoire*) to a competent judicial authority in a foreign country or to French diplomatic officers abroad. These letters, which are again delivered via the *ministère public* and the Ministry of Justice, authorise the taking of whatever investigative or judicial actions are deemed necessary by the judge. Articles 736 to 748 deal with the converse situation, where *une commission rogatoire* is sent to France from abroad. The French judge cannot refuse to comply with the letters rogatory on the grounds that French law claims exclusive jurisdiction over the matter, that it has no legal procedure meeting the aims of the foreign request or that it would arrive at a different result in the case from the one likely to be reached abroad. However, the judge can refuse compliance if he or she believes the request made is outside his or her jurisdiction and compliance must be refused if otherwise French sovereignty or security would be compromised.

For further information about the international recognition and enforcement of judgments, see Chapter 14.

FURTHER READING

The best accounts in English of French civil procedure are in West *et al.*, *The French Legal System: An Introduction* (1992), Chapter 6 (which also contains sample documents which might have been used in a typical *tribunal d'instance* action) and in C. Dadomo and S. Farran, *The French Legal System* (1993), pp. 155–81. Less systematic is the information supplied by G. Danet and B. Weiss-Gout, in M. Sheridan and J. Cameron (eds), *EC Legal Systems: An Introductory Guide* (1992). For an annotated translation in English of the *nouveau Code*, see de Kerstrat and Crawford, *The New Code of Civil Procedure in France* (1978). Learned articles include those by Sloan, 'Games French people play with class actions' (1972) 45 *Temple Law Quarterly* 210; Wesley, 'Litigating personal injury and other cases in France' (1985) 129 Sol Jo 863; J. Beardsley, 'Proof of Fact in French Civil Procedure' (1986) 34 Am Jo Comp L 459; J. A. Jolowicz, 'Comparative law and the reform of civil procedure' (1988) 8 *Legal Studies* 1; and C. N. Ngwasiri, 'The role of the judge in French civil proceedings' [1990] *Civil Justice Quarterly* 167.

In French the best books are G. Goubeaux and P. Voirin, *Les épreuves écrites de droit civil* (7th edn, 1993); A. Jauffret and J. Normand, *Manuel de procédure civile et voies d'exécution* (15th edn, 1992); G. Couchez, *Procédure civile* (7th edn, 1992); J. Vincent and S. Guinchard, *Procédure civile* (22nd edn, 1991); and H. Croze and C. Morel, *Procédure civile* (1988). Books entitled *Droit judiciaire privé* contain information not just about civil procedure strictly so called but also about the jurisdiction of each of the civil courts; a good one is by L. Cadiet (1992).

CHAPTER 8

Contract law

INTRODUCTION

In France contract law is studied as part of the law of obligations. The *Code civil* itself views a contract as simply one method whereby property can be acquired. Articles 1101–1369 are devoted to the general principles relating to the subject, while several later parts of Book 3 deal in detail with specific forms of contract, such as sales (Articles 1582–1701), hire (Articles 1708–1831), loans (Articles 1874–1914) and charges (Articles 2092–2203). Outside the *Code civil* French law recognises two types of special contracts – *contrats commerciaux* and *contrats administratifs*. Indeed, in France the concept of contract is wide enough, and flexible enough, to embrace what in England are usually treated as discrete subjects, namely bailments, trusts and leases. This chapter will explain the general features of French contract law, including the protections available to consumers, leaving to Chapter 10 a description of more particular commercial law transactions. Administrative contracts are discussed in Chapter 4.

At the heart of a valid contract in the eyes of English law is the notion of a bargain. The concepts which that law has developed to substantiate this notion are offer, acceptance, consideration, intention to create legal relations and contractual capacity. Most commentators now acknowledge the artificiality of the concepts of offer and acceptance (it is certainly impossible to analyse the formation of every bargain in those terms, especially the so-called standard form contracts) but the requirement of consideration is still taken fairly seriously. It has been under attack at least since the damning, but still unimplemented, report by the Law Revision Committee of 1937, and it has been severely undermined both by the doctrine of promissory estoppel (which, regrettably, has not advanced since the retirement of Lord Denning in 1982) and by isolated decisions such as *Williams* v *Roffey Bros and Nicholls (Contractors) Ltd* (1990). But it has nevertheless remained intact.

In France the rules on contracts which were enshrined in the 1804 *Code civil* were largely adopted from the work of Pothier, whose *Traité des Obligations* was published in 1761. In the 19th century the writings of the German Roman law expert Savigny greatly influenced the way in which the rules were applied by the courts. The principles established during that period, as can also be said for English law, still largely reflect the legal position today. As regards the formation of contracts, French law applies a more subjective approach than English law: rather than look for what might appear to third-party observers to be the *indicia* of a contractual relationship it hunts for evidence of a real agreement between the parties. There are of course several requirements to be fulfilled before a transaction will be recognised as a valid contract in French law, but the concepts embraced by those requirements are not reified to the same fictitious degree as they are in English law. In addition, one party's innocent mistake, or the other party's absence of good faith, play roles in French contract law which do not exist in English contract law. However, *contrats d'adhésion* – standard form contracts – are just as common in France as they are in England.

FORMATION OF A CONTRACT

By Article 1101 of the *Code civil*:

> *Le contrat est une convention par laquelle une ou plusieurs personnes s'obligent, envers une ou plusieurs autres, à donner, à faire ou à ne pas faire quelque chose.*

> (A contract is an agreement by which one or more persons bind themselves to one or more other persons to give, do or not do something.)

Then Article 1108 categorically states:

> *Quatre conditions sont essentielles pour la validité d'une convention: le consentement de la partie qui s'oblige; sa capacité de contracter; un objet certain qui forme la matière de l'engagement; une cause licite dans l'obligation.*

> (Four conditions are essential for the validity of an agreement: the consent of the party binding himself or herself; his or her capacity to contract; a definite subject-matter for the arrangement; a legitimate purpose for the binding obligation.)

In English law, of course, considerable attention is paid to the need for an agreement to be properly formed; there is a lot of case law, for instance, on the difference between an offer and an invitation to treat and on when an acceptance becomes effective. As regards acceptances sent through the post, the so-called theory of emission applies, whereby the acceptance is effective the moment the letter is sent. The French, by and large, are not as perplexed by these problems, usually treating them as matters of fact, not of law, and so the *Cour de Cassation* does not attempt to lay down general rules in respect of them. As far as the definition of an offer is concerned, to the French the important requirement is that the maker of what appears to be an offer must have been willing to enter into a contract on a specific set of terms. To be an offer (*offre* or *pollicitation*) a statement must have been precise, definite and unequivocal (*précise, ferme* and *non équivoque*). Anything short of an offer can be termed *une invitation à des pourparlers* (an invitation to enter negotiations).

An offer will lapse in French law (*causes de caducité*) if the time fixed for acceptance runs out, if the offeror dies or if the offeree replies with a counter-offer (*contre-proposition*). What is innovatory from an English viewpoint is the principle that an offeree can still sue an offeror on an offer if it is withdrawn prior to the elapse of a specified time, or if a reasonable time has not yet elapsed since the offer was first made. In England such an action would be possible only if there were consideration for a promise, express or implied, to keep the offer open. There would also have to be an intention to create legal relations on the part of the maker of the offer. The cause of action in France, however, would be seen not as a purely contractual one (no contract has actually come into existence) but as a non-contractual (i.e. tortious) one arising under Article 1382 of the *Code civil*. This way of dealing with the matter (known as the doctrine of *culpa in contrahendo*) is facilitated by contract and tort law being seen by the French as simply separate parts of the all-embracing law of obligations. Although there are indications that some commentators are now adopting a similar frame of reference for English law (see recent books on the law of obligations by Tettenborn and by Cooke and Oughton), the strong tradition is to maintain a clear distinction between the two 'branches' of law.

As far as letters of acceptance go, there is no clear position in French law as to whether the sending or the receiving of the letter determines the conclusion of the contract. For a while it seemed that the former was preferred (*théorie de l'expédition*) in situations where the question was *where* the contract was concluded, while the latter was preferred (*théorie de la réception*) in situations where the question was *when* the contract was concluded; but in the most recent cases the *Cour de Cassation* seems to have almost always opted for the first theory, while saying that of course the parties themselves retain the freedom to agree otherwise.

French contract law knows nothing of the notions of consideration and intention to create legal relations. To an extent it incorporates them into its very concept of an offer. It employs, however, two supplementary concepts which complicate the picture almost as much as consideration does in English law. These are *cause* and *objet*.

Zweigert and Kötz define *cause* as 'simply the generalised motive behind a promise' and conclude that today the concept lacks meaningful content. David, on the other hand, writing in 1980, said that 'No criticism is raised at present in France against that doctrine'. Although it is often pointed out that the German Civil Code, enacted in 1896, manages to do without the idea of *cause*, David and others would argue that the role it plays in French law is still necessary in other legal systems, which consequently adopt alternative devices for fulfilling that role. In France every contract is meant to be supported throughout its life by *une cause licite*, but in practice very few contracts are held invalid because of its absence. Promises to do something because it is the honourable or decent thing to do have been sustained as lawful and enforceable, though in early cases (before it was accepted that the stipulation of a 'symbolic' price can achieve the same end) this was sometimes because in France a gratuitous gift can be invalid unless it is recorded by a *notaire* and so courts have an incentive to label unnotarised gifts as contracts in order to preserve their validity. One might draw an analogy here with the reasoning sometimes employed in English cases: if a promise would be enforceable if contained in a deed under seal, why let it be held unenforceable due to the absence of something that can easily, if artificially, be labelled consideration? The purpose of the doctrine of consideration is, in effect, to distinguish those promises which the law deems worthy of enforcement from those it does not: it reflects the idea, always central to the English law of contract, that only bargains, or exchanges, should be legally enforceable. The function of *cause* in French law, however, is different: it is to provide evidence of what kind of transaction the parties intended to enter into, so that if their final agreement does not embody their joint original intentions, or if the parties turn out to be at cross-purposes in respect of their intentions, the contract can be said to be *sans cause* or based on *une fause cause* (Article 1131).

The requirement that every contract in French law must have an *objet* is nowadays of little significance. In effect it is equivalent to the English requirement of certainty: if the parties have not reached agreement on all the important terms of their contract it cannot yet be said to exist. Likewise if, prior to agreement being reached, the subject-matter of the proposed contract has been destroyed, there is no longer an 'object' to be dealt with by the parties. In some of these latter cases English law will nevertheless hold a promisor liable for failing to perform the impossible, whereas in French law the promisor is liable, if at all, only for pre-contractual fault (*culpa in contrahendo*). In cases where the 'object' of a contract is illegal, French law now prefers to strike down the agreement, not for lack of *objet* but for lack of *cause licite*.

The absence of a doctrine of consideration in French law means, for a start, that the rule against past consideration plays no part in France: a promise made in return for services already rendered is just as enforceable as one made for services agreed to be rendered in the future. It also means that what to the English is termed a unilateral, or executory, contract – one consisting of a promise in return for an as yet unperformed act – is in France viewed as an ordinary bilateral (or what the *Code civil* also calls a synallagmatic) contract:

Le contrat est synallagmatique ou bilatéral lorsque les contractants s'obligent réciproquement les uns envers les autres.

(A contract is synallagmatic or bilateral when the contracting parties bind one another reciprocally.) (Article 1102)

In French eyes a unilateral contract is one where one or more persons are bound *vis-à-vis* one or more others without these others themselves having to fulfil any requirements (Article 1103). An agreement to make a gift would be an example. In de Moor's words:

> there is thus a difference between the French *contrat unilatéral*, by which one party only is bound from the moment of agreement, and the English unilateral contract which, because of the requirement of consideration, only becomes binding upon completeion of the act required. (p. 282)

To help fill the gap in English law in this regard the courts, particularly through the interventions of Lords Denning and Goff, have developed the doctrine of promissory estoppel. In France such a doctrine has not been necessary because the courts have been able to construe a serious promise as creative of a contract, the mere silence of the promisee not being an objection to the enforcement of the promise in the way that silence would be seen by English law as not tantamount to acceptance. Just a few years before the *High Trees* case in England (1947), a case with similar facts arose in France. The *Cour de Cassation* held that the landlord was bound by his promise to reduce the rent because the offer he had made to the tenant was in the latter's exclusive interest.

THIRD PARTIES

English law's obsession with the doctrine of consideration has also made it more difficult for the principle of privity to be fully abandoned, even though there are now a great many exceptions to it. In Articles 1119 and 1165 of the *Code civil* there are similar prohibitions on third party involvement:

> *On ne peut, en général, s'engager, ni stipuler en son propre nom, que pour soi-même.*

> (In general one can bind only oneself or make promises only on one's own behalf.) (Article 1119)

> *Les conventions n'ont d'effet qu'entre les parties contractantes.*

> (Agreements can affect only the parties to them.) (Article 1165)

But the French notion that a contract is simply an agreement, rather than a bargain, has allowed the courts to create a high number of exceptions to this general principle, and the kind of serpentine reasoning with regard to the requirement of consideration in which the courts have had to indulge in order to allow exceptions in English law has not been necessary. The French judicial approach has been aided by the fact that Article 1121 of the *Code civil* already drives a coach and horses through the privity rule in Article 1165:

> *On peut . . . stipuler au profit d'un tiers, lorsque telle est la condition d'une stipulation que l'on fait pour soi-même ou d'une donation que l'on fait à un autre.*

> (One can promise something to a third party if this is the condition upon which something was promised to oneself or upon which one has made a gift to another.)

Even so, the French judges have devised the notion of an *action directe* to allow third parties to sue a contracting party without having to rely upon the other party's assistance: if *Beswick* v *Beswick* (1968) or *Jackson* v *Horizon Holidays* (1975) were to occur in France, there would be no need for convoluted arguments supporting a direct cause of action for the wives and children concerned.

MISTAKES

As regards the requisite consent for a valid contract, the French courts will assume there is an agreement unless one of the parties can prove a *vice du consentement* (a defect in the agreement). It is no longer even necessary for a particular *vice* to be specified in the claim, but the law actually categorises them into *erreur*, *violence* and *dol*:

> *Il n'y a point de consentement valable, si le consentement n'a été donné que par erreur, ou s'il a été extorqué par violence ou surpris par dol.*

> (There is no valid agreement if consent has been given only by mistake or if it has been extorted by duress or fraud.) (Article 1109)

As has been ably demonstrated by Nicholas, the concept of *erreur* is much wider than the concept of mistake in English law. It is enough, in France, if, had the mistaken party not been mistaken, he or she would not have entered into the contract. If one party can show that he or she had not expressly agreed to one of the suggested terms of the contract then the whole contract can be declared void. So the English idea that the mistake has to be really fundamental before it can have any effect in law is not mirrored in the French rules; a mistake as to the identity of the person with whom one is contracting, or even as to his or her creditworthiness, and even a mistake as to the state of the law on a certain point, can be enough in France. All that is required is that the thing about which a party is mistaken should be a principal motive for that person in concluding the contract and that the mistake should concern basic qualities of the object of the contract. In the terms of the first paragraph of Article 1110 of the *Code civil*:

L'erreur n'est une cause de nullité de la convention que lorsqu'elle tombe sur la substance même de la chose qui en est l'objet.

(A mistake annuls an agreement only if it relates to the very substance of the object of the agreement.)

What in England would sometimes be dealt with under the rubrics of innocent misrepresentation or breach (in contract law), or negligent misrepresentation (in tort law), will in France often be dealt with as examples of *erreur*. But in both legal systems a mistake merely as to the value of an article, or as to the motive for entering into a contract, would not be enough to constitute an operative mistake, for just as a person's negligence will prevent him or her from relying upon a mistake in English law, so in France an 'inexcusable' mistake will not be allowed to have any legal effect.

French law does not categorise mistakes in the rather confusing way that English law chooses to do (distinguishing between common, mutual and unilateral mistakes – though judges and academics disagree over how to use these labels – and adding, for good measure, documents mistakenly signed). The closest French law comes to this division is in its distinction, now considered somewhat old-fashioned, between an *erreur obstacle*, which concerns some barrier to the very existence of the agreement in the first place (the preference of some English commentators for the label of mistakes negativing consent is comparable) and an *erreur sur la substance*, which is referred to specifically in Article 1110, cited above. Today the books tend simply to examine how the general principle of *erreur sur la substance* applies in practice to typical situations (mistake of law, mistake as to the authenticity of a work of art, mistake as to the price or value of something, or as to one's reasons for making the contract, etc.). It should be remembered, also, that one reason why French courts may be more willing to allow a party to rescind a contract on the basis of mistake is that they retain a power to balance the rescission with an award of damages to the non-mistaken party so that he or she does not suffer any loss as a result of the other party's mistake. No such compensatory power exists in English law.

It is worth illustrating the French law on mistake by reference to one important case which received coverage even in English newspapers. It also serves as an example of the manner in which litigation can be prolonged in France. In 1968 a mining engineer named Monsieur Saint-Arroman took a painting which his family had owned for some time to a firm of auctioneers in Paris, where it was identified as being of the Carracci school. It was bought at the auction for 2,200 francs by a London gallery, but at the last minute the *Réunion des musées nationaux* stepped in to exercise its right of pre-emption for the French nation, one of its experts having identified the painting as an early masterpiece by the 17th-century French artist Poussin. The painting was then put on display in the Louvre. In 1972 the *tribunal de grande instance de Paris* allowed Monsieur and Madame Saint-Arroman to invoke their own mistake so as to get the sale rescinded. On appeal, in 1976, the *cour d'appel de Paris* overturned the lower court's decision, on the basis that the picture's attribution had been uncertain and that therefore the sellers' mistake could not bear on the *substance* of the contract. In turn, however, the *Cour de Cassation* quashed this decision in 1978 because the appeal court had not established whether, at the time of the sale, the sellers' consent had actually been vitiated by an erroneous belief that the picture could not have been by Poussin. The case was therefore sent back to another *cour d'appel*. In 1982 the *cour d'appel d'Amiens* held that it was important to consider the time at which the reality of the situation had to be compared with the sellers' belief; that court thought that the relevant time was the moment at which the contract was made and here, because in 1968 attributing the picture to Poussin was not taken to be 'a serious possibility', there was no operative mistake. Back in the *Cour de Cassation*, in 1983, the relevant time was held to be the day on which the original judges had had to decide the case, in 1972. The *cour d'appel de Versailles* then applied this ruling in 1987 and the painting was ordered to be returned to its original owners. In December 1988 it was again auctioned, this time as a Poussin; it fetched approximately £600,000.

In England it is much more difficult for a party to get out of a contract concerning a work of art which turns out to be much more or less valuable than anticipated. There are *dicta* to that effect by the House of Lords in *Bell* v *Lever Bros* (1932) and decisions in *Leaf* v *International Galleries* (1950) and *Harlingdon & Leinster Enterprises Ltd* v *Christopher Hull Fine Art Ltd* (1990).

DURESS, FRAUD, UNFAIRNESS AND ILLEGALITY

Duress

Duress (*violence*) is dealt with by Articles 1111–1115 of the *Code civil*. The immediate difference from English law is that (by Article 1111) *violence* is operative in France even though the duress emanates from a person who is not a party to the contract. The actual definition of duress is similar in both countries, Article 1112 saying that it exists:

> *lorsqu'elle est de nature à faire impression sur une personne raisonnable, et qu'elle peut lui inspirer la crainte d'exposer sa personne ou sa fortune à un mal considérable et présent.*

> (when it is such as to affect a reasonable person and to make him or her fear that his or her person or possessions will be exposed to considerable and imminent risk.)

It is also enough in France if the duress has been exercised on the spouse or close family relative of a contracting party, but a threat to exercise one's proper legal rights will not be duress, subject to the operation of the abuse of rights doctrine (*abus de droits*). Recent cases suggest that, as in English law, economic duress may qualify for relief. There are at least two reported cases where an employee has been allowed to escape from a contract on the basis that he accepted a low wage because of his straitened financial circumstances at the time, and there is a 1984 decision concerning the blacking of a ship comparable to the two House of Lords cases of *The Universe Sentinel* (1982) and *The Evia Luck* (1991).

Fraud

There is only one provision in the *Code civil* devoted to fraud (*dol*) (Article 1116):

Le dol est une cause de nullité de la convention lorsque les manoeuvres pratiqueés par l'une des parties sont telles, qu'il est évident que, sans ces manoeuvres, l'autre partie n'aurait pas contracté. Il ne se présume pas, et doit être prouvé.

(Fraud annuls an agreement whenever one party's conduct is such that it is clear that, if that conduct had not occurred, the other party would not have entered into the contract. It is not presumed but must be proved.)

As in England, the courts in France have found it difficult at times to distinguish between simple hard bargaining, which is perfectly commercially acceptable, indeed to be respected, and artifice, deceit, lies, dishonesty and cheating, all of which are *manoeuvres dolosives*. One of the topical issues is whether mere silence can constitute fraud (*dol par réticence*). It seems that it can, especially in cases involving the transfer of land or involving professional salespeople. In credit sales there is frequently an obligation to supply certain information to the buyer, and in one recent case a contract for the sale of a second-hand car was rescinded on this basis. Unlike *violence*, however, *dol* can affect a contract only if it is exerted by a contracting party (or someone for whom that party is vicariously liable). In English law this is also the case for purely innocent misrepresentation (for which of course rescission is available, though not damages as of right), but not for negligent or fraudulent misrepresentation, which are really concepts regulated by the law of torts.

Unfairness and illegality

What remains true in France, just as in England, is that mere unfairness in a transaction is not enough by itself to justify the rescission of a contract.

Inequalities in exchange are taken to be part and parcel of the rich tapestry of contractual life. Nor is there anything comparable to the doctrine of inequality of bargaining power which Lord Denning tried to create in decisions such as *Lloyds Bank Ltd* v *Bundy* (1974). The nearest thing to this is probably the French doctrine of *lésion*. According to Article 1118, this doctrine does not vitiate contracts except in the situations specified elsewhere in the *Code civil*, the three principal examples of this being acceptance of a legacy, contracts entered into by minors, and sales of immovable property (Articles 783, 1305 and 1674). For the last of these three situations there is a particularly definite principle: if the seller has sold land for less than five-twelfths of its true value, he or she can ask (provided this is prior to the elapse of the two-year limitation period) for the contract to be rescinded; this applies even if the seller had expressly given up this right in the contract itself.

Also worth mentioning in the context of illegal, immoral or simply unfair contracts are Articles 6 and 1133 of the *Code civil*. These provide as follows:

> *On ne peut déroger, par des conventions particulières, aux lois qui intéressent l'ordre public et les bonnes moeurs.*

> (Contracting parties cannot violate statutes which represent public policy and good practice.) (Article 6)

> *La cause est illicite, quand elle est prohibée par la loi, quand elle est contraire aux bonnes moeurs ou à l'ordre public.*

> (A contract is unlawful if it is prohibited by statute or contrary to good practice or public policy.) (Article 1133).

From time to time these provisions are invoked, especially in consumer contracts, to protect parties who are being exploited.

In both England and France the general principle holds that parties are free to agree whatever they like in their contracts, subject of course to the law's views on public policy. In French this is known as *l'autonomie de la volonté*. In reality, of course, 20th-century contract law has moved significantly away from such untrammelled liberalism; a more paternalistic approach has had to be adopted in several areas in order to protect the weak against the strong, the vulnerable against the exploitative. Consumers have benefited particularly from this more caring legal attitude. But even the original version of the *Code civil* laid down precise obligations on parties to special types of contract. French law does not utilise the concept of implied terms – a great favourite with English judges when they can find no other rational way of reaching the decision they wish to arrive at without completely ignoring the freedom of contract principle – preferring instead to rely on such doctrines as *abus de droits*, *ordre public* and *bonnes moeurs*. But judicial creativity has not been lacking when required. As early as 1911, for instance, the *Cour de Cassation* succeeded in imposing more or less strict liability on passenger transport companies if they killed or injured their passengers: it was not so much that a term was implied to that effect but that the very nature of the transport contract was held to entail an *obligation de sécurité* (or *obligation de résultat* or *obligation déterminée*), rather than an *obligation de moyens* (or *obligation de prudence et de diligence*).

To a certain extent it would help an English lawyer to think of these *obligations de sécurité* and *obligations de moyens* as roughly equivalent to conditions and warranties. Breaches of the former have more serious consequences than breaches of the latter. The French, however, have found it as difficult as the English to devise a reliable test for deciding when an obligation falls into one or other of the two categories. An influential factor in France is the doctrine of *non-cumul*, which in this context means that an action in tort cannot be brought if an action in contract is also available: if relatives and friends of contracting parties can sue in tort under Article 1382 or, more likely, Article 1384 (*see* Chapter 9), the courts have an incentive to allow a contractual claim to the contracting parties as well. There is no real equivalent to the 'wait and see' test which is applied in English law in order to categorise so-called innominate or intermediate terms (see *Hong Kong Fir Shipping Co.* v *Kawasaki Kisen Kaisha Ltd*, 1962).

TERMINATION OF A CONTRACT

One of the most difficult statements for an English lawyer to swallow is that French law does not use the notion of discharge of contract. There is no direct equivalent to the idea of frustration, although in administrative contracts the doctrine of *imprévision* comes very close to it (*see* Chapter 4). Instead the French rely on absence of *cause*, already alluded to, and on the principle of *force majeure*, enshrined in Article 1148 of the *Code civil*:

> *Il n'y a lieu à aucuns dommages et intérêts lorsque, par suite d'une force majeure ou d'un cas fortuit, le débiteur a été empêché de donner ou de faire ce à quoi il était obligé, ou a fait ce qui lui était interdit.*

> (No compensation can be claimed if, following an act of God, a contracting party has been prevented from giving or doing what he or she was obliged to give or do, or has done something which he or she was prohibited from doing.)

But the doctrines of *cause* and *force majeure* are not as wide-ranging as the doctrine of frustration in English law. In particular, they seem to cover only cases of physical or legal impossibility, not the sort of commercial impossibility evident in cases such as *Krell* v *Henry* (1903). The standard illustration of this is the *Canal de Craponne* case, decided by the *Cour de Cassation* in 1876. The case concerned contracts dating from 1560 and

1567, according to which a company operating a canal was to irrigate landowners' orchards for an annual sum of money. This sum had of course become derisory by the 1870s. Nevertheless, the *Cour de Cassation* maintained the principle that the courts could not interfere with the contract. This attitude may be contrasted with the decision of the English Court of Appeal in *Staffordshire Area Health Authority* v *South Staffordshire Waterworks Co.* (1978).

In instances where the French courts are able to excuse a party's performance because of the absence of *cause* (and it need not be a total absence), the other party is granted restitution of whatever performance he or she has already delivered, or the monetary equivalent thereof. If there is no excuse for non-performance (*inexécution*) the other party is entitled to refuse to carry out his or her performance (the so-called defence of *non adimpleti contractus*) or, if it is too late for that, to ask a court to order what English lawyers would call specific performance. As such performance may not be possible, the remedy, as in England, inevitably becomes one of damages. Indeed, Article 1142 of the *Code civil* provides:

> *Toute obligation de faire ou de ne pas faire se résout en dommages et intérêts, en cas d'inexécution de la part du débiteur.*

> (Every obligation to do or not to do something leads to compensation if the person who is under the obligation does not perform it.)

Immediately following this provision, however, there are two more which considerably qualify it. By Article 1143, if a contracting party has done something which he or she promised not to do, the other party can get a court order authorising what has been done to be 'destroyed' (*détruit*), at the first party's expense and without prejudice to a claim for damages. The courts are more willing in France than in England to order such destruction, even of buildings. Article 1144 allows a contracting party who has waited in vain for the other party to perform to seek a court order authorising him or her to engage a third party to carry out the performance at the expense of the defaulting party. The combined effect of Articles 1143 and 1144 is to deprive Article 1142 of most of its teeth; it tends today to be confined to personal obligations, which it is against public policy both in France and in England to seek to be specifically performed by order of a court. The famous case involving Whistler's portrait of Lady Eden, recounted by Nicholas (pp. 213–4), provides a typical illustration of the limited operation of Article 1142.

No account of remedies in the French law of contract would be complete without a reference to the peculiarly French concept known as *astreinte*. It is explained in Chapter 7.

CONSUMER LAW

Like all other developed countries, France has experienced a tremendous growth in consumerism in the past 40 years, and alongside this has come a sophisticated body of laws to protect consumer interests. Some older laws have been made to serve a more modern function, but completely new legislation has also been passed, especially since 1970. A consumer, generally speaking, is someone who obtains or uses goods or services for personal, not professional, purposes. Consumer contracts are therefore often contrasted with commercial contracts. English law recognises this distinction not just by enacting legislation which applies mainly to consumer contracts, such as the Consumer Credit Act 1974 and the Consumer Protection Act 1987, but also by inserting special protections in legislation applying to a broader range of contracts, such as the Unfair Contract Terms Act 1977 and the Sale of Goods Act 1979.

In the *Code civil* itself, Articles 1641–1649 make all sellers strictly liable for latent defects in the goods they sell, whether the buyer is a consumer or not. This is a more extensive liability than that imposed upon English sellers by virtue of the terms concerning description, merchantability and fitness for purpose implied into contracts by the Sale of Goods Act 1979. In France an important statute was passed in 1905 imposing criminal liability on persons who use fraud when selling food; it has since been extended to cover many other products and services; a law of 22 December 1972 grants persons who buy from door-to-door salespeople a right to change their mind within seven days (*un délai de réflexion*); Article 44 of the *loi Royer* (1973) prohibits deceitful advertising (*la publicité trompeuse*), while Article 46 (amended in 1988) allows consumer associations to take court actions to defend consumer interests; a law of 4 January 1978 amends Articles 1972 *et seq.* in the *Code civil* so as to impose greater duties on building contractors; two statutes passed on 10 January 1978, each referred to as the *loi Scrivener*, grant a seven-day change-of-mind period to consumers taking credit to buy movable goods and lay down new laws on unfair clauses (*clauses abusives*); a statute of 1979 gives greater protection to persons taking credit to purchase land; in 1982 the *loi Quillot* regulated landlord and tenant agreements, and this was further amended both in 1986 (the *loi Méhaignerie*) and 1989 (the *loi Mermaz*); a decree of 1984 governs the labelling of prepackaged food products; an ordinance of 1 December 1986 and an *arrêté* of 3 December 1987 contain provisions on pricing information; a law of 6 January 1988 confers the seven-day change-of-mind period on persons who buy on a mail order basis (*la vente à distance*); a decree of 4 March 1988 amends the *Code de procédure civile* to make it easier for a consumer to obtain a court order requiring the other contracting party to do something, such as deliver goods or perform a service (*l'injonction de faire*); two statutes, each referred to as the *loi Neiertz*, contain measures to help persons who are heavily in debt (law of 31

December 1989) and to allow joint actions by individual consumers (*l'action en représentation conjointe*) (law of 18 January 1992).

It is clearly apparent that, as is the case in England, consumer law in France has a great variety of sources. Given the French predilection for codification, it should come as no surprise that a statute of 26 July 1993 makes provision for all the exisiting statutory measures to be codified. This has now been achieved, with a *partie réglementaire* to follow. The *Code de la consommation* consists of five books. Book 1 deals with consumer information and the formation of consumer contracts; Book 2 with the quality and safety of products and services; Book 3 with consumer credit; Book 4 with consumer organisations; and Book 5 (not yet complete) with institutions operating in the consumer field, such as *Le Conseil national et les comités départmentaux de la consommation*, the intra-governmental committees concerned with consumer matters, *L'Institut national de la consommation* and *Le Conseil national de l'alimentation*. The Code is consolidatory only – it does not add to the existing law – and its content therefore still falls far short of what some campaigners want. In particular, the Commission on the Reform of Consumer Law (*Commission de refonte du droit de la consommation*), appointed by the government in 1982, has issued two lengthy reports proposing a fairly radical overhaul of legal protection for consumers. Whatever reforms are eventually introduced, account will of course have to be taken of European Community initiatives, which are growing increasingly common in this area. Directives have already been issued on the marking of prices on foodstuffs (1979), misleading advertising (1984), product liability (1985), doorstep selling (1985) and consumer credit (1986). Others in the pipeline include those on general product safety, package tours and unfair terms. To date the EC measures have not required France to alter its own relatively high standards in consumer protection, but that day may soon come.

It is worth looking in a little more detail at the provisions of one of the pieces of legislation mentioned above, the second *loi Scrivener* in 1978, and comparing them with those in the Unfair Contract Terms Act 1977. In the first place the French law is wider in scope, since it is not confined to certain types of contracts as is the English Act (Schedule 1 excludes contracts such as those involving land, insurance or shares). The French law does, though, seem to be limited to written contracts (since one of the sanctions it imposes is that the clause in question should be regarded as unwritten – *réputée non écrite*); the English Act extends to all contracts which are made on one party's 'written standard terms of business', while also applying to every contract made by a consumer as such. But the two laws affect very similar categories of individual. In France the category consists of those who contract with professionals as consumers or non-professionals (Article 35); in England it comprises those persons who, while not operating in the course of a business, contract with those who do (s. 12). The French provision is clearer in that it more obviously applies to persons who, while they may be professionals on some occasions, certainly act in a non-professional capacity on other occasions (e.g. a dentist who buys a carpet for the surgery). Two recently reported cases on the point suggest that this is indeed the intention behind the wording of Article 35: one involved an estate agent who was buying an alarm system for his office (1987), the other a jeweller who was getting advertising material printed (1990). However, the opposite view is taken by one of the leading French commentators on consumer law, Jean Calais-Auloy, and also by the Commission on the Reform of Consumer Law in its 1990 proposals. The French law on unfair terms applies to only particular types of term, namely those relating to the fixing of the price, the payment of the price, the nature of the goods, the delivery of the goods, the bearing of the risks, the extent of liabilities and the conditions for performing, varying or terminating the contract. The English Act is not quite as restricted, because ss. 2 and 3 are worded in general terms and s. 13 defines 'exclusion clause' very broadly (a point confirmed by the Court of Appeal in *Gill (Stewart) Ltd* v *Horatio Myer Ltd*, 1992). Both laws, however, fall short of controlling unfairness in the formation of a contract or of requiring fairness in the actual exchange.

Where the two pieces of legislation differ significantly is in the methods they adopt for ensuring that unfair terms are not actually used in contracts. The English approach is to give courts a power to strike down any term which they deem unfair within the constraints of the 1977 Act: some terms, especially those attempting to deprive consumers of their rights under the Sale of Goods Act 1979, are always void, others are void if held to be unreasonable, with s. 11 and Schedule 2 giving further guidance as to how this test of unreasonableness is to be applied. The English approach, therefore, is retroactive: it waits until a dispute comes to court and then considers whether the term in question should be struck out. The only clauses which it is a crime for a seller to try to insert into a contract of sale are those prohibited under the Consumer Transactions (Restrictions on Statements) Order 1976; these include clauses purporting to exclude rights under the Sale of Goods Act.

The French approach is generally more preventative in character. However, suspicious as French law is of judicial power, the 1978 statute confines to the government the authority to strike down a clause by the issue of a decree. Sadly, only one such decree has to date been issued, that of 24 March 1978. It outlaws two types of unfair clause – those in contracts for the sale of goods which reduce a consumer's remedies if the seller fails to comply with his or her legal duties, and those which purport to confer on the 'professional' party to a contract the right to modify unilaterally the character of the goods or services in question. Such clauses are void but, as in England under the 1977 Act, there is no criminal sanction attached to continuing to insert them in contracts even though they then deter many consumers from enforcing their legal rights. By Article 4 of the 1978 decree a fine can, however, be imposed in France if a professional seller does not expressly inform the consumer that he or she has the right to sue for latent defects under Articles 1641–1649 of the *Code civil*.

The fact that only one decree has so far been issued under the 1978 law has led some judges to try to develop their own jurisprudence in this context. Some recent decisions of the *Cour de Cassation* betoken greater activism in this regard. In fact some commentators would wish the courts to go further by making use of their power to alter obligations on the basis of Article 6 (*ordre public* – public policy) or Article 1134 (*bonne foi* – good faith) of the *Code civil*.

An innovatory feature of the 1978 *loi Scrivener* was the creation of the *Commission des clauses abusives* (the Commission on Unfair Terms). This is a body acting under the aegis of the Minister responsible for consumer affairs; it has 15 members, comprising representatives of judges (one of whom acts as chairperson), administrators, lawyers, consumer associations and the professions. One of its tasks is to examine commonly encountered consumer contracts with a view to recommending that legislative action be taken to counter terms which it believes to be unfair. These recommendations have no binding force, but are meant to persuade professional groups to change their practices. Some are general in character, others are directed at particular professions (e.g. furniture removers, car dealers or educational institutions). They embrace proposals not just for the removal of unfair terms but also for the insertion of fair ones, and they deal with the process of negotiating a contract as well as with the content of contracts already agreed. The Commission publishes an annual report, as of course do other bodies in the consumer field such as the *Commission de la sécurité des consommateurs*.

In addition to the work of the Commission on Unfair Terms, it should be noted that a law of 5 January 1988 has greatly facilitated the taking of court actions by consumer associations in situations where the associations believe that a standard form contract used by a professional when dealing with a consumer contains unfair terms. The association can simply bring the action to the local *tribunal de grande instance*, which will decide whether or not to strike down the term in question. If it does strike it down the defending professional will not be able to use that clause again in contracts with consumers. The judgment is not binding on other professionals (given the absence of a doctrine of precedent in French law) so the consumer association should ensure that as many defendants as possible are made parties to the original action. The professions can pre-empt such damaging court actions by adopting uniform standard form contracts negotiated directly with consumer associations, though there then remains the problem of compelling individual professionals to abide by these agreed standards. Collective agreements of this type have been created dealing with the sale of household appliances and used cars, but even these do not appear to be frequently adhered to in practice. It has therefore become necessary for legislation to be passed settling the standard terms of particularly common contracts; the rules do not cover everything but they go a long way towards protecting consumers from the commonest forms of exploitation. The sectors covered to date by such legislation include insurance contracts (law of 10 January 1978), credit agreements (law of 13 July 1979), contracts with travel agents (*arrêté* of 14 June 1982) and residential leases (law of 23 December 1986). The last-mentioned is not a variety of contract which tends to be thought of as a consumer contract in English law, but there is no good reason why it should not be.

FURTHER READING

A good, if at times difficult, account of this subject is provided by Barry Nicholas in *The French Law of Contract* (2nd edn, 1992). Much can be learned about Nicholas's overall approach by reading the review article by Anne de Moor, 'Contract and Agreement in English and French Law' (1986) 6 *Oxford Journal of Legal Studies* 275. A much briefer comparison is to be found in Chapter 8 of *English Law and French Law* by René David (1980) and an even deeper analysis appears in Donald Harris and Denis Tallon (eds), *Contract Law Today: Anglo-French Comparisons* (1989).

Extracts from and commentary on many cases and articles dealing with contract law are included in Part II of *A Source-book on French Law* by Kahn-Freund, Lévy and Rudden (3rd edn, 1991). Serious scholars wishing to appreciate the features of French contract law differentiating it from Anglo-American and German law should consult *An Introduction to Comparative Law* by Konrad Zweigert and Heinrich Kötz (2nd edn, 1987), vol. 2, Chapters 1 to 14 (translated by Tony Weir). Particularly useful journal articles on specific topics within the law of contract include Markesinis, '*Cause* and Consideration: A Study in Parallel' (1978) Camb LJ 53, Legrand, 'Pre-Contractual Disclosure and Information: English and French Law Compared' (1986) 6 *Oxford Journal of Legal Studies* 322, and Legrand, 'Judicial Revision of Contracts in French Law: A Case Study' (1988) 62 Tulane L Rev 963. On consumer law, see the now somewhat dated Calais-Auloy and others, *Consumer Legislation in France* (1981), Minor, 'Consumer Protection in French Law: General Principles and Recent Developments' (1984) 33 ICLQ 108, and Berlioz, 'The Protection of the Consumer in French Law' [1985] JBL 342.

For material in French on general contract law, see H. and L. Mazeaud, J. Mazeaud and F. Chabas, *Leçons de droit civil*, vol. 2, Part 1 (8th edn, 1991), 'Obligations', pp. 49–339; F. Terré, Y. Lequette and P. Simler, *Droit civil: Les Obligations* (5th edn, 1993); B. Starck, H. Roland and L. Boyer, *Droit civil. Les Obligations*, vol. 2, 'Contrat' (1992); M. de Juglart and A. Piedelièvre, *Cours de droit civil*, vol. 2, 'Biens/Obligations' (12th edn, 1992); J. Hauser, *Les contrats* (3rd edn, 1992). Among the more specialist works are F. Collart Dutilleul and P. Delebecque, *Contrats civils et commerciaux* (2nd edn, 1993); A. Benabent, *Droit civil: Les contrats spéciaux* (1993); J. Ghestin, *Droit civil: La formation du contrat* (3rd edn, 1993); CNRS, *Les modifications du contrat au cours de son exécution en raison de circonstances nouvelles* (1986), pp. 13–49 (France) and pp. 145–56 (England). On consumer law it is worth referring to Calais-Auloy, *Droit de la consommation* (3rd edn, 1992) and Bihl, *Le droit pénal de la consommation* (1989).

CHAPTER 9

Tort law

INTRODUCTION

In Anglo-American legal systems tort law is viewed as the pendant to contract law: it provides compensation to people who suffer loss in some way other than through an agreement going wrong. Historically, of course, contract law grew out of tort law, more precisely out of that part of tort law which catered for indirectly caused losses (i.e. not those caused by direct trespass). Contract law (or *assumpsit*) dealt with one particularly common way in which a person could cause loss to another, namely by failing to do something which he or she had undertaken to do. By the 19th century tort law had become an amalgam of separate causes of action – a law of torts rather than a law of tort. Today, following the decision in *Donoghue* v *Stevenson* in 1932 and the consequential growth in the number and range of actions for negligence, it is more accurate to see English tort law as basically a collection of rules imposing liability for fault, but with some exceptions where even faultless behaviour can give rise to liability or where, despite the presence of fault, the loss suffered is not such as to be deemed protectable by the law. In the 1960s and 1970s English courts were very ready to expand liability for negligence, but in the last 10 years or so there has been something of a retreat from this position; while Parliament has been imposing ever greater duties on various sectors of society, judges have been holding back. Even quite recent and authoritative precedents have been overruled and attempts to create new forms of liability have come to naught. Central to the question whether tortious liability should be imposed or not in English law is the issue of whether a 'duty of care' can be said to exist. This, together with the notions of 'standard of care' and 'damage', is one of the conceptual devices used by English law to justify policy decisions on the existence of liability.

In French law it has not been customary to recognise the existence of a separate branch of civil law comparable to England's tort law. Instead the relevant rules have been viewed as part and parcel of the law of obligations; students take one or more courses in that law rather than one in the law of contract and then another in the law of tort or *vice versa*. In the *Code civil* the relevant legal rules are contained in Book 3, which is entitled '*Des différentes manières dont on acquiert la propriété*'. Part 3 of this book

(Articles 1101–1369) contains provisions dealing in general with contracts and other obligations arising out of agreements; Part 4 (Articles 1370–1386) deals with obligations (here called *engagements*) arising in the absence of any agreement. This category is in turn sub-divided into provisions on quasi-contracts, a category now known in England as the law of restitution (Articles 1371–1381), and provisions on *délits et quasi-délits* (Articles 1382–1386). Recently, however, it has become common to refer to the non-contractual rules as if they constituted a separate body of law. Self-contained books are being published on *La responsabilité civile délictuelle* or on *Les obligations non-contractuelles*. Discrete statutory schemes have been established to deal with particular areas of this 'tortious' liability, though it is still premature to talk of French law recognising a variety of different torts.

Perhaps the most remarkable aspect of French tort law – if we may now concede that there is such a separate body of law – is that it is virtually entirely judge-made, or *loi praetorienne* as the French sometimes say. As already mentioned, the *Code civil* contains only five short articles on the subject (Articles 1382–1386); the rest of the law has been left to judicial expansion. Academic opinion (*doctrine*) has had an important role to play as well, the leading lights being such as Saleilles and Josserand.

THE MAIN PRINCIPLE

Our starting-point has to be Article 1382:

> *Tout fait quelconque de l'homme, qui cause à autrui un dommage, oblige celui par la faute duquel il est arrivé, à le réparer.*

> (Loss which is caused to a person by another's behaviour must be redressed by the person whose fault it was that the loss occurred.)

As ever with articles in the *Code civil*, it is vital to pay close attention to the precise wording of this provision. It begins by using the term *fait*, which immediately differentiates this area of law from contract law, where the main trigger for legal involvement is not a *fait juridique* but an *acte juridique*. A *fait* can be something omitted as well as committed, though as in English law there is a general judicial reluctance to impose tortious liability for a pure omission. The article goes on to introduce the ideas of *cause*, *dommage* and *faute*, which are roughly equivalent to English law's causation, damage and standard of care. But these terms are not defined in the *Code civil*, it being left to judges to distinguish, for example, between personal injury and property damage (*dommage* or *préjudice matériel*) and non-pecuniary losses (*dommage* or *préjudice moral*). There is no automatic exclusion of claims based only on economic loss, such as exists in English law, except in cases based on a negligent misrepresentation or on a negligent action which has also caused property damage or physical injury upon which the economic loss is 'parasitic'. In a case where the facts were similar to those in *Spartan Steel & Alloys Ltd* v *Martin & Co.* (1973), the plaintiff's electricty being cut off due to the defendant's negligence, the *Cour de Cassation* allowed recovery quite readily without requiring the economic loss to be parasitic on property damage.

It would be wrong, moreover, to equate *tout fait quelconque* in Article 1382 with the notion of duty of care: in theory any relationship can give rise to liability in French law. A decision such as *Donoghue* v *Stevenson* has not been necessary in France because in the first place the French law of contract has never had such a strict privity of contract rule as the one which prevented a contractual remedy being applied in that case, and in the second place the problem of non-contracting parties not being in a sufficiently 'proximate' relationship with the manufacturer or retailer of an article has never existed in French delict law.

But inevitably French law has had to find some device for limiting the apparent generality of Article 1382. Lawson, indeed, was of the opinion that 'there is latent in the [civil] law a need to establish a duty of care'. What French law substitutes, perhaps, is the notion of *cause*, i.e. the requirement that there be a *lien de causalité* (a causal link) between one person's behaviour and another's loss (the word is not being used here with the specific meaning it has acquired in the law governing contractual obligations). If the chain of causation is broken the French refer to *une cause étrangère* (a 'foreign' cause), a generic concept embracing the more particular notions of *force majeure* (act of God) and contributory negligence. English law also requires causation of damage, but because of the duty of care concept fewer decisions are made to turn on the causation requirement than in France. Until fairly recently, for example, French law used the causation argument to deny a remedy to persons who had cohabited with the victim of an accident, even if they were dependent on that victim for financial support. But in 1970 the *Cour de Cassation* reversed this rule, extending the reversal in 1976 to cover partners in adulterous relationships. In one 1978 case both the victim's wife and his mistress received compensation from the defendant, though in 1984 the Social Security Division of the *Cour de Cassation*, following a provision in the *Code de sécurité sociale*, maintained the original rule in a case of an accident at work. Occasionally even the employer of someone injured by another's negligence has been able to sue in respect of his or her economic loss 'ricocheting' from the accident. By and large the courts in France have been more willing than their English counterparts to compensate third parties: England has maintained a fairly rigid rule prohibiting someone who has merely a contractual interest in goods from suing in respect of their loss (see most recently *Leigh and Sillivan Ltd* v *Aliakmon Shipping Co. Ltd*, 1986), largely because special statutes, such as the Bills of Lading Act 1855, usually ensure that property in goods passes to a buyer only whenever the risk passes, and *vice-versa*.

As regards the need to draw a line between losses directly attributable to a person's fault and those which are too 'remote', the French rule is closer to that formerly applied in England under the test in *Re Polemis* (1921) than to that substituted by *The Wagon Mound* (1961): there is recovery for losses which are the immediate and direct consequence of the incident (*une suite immédiate et directe*), not just for those which are foreseeable. This is the test expressly laid down for contract claims by Article 1151 of the *Code civil*, and in France contract law covers some of the ground normally covered by tort law in England. The French also maintain the principle of *non-cumul*, according to which a plaintiff who has both a contractual and a tortious claim available (to put it in English terms) must opt to sue in contract. In England the plaintiff can pick and choose according to whether on the particular facts of the case the contractual 'reasonable contemplation' test is more or less generous in terms of the compensation that can be claimed than the tortious 'reasonable foreseeability' test.

French judges have also controlled the potential floodgates of litigation by requiring the *tout fait quelconque* of Article 1382 to be unlawful (*illicite*). If an action, or omission, is not unlawful there can be no tortious liability flowing from it. Thus, opening one restaurant close to another, thereby taking customers away from the latter, is not a tort because there has been no recognised illegality. Conduct is clearly *illicite* if it is criminal, but a breach of the civil law can suffice too, or even a violation of a customary rule (*bonnes moeurs*) or of 'normal reason' (*la sagesse moyenne*). Napoleon himself thought the law should require people to act *comme un bon père de famille* (like a good head of the household). Sometimes the phrase *homme avisé* is used, just as English judges occasionally refer to 'the man on the Clapham omnibus'.

Also relevant here is the requirement, again developed by the judges rather than enshrined in the *Code civil*, that a person must not abuse his or her rights (the doctrine of *abus de droits*). Whether there has been such an abuse depends on the reason a person had for behaving as he or she did; if the only reason was to cause loss to the plaintiff then liability for ensuing loss will be imposed. One famous example of this is the *Clément-Bayard* case in 1915, where a landowner erected a wooden tower on his land, topped with spikes, in order to dissuade his neighbour from using his land as an airfield for Zeppelin airships. Liability can even arise under Article 1382 where the *abus de droits* was unintentional, a situation sometimes referred to as *faute quasi-délictuelle*, and the initiation of 'vexatious' litigation can also constitute an *abus*. Such an approach contrasts with that in England, as illustrated by the notorious decision of the House of Lords in *Bradford Corp.* v *Pickles* (1895), where the court refused to impose tortious liability on Mr Pickles for extracting water from under his land simply in order to deprive a neighbouring landowner (the local council) of access to that water. To some extent the *abus de droits* doctrine in French law fulfils the role played by the tort of nuisance in English law; the French call neighbour disputes *trouble de voisinage*.

The generality of Article 1382 owes something to the work of two 17th-century jurists, the Dutchman Grotius and the Frenchman Domat. Article 1383 confirms that it extends to both intentional and non-intentional behaviour, provided always there has been *faute*:

> *Chacun est responsable du dommage qu'il a causé non seulement par son fait, mais encore par sa négligence ou par son imprudence.*
>
> (Every person is liable for the damage caused not only through his or her fault but also through his or her negligence or imprudence.)

Despite the presence of *faute* depending on the particular facts of each case, the *Cour de Cassation*, normally only concerned with questions of law, will quash a decision if it believes that the lower court has misconstrued the concept. Usually it looks for an exercise of will on the part of the defendant, and in this context minors and persons who are mentally unwell are assumed to have a 'will' just as much as if they were of full age and mental fitness. As in England, in the 19th century *faute* tended to mean culpable blameworthiness, fault in the moral or subjective sense. In the 20th century the pendulum has swung more towards social or objective fault: a person tends to be held liable not on account of his or her own personal blameworthiness but because he or she is the better risk-bearer. Today French law, on the basis of Articles 1382–1386, distinguishes between three types of tortious liablity. It speaks of personal liability (*responsabilité du fait personnel*), vicarious liability or liability for others (*responsabilité du fait d'autrui*), and liability for things (*responsabilité du fait des choses*). The third of these categories is the one where there has been the most definite trend towards imposing strict liability.

EXTENSION OF THE MAIN PRINCIPLE

While personal liability arises squarely from Articles 1382 and 1383, vicarious liability derives in the first instance from Article 1384:

> *On est responsable non seulement du dommage que l'on cause par son propre fait, mais encore de celui qui est causé par le fait des personnes dont on doit répondre, ou des choses que l'on a sous sa garde.*
>
> (A person is responsible not just for loss caused by his or her own actions but also for that caused by the actions of persons for whom he or she is responsible or by things over which he or she exercises control.)

Originally this provision was simply supplemented by two further paragraphs, one saying that employers (*maîtres et commetants*) are liable for loss caused by their employees (*domestiques et préposés*) provided the latter were acting in the course of their employment (*dans les fonctions auxquelles ils les ont employés*), the other saying that teachers and craftsmen (*instituteurs et artisans*) are liable for loss caused by their pupils and apprentices (*élèves et apprentis*) while they are under their care (*pendant le temps qu'ils sont sous leur surveillance*).

When deciding whether a person is an employee of another, French law adopts a test closer to the control test favoured by the English case of *Mersey Docks and Harbour Board* v *Coggins & Griffiths (Liverpool) Ltd* (1947) than to the 'integration' test favoured by more recent cases. But the distinction is in any event not so important because Article 1384 extends to liability for persons other than employees. French law also tends to be more plaintiff-orientated than English law as regards employees who, as English law would put it, are on a frolic of their own. While not going so far as to hold employers vicariously liable for an employee's negligence occurring on the way to or from work, the courts have held them liable for employees' acts ranging from theft and criminal damage to murder. There are, again, French cases with facts very similar to well-known English decisions. In a case in 1950 an employer was held liable for an agricultural worker's carelessness in the use of his cigarette lighter, just as the Northern Ireland Road Transport Board were held vicariously liable when one of their drivers threw away a cigarette butt and caused a serious fire at a petrol station (the *Century Insurance Co.* case, 1942). In *Photo Productions Ltd* v *Securicor* (1978) the defendants were held not liable for their employee's arson, and in an almost identical French case in 1985 the same result was reached.

As well as many important judicial decisions expansively interpreting Article 1384, three further statutes have added significantly to the original basic principle. First, in 1922 a paragraph was inserted into the *Code civil* by the law of 7 November; it provides that the occupier of property (*celui qui détient*), whether immovable or movable, is liable for losses caused by fire which breaks out on that property only if it is proved that the fire is attributable to his or her fault or to the fault of persons for whom he or she is responsible. Secondly, in 1937 a statute of 5 April said that, whereas parents and craftsmen are not liable under Article 1384 if they can prove that they could not have prevented the action giving rise to the liability, teachers are liable only if their fault is proved by the plaintiff. Thirdly, a law of 4 June 1970 added a provision saying that after 1 January 1971 parents are jointly liable (*solidairement responsables*) for loss caused by their children who are living with them.

The judicial conservatism of the greater part of the 19th century is well illustrated by the case of *Painvin* v *Deschamps* (1870), where the *Cour de Cassation* held that a plaintiff who had been injured by an exploding boiler while working in the defendant's laundry could not recover damages because he was not able to show that the owner of the laundry had in any way been at fault, as required by Article 1382. The *volte face* in the judicial approach really began in 1896, and Article 1384 of the Code was used as the catalyst. On 4 June 1891 a steam engine on a barge exploded, killing a mechanic nearby, Monsieur Teffaine. When his widow's claim for compensation finally reached the *Cour de Cassation* (even in those days this took five years), the court ruled that the barge-owners were liable because it had been shown that there was faulty soldering on a pipe on the steam engine, even though the owners did not know this and so could not have avoided the explosion. The judges said that Article 1384 was not to be confined to cases involving animals and buildings, the two situations expressly mentioned in the article.

But lest it be thought that even in the 1890s the French courts were in favour of imposing strict liability on, say, all transport operators, it should be noted that reported a year after the *Teffaine* case was the *Grange* case, where the *chambre des requêtes* of the *Cour de Cassation* held (in 1897), in a case where an explosion had occurred on a steamer, that there was no liability on the facts because there was no proof as to how the accident happened: it was a case of *cas fortuit* (act of God). In the year following this decision the French Parliament passed a Workmen's Compensation Act which dispensed altogether with the need for workers to prove fault if they were injured during the course of their work but allocated a lower level of damages in place of that available under the *Code civil* (*loi concernant les responsabilités des accidents dont les ouvriers sont victimes dans leur travail,* 9 April 1898). Since the statute of 30 October 1946, injuries suffered at work are considered to be the concern of social security law and are compensated out of a fund financed by employers. In England very similar statutes were passed at almost exactly the same time in the shape of the Workmen's Compensation Act 1897 and the National Insurance (Industrial Injuries) Act 1946.

It was made clear in a decision of the *Cour de Cassation* in 1919 (*Chemins de Fer de l'Ouest* v *Marcault*), where a railway engine had exploded, smashing two stained-glass windows belonging to Marcault, that a mere absence of explanation for an accident was not enough to exonerate the defendant: he or she had positively to show that there was no fault on his or her part. Some commentators still maintained the view that this fairly strict liability should be imposed only if the defendant was in control of the manufacture of the object in question (*garde de la structure*), but not if he or she was simply in control of how the object was handled (*garde du comportement*). It was in the famous case of *Jand'heur* v *Les Galéries belfortaises,* decided in 1930 by the *chambres réunies* of the *Cour de Cassation* (i.e. all the chambers sitting in a plenary session), where a lorry had mounted a footpath and seriously injured a young girl, that confirmation was given that Article 1384 applied to *all* things under a person's control, whatever the object and whatever the nature of the control.

Although widely welcomed, the *Jand'heur* decision left some lawyers wondering what scope was left for liability under Article 1382, for some 'thing' would almost always be involved in the causation of loss. Ripert stated: 'It would . . . be necessary to imagine a collision between two persons practising nudism before Article 1382 would apply.' Of course Article 1382 is still required for cases of negligent omissions and negligent misrepresentations. The judges have therefore discovered in Article 1384 a general principle of fairly strict liability for inanimate objects: liability exists not if fault is proved but unless fault is disproved in the form of *cas fortuit*, *force majeure* or *une cause étrangère*. (*Force majeure* is really a synonym for *cas fortuit*, referring to an event which is unpredictable and beyond anyone's control.)

Such remarkable judicial creativity is certainly comparable to that of the English courts in such cases as *Donoghue* v *Stevenson* (1932), *Hedley Byrne* v *Heller and Partners* (1964) and *Anns* v *London Borough of Merton* (1977). It means that some of the specific torts known to English law (such as nuisance and *Rylands* v *Fletcher*) find their French counterpart in the judicial excrescence to Article 1384. It means too that in both countries relatively few statutes have had to be passed dealing with particular forms of tortious liability. In England these now include the Defamation Act 1954, the Occupiers' Liability Act 1957, the Employers' Liability (Defective Equipment) Act 1969, the Animals Act 1971, the Defective Premises Act 1972, the Congenital Disabilities (Civil Liability) Act 1976, the Torts (Interference with Goods) Act 1977, the Highways Act 1980, the Occupiers' Liability Act 1984 and the Consumer Protection Act 1987. Any gaps in protection can sometimes be filled by granting the plaintiff a right to sue not for the tort of negligence *per se* but for breach of statutory duty; this has been resorted to in matters of environmental concern (see e.g. the Public Health Act 1936 and the Environmental Protection Act 1990). In France the most important statutes apart from those already mentioned have dealt with losses caused by civil aviation (part of the *Code de l'aviation civile*, compiled under a decree issued in 1967) and road traffic accidents (statute of 5 July 1985). There are also several very important legislative provisions, as in English law, dealing with insurance obligations. All of these laws are, in the Dalloz version at least, reprinted immediately following Article 1384 in the *Code civil*. The statute on road trafic accidents is one which deserves more detailed examination.

ROAD ACCIDENTS

Legislation providing compensation for road accident victims was considered as early as 1907, in the wake of the successful legislation dealing with accidents at work, but nothing reached the statute book for fear of suppressing further technical progress. It was only after compulsory liability insurance for motor vehicles was introduced in France in 1958 (nearly three decades after England's Road Traffic Act 1930) that the matter of no-fault liability again became topical, for despite the insurance law there was still considerable confusion as to when liability existed in the first place. In an attempt to clarify matters one of France's leading legal scholars, André Tunc, an expert in comparative law, published a proposal for reform in 1966, but it was rejected by the Ministry of Justice. He tried again in 1983, this time being impelled to do so by the decision of the *Cour de Cassation* in the *Desmares* case a year earlier. Here two pedestrians had been knocked down while crossing a busy four-lane highway during the rush-hour; the court held that the defendant driver was fully liable despite the apparent contributory negligence of the victims. While some lower courts followed this lead given by the *Cour de Cassation*, even extending it at times, half of the *cours d'appel* refused to follow it, as they were of course entitled to do because of the absence of any doctrine of binding precedent in French law.

In 1985, largely due to the pressure exerted by the then Minister for Justice, Robert Badinter, a statute was passed entitling victims of road accidents to automatic damages for personal injury provided that their 'inexcusable' fault was not the exclusive cause of the accident. *Force majeure* and *causes étrangères* are no longer defences, although some courts have tended to give an unfortunately wide interpretation to *faute inexcusable*, thereby limiting the instances of recovery. The *Cour de Cassation* has had to step in to stress that *faute inexcusable* really means:

la faute volontaire, d'une exceptionnelle gravité, exposant sans raison valable son auteur à un danger dont il aurait du avoit conscience.

(voluntary and exceptionally serious negligence, exposing its perpetrator for no good reason to a danger of which he or she ought to have been aware.)

In addition, the *faute inexcusable* of the claimant, if it is to exonerate the defendant from having to pay compensation, must have been the sole cause of the ensuing accident. While victims who are drivers involved in the accident are excluded from the automatic compensation scheme (their damages will be reduced in proportion to their own share of the blame for the accident, as in England under the Law Reform (Contributory Negligence) Act 1945), victims who are under 16, or over 70, or who have a greater than 80 per cent disability, recover compensation even if they are themselves exclusively at fault. Only claims for property damage will be reduced by evidence of contributory negligence on the part of such victims.

The main provisions of the statute came into force immediately, and even extended to accidents occurring in the previous three years. It was supplemented by a decree dated 6 January 1986, most of which has been incorporated into the Code of Insurance Law (*Code des assurances*). A victim of a road accident involving *un véhicule terrestre à moteur* (a motorised land-based vehicle) must now sue under the 1985 statute and not under Articles 1382–1386 of the *Code civil*, but the statute does not apply to losses caused by cyclists, by pedestrians or at railway level-crossings.

LIABILITY FOR ANIMALS AND BUILDINGS

Animals

Article 1385 of the *Code civil* provides as follows:

> *Le propriétaire d'un animal, ou celui qui s'en sert, pendant qu'il est à son usage, est responsable du dommage que l'animal a causé, soit que l'animal fût sous sa garde, soit qu'il fût égaré ou échappé.*

> (The owner of an animal, or whoever is making use of it (while it is being so used), is liable for the loss caused by the animal, whether the animal was under his/her control at the time or whether it had got lost or escaped.)

The judges in France have held that a veterinary surgeon is 'making use of an animal' while treating it and a kennel-owner likewise while looking after it. The principle in the *Desmares* case, mentioned above, whereby a person is liable for his or her control of a thing (including an animal) regardless of the contributory fault of the person who suffers loss thereby, has now been abandoned by the *Cour de Cassation*, as far as losses other than those caused by road accidents are concerned, in a decision issued on 6 April 1987. The *Code rural* contains further provisions dealing with the control of domestic animals, liability for dangerous and wandering animals, the destruction of harmful animals and compensation for losses caused by animals being hunted (such as boars). The range of legislative provisions is comparable to that in England's Animals Act 1971, the Guard Dogs Act 1975, the Dangerous Wild Animals Act 1976 and the Dangerous Dogs Act 1989, though some of these impose criminal as well as civil liabilities; as far as the law is concerned there is little justification for the claim that the English are unusually indulgent towards their animals.

Buildings

According to Article 1386 of the *Code civil*:

> *Le propriétaire d'un bâtiment est responsable du dommage causé par sa ruine, lorsqu'elle est arrivée par une suite du défaut d'entretien ou par le vice de sa construction.*

> (The owner of a building is liable for the loss caused by its collapse when this is due to a lack of maintenance or to a defect in its construction.)

It must be noted straightaway that this provision has to be read in conjunction with Articles 1382 to 1384 if one wants an overall view of the tortious liability of occupiers of premises in French law. A plaintiff has the choice of suing under Articles 1382 and 1383, under Article 1384 or under Article 1386. The main differences are that while Articles 1384 and 1386 apply only to the controllers (*gardiens*) and owners of buildings, Articles 1382 and 1383 apply more generally; and while the plaintiff must prove fault if suing under Articles 1382 and 1383 he or she can rely upon a presumption of fault if suing under Articles 1384 and 1386.

Article 1384 was first held to apply in cases involving buildings in *Vidal* v *de Taiguy*, where the plaintiff had been injured in a hotel lift (*Cour de Cassation*, 1928). Because of its generality it represents a preferred cause of action to that provided by Article 1386, which is limited to cases involving *bâtiments* and their *ruine*. The predominant view at the moment, however, is that if the plaintiff is able to sue under Article 1386 he or she must do so and cannot resort to Article 1384 (there is a decision of the *Cour de Cassation* to this effect in 1988). This is because the *ruine* presupposed by Article 1386 contemplates the unplanned destruction of, or damage to, the fabric of a building, not something which is a *chose* within the terms of Article 1384. Thus, a door would be covered by Article 1386, but not a tree in a garden or snow falling from a roof; nor is damage caused during the construction or demolition of a building covered. As explained above, the law of 7 November 1922 excludes damage caused by fire, regulating that matter as part of Article 1382.

UNJUST ENRICHMENT AND OTHER MEANS OF COMPENSATION

Unjust enrichment

The *Code civil* (unlike other national codes such as those in Germany and Italy) does not contain any general principle requiring a person who has been unjustly enriched at the expense of another to disgorge the benefit obtained. But it does have a few articles which impose such a duty in particular circumstances. One example is Article 555, which requires the owner of land on whose property another person has built or planted something to reimburse this person if the owner decides to keep the building or plants; the owner can choose to pay either a sum equal to that by which the property has increased in value as a result of the work done, or the cost of the materials and labour involved in the work calculated as of the date of reimbursement. Also pertinent is Article 1371, which reads:

> *Les quasi-contrats sont les faits purement volontaires de l'homme, dont il résulte un engagement quelconque envers un tiers, et quelquefois un engagement réciproque des deux parties.*

> (Quasi-contracts are purely voluntary human acts which give rise to an obligation towards another person, and sometimes to reciprocal obligations between two parties.)

This provision has been applied many times to permit deserted wives to claim an interest in the assets of their husbands after separation. A similar restitutionary duty is imposed by Article 1376:

> *Celui qui reçoit par erreur ou sciemment ce qui ne lui est pas dû s'oblige à le restituer à celui de qui il l'a indûment reçu.*
>
> (A person who mistakenly or knowingly receives something which is not owing to him or her is under a duty to make restitution to the person from whom it was improperly received.)

Towards the end of the 19th century some academics, in particular Aubry and Rau, tried to develop a general theory of unjust enrichment on the basis of these scattered texts, but none of the suggestions captured the imagination of the judges. They preferred to look outside the *Code civil*, proof, if more were needed, of their creativity. Conscious of the restricted scope of both standard contract claims and those based on *responsabilité civile*, judges have devised a whole new category of tort-like obligations grouped around the central concept of unjust enrichment (*enrichissement sans cause*). The starting point for this development was *Patureau v Boudier* in 1892. Here the plaintiff was the supplier of manure; the initial recipient of the manure was a tenant who went bankrupt before paying for it but his landlord gave him an allowance for it when taking over the land. The plaintiff successfully sued the landlord for the cost of the manure and the *Cour de Cassation* based its decision on a principle of equity which prohibits someone from enriching him- or herself at another's expense (*un principe d'équité qui défend de s'enrichir au détriment d'autrui*).

As a result of the numerous decisions made in similar cases during the past 100 years French law now requires four conditions to be satisfied before a court can allow a claim based on unjust enrichment:

(a) there must be a direct or indirect connection between the plaintiff's loss and the defendant's enrichment;

(b) there must be no legal justification for the enrichment (or, putting this another way, no *cause* for it and no *faute* on the part of the plaintiff);

(c) the remedy must be sought only when there is no other remedy available (*la condition de subsidiarité*): if such a remedy was available but no longer is (perhaps because it has become statute-barred) then a claim based on unjust enrichment is disallowed too;

(d) the enrichment must still exist at the time of the claim: if it has disappeared (because, say, the defendant has already spent the windfall) no claim is possible.

Even if all these requirements are met in a particular case, the amount of money which is to be reimbursed can be no higher than the amount lost or the amount gained, otherwise the plaintiff would in turn be unjustly enriched at the expense of the defendant.

In English law the struggle for recognition of a general principle against unjust enrichment has been long and hard, but in *Lipkin Gorman* v *Karpnale Ltd* (1992) the House of Lords eventually conceded its existence. The Lords even held that the defendant could raise the defence of change of position, meaning that he or she has so altered his or her position on the strength of the benefit received that to oblige restoration of the benefit would be unjust. The case involved a solicitor who gambled away, in the Playboy Club, money belonging to his firm's clients; the firm was allowed to recover most of the lost cash from the Club. The principle has also been applied in a case involving overpayment of taxes (*Woolwich* v *IRC*, 1992) and, most recently, in a case where a lesbian sued her lover for a share in the proceeds of the sale of their house (*Tinsley* v *Milligan*, 1993). In many earlier cases English law managed to accord restitutionary remedies without expressly basing the decision on unjust enrichment: for instance the so-called action for money had and received, and the action for money paid, are approximate English equivalents to France's *paiement de l'indû*.

Other means of compensation

As has been so ably demonstrated for English law by Atiyah and others, civil liability in tort or in restitution is just one method available for the compensation of accident victims or losers of assets. It is worth remembering that as well as, or instead of, suing an alleged tortfeasor a claimant may find it easier to seek compensation under an insurance arrangement, under the social security system or under a special state-sponsored scheme. Three of these schemes have been created in recent years in France. In 1983 a statute was passed obliging the state to compensate the victims of tortious behaviour which is also criminal, provided the behaviour causes personal injury and serious difficulties in the victim's life (*un trouble grave dans les conditions de vie de la victime*); this may be compared with England's Criminal Injuries Compensation Scheme, placed on a statutory footing by the Criminal Justice Act 1988. In 1986 a statutory fund was set up guaranteeing compensation to victims of hunting accidents, road accidents and terrorist incidents, though only if the person responsible for the losses is unknown or insolvent; in England the Criminal Injuries Compensation Scheme and the Motor Insurance Bureau Scheme would cover much the same ground. Finally, at the end of 1991 another statutory fund was established to ensure compensation for persons who contract AIDS after receiving infected blood in a transfusion.

FURTHER READING

For accounts in English, *see* Chapter 10 of René David, *English Law and French Law* (1980) and Konrad Zweigert and Heinrich Kötz, *An Introduction to Comparative Law* (2nd edn, 1987) (translated by Tony Weir), vol. 2, Chapters 17–20. Useful journal articles include those by Tunc, 'The 20th Century Development and Function of the Law of Torts in France' (1965) 14 ICLQ 1089; McMahon, 'Delictual Liability in France: A Case Study in the Liability of Owners of Premises to Injured Entrants' (1973) 24 *Northern Ireland Legal Quarterly* 491; Markesinis, 'The Not So Dissimilar Tort and Delict' (1977) 93 LQR 78; Redmond-Cooper, 'The Relevance of Fault in Determining Liability for Road Accidents: The French Experience' (1989) 38 ICLQ 502; and Palmer, 'A Comparative Study (From a Common Law Perspective) of the French Action for Wrongful Interference With Contract' (1992) 40 Am Jo Comp L 297. There are useful extracts from numerous French cases in F.H. Lawson, Negligence in the Civil Law (1950) pp. 201–305.

For a comparison of laws on product liability see the section on France by Warren Freedman in *Products Liability: An International Manual of Practice*, vol. 1 (looseleaf, 1990). The English law on unjust enrichment is concisely explained in Andrew Burrows, *The Law of Restitution* (1993), while fascinating material on comparative unjust enrichment law (mostly England, France and Germany) is contained in Chapters 15 and 16 of Zweigert and Kötz (cited above). On compensation in general, see *Accidents, Compensation and the Law* by Patrick Atiyah and Peter Cane (5th edn, 1993).

French works on this area include P. le Tourneau and L. Cadiet, *La responsabilité civile* (1994); Sériaux, *Droit des obligations* (1992), pp. 305–506; B. Starck, H. Roland and L. Boyer, *Droit civil. Les Obligations*, vol. 1, 'Responsabilité délictuelle' (1991); Malinvaud, *Droit des obligations: Les mécanismes juridiques et des relations économiques* (5th edn, 1990), pp. 231–337 (this includes extracts from law reports); Malaurie and Aynès, *Droit civil: Les obligations* (2nd edn, 1990), pp. 21–163. Now somewhat dated but still illuminating because of its concentration on the judicial contribution to this area of law is R. Rodière, *La responsabilité délictuelle dans la jurisprudence* (1978). On unjust enrichment, see G. Bonet, *Enrichissement sans cause: droit privé et droit public* (1990) and M. Malaurie, *Les restitutions en droit civil* (1991).

CHAPTER 10

Commercial and company law

INTRODUCTION

Given the diversity of subject-matter falling under the rubric commercial law it is difficult to identify features which particularly distinguish a French approach from an English approach. Finding the law is that much easier in France, but the preference for codification makes that an advantage in almost every legal field. While the use of concepts such as *acte de commerce* perhaps unnecessarily complicates French law, this is more than compensated for by the flexibility achieved through an imaginative approach to the permitted forms of business organisation. The substance of and procedures used in competition law and insolvency law are remarkably similar in the two jurisdictions, again due in no small measure to the harmonising influence of EU standards.

English law has long had difficulty in knowing what topics to include under the heading 'commercial law'. In France the task is easier because there has been a separate *Code de commerce* from as early as 1807. Indeed there were important codifications of particular commercial matters long before the Napoleonic era. As mentioned in Chapter 1, Jean Baptiste Colbert ensured the issuing of a law governing overland commerce in 1673 (*Ordonnance sur le commerce par terre*), and in 1681 he passed a law dealing with marine commerce (*Ordonnance sur le commerce par mer*). The *Code de commerce* itself comprised four Books: the first regulated commerce in general, the second marine law, the third insolvency and the fourth jurisdiction in commercial cases.

Needless to say, economic developments have entailed numerous and extensive amendments to the original Code. In Book 1 (Articles 1–189) Articles 18–70 have been repealed; all but Article 433 (on prescription) has been repealed in Book 2; Book 3 has been entirely replaced by new laws on bankruptcy and insolvency; and only Articles 631–41 remain in place of the original Articles 615–648 in Book 4. The *Code de commerce* is therefore much less at the heart of today's *droit commercial* than the *Code civil* is at the heart of *droit civil*. In most cases it has not been possible to substitute new provisions in the *Code de commerce* itself; instead the supplementary laws are now usually published as an Appendix to the Code. In the Dalloz version the Appendix has 43 headings, arranged alphabetically; they include such topics as *banques*, *chèques*, *commerce maritime*, *concurrence* (competition), *fonds de commerce* (trading assets), *propriété industrielle*, *redressement et liquidation judiciaire* (arangements and insolvency), *sociétés commerciales* and *ventes commerciales*. In this chapter we will look at only a few of the most important topics embraced by the term *droit commercial* in France. In particular we will omit discussion of the financing of commercial transactions and international trade law.

In the field of company law the *Code civil* contains several important provisions, some of them inserted quite recently in order to comply with European Community initiatives. In 1858 France abandoned its system of granting concessions to persons involved in trade, and in 1867 it passed a law regulating the granting of shares in companies. This remained in force for 99 years to the day, though in 1925 the concept was accepted of a company having limited liability (several decades later than in England). The statute in 1966 radically altered French company law and it has been amended on many subsequent occasions. In 1978 Parliament reformed the provisions in the *Code civil* itself. These now constitute Title 9 of Book 3 (Articles 1832–1873): chapter 1 (Articles 1832–1844) contains general provisions applying to all companies, chapter 2 (Articles 1845–1870) specifically regulates non-commercial companies (*sociétés civiles*), while chapter 3 (Articles 1871–1873) deals with what an English lawyer might call 'silent partnerships' (*sociétés en participation*).

More important than this growth in the quantity of formal legal provisions has been the change in the substance of French commercial and economic law. There has been a shift away from liberalism to interventionism, most noticeable perhaps in the rising influence which public law has had on the area. As in most Western democracies there are now state controls not just on export law and currency law but also on purely internal matters such as banking, the stock exchange, the insurance industry and transport enterprises. Certainly under the socialists in the 1980s the state played a greater part in the economic life of the country. This was not just because of the creation of various public sector enterprises, as in the energy field, but also because of the nationalisation programme undertaken by the government. Since the founding of the Fifth Republic France has generally favoured a more planned approach to economic policy than most other European states (*planification*).

French commercial law is also increasingly influenced by international agreements. The country is a signatory to the main treaties on international transport, patents and trade marks. It has also brought its law on negotiable instruments into line with the draft uniform law on that topic agreed in Geneva in 1930. But today the most important international impetus is undoubtedly provided, as it is in England, by the country's membership of the European Union. This has affected not just international traffic in goods but also the freedom of individuals to establish themselves in a trade or

profession and the freedom to provide services (Article 85 of the Treaty of Rome).

TRADING AS A BUSINESS

In France the key to the application of commercial law is the presence on the scene of *un acte de commerce*. Articles 632 and 633 of the *Code de commerce* specify a total of 17 varieties of activities which are to be regarded as commercial, and the lists are not meant to be exclusive. They include purchases for the purpose of resale, agency agreements, factoring agreements and banking activities. But these types of activity are held by the courts to attract the application of commercial law only if they are carried out by a person engaged in commerce (*un commerçant*). Likewise, any incidental acts which a trader undertakes in the context of his or her trade or profession are nevertheless classified as commercial acts (*actes de commerce par accessoire*). As Article 1 of the *Code de commerce* puts it:

> *Sont commerçants ceux qui exercent des actes de commerce et en font leur profession habituelle.*

> (Traders are those persons who engage in trade and make this their usual profession.)

There is obviously a circularity in the definitions here but this has not led to practical difficulties in delimiting the scope of commercial law. The crucial deciding factor is always whether the acts in question are typical of commercial behaviour. Probably the nearest equivalent in English law to *un acte de commerce* is the notion of 'acting in the course of a business', but whereas members of professions in England can be recognised as acting in the course of a business this is not permitted for many professions in France, in particular doctors and lawyers. French law also recognises as commercial acts those which may be commercial in appearance only, such as exchange agreements, the formation of companies and dealings in shares; it makes no difference that they are agreements between private individuals. The reason for this classification is that there is merit in subjecting such acts to the, at times, stricter and, at times, more liberal provisions of the commercial law as well as to the jurisdiction of the special commercial courts.

Classifying an act as *un acte de commerce* means not just that the *tribunal de commerce* will have jurisdiction over the matter but also that a different rate of interest will be payable (Article 1153 of the *Code de commerce*: 6 per cent as opposed to 5 per cent) and a different limitation period will apply (generally speaking, 10 years as opposed to 30 years: Article 189 of the *Code de commerce*). It also avoids the application of some provisions of the *Code civil* which would otherwise govern the situation: Article 109 of the *Code de commerce*, for instance, contrary to the standard rule in Article 1341 of the *Code civil*, allows proof of a commercial agreement to be adduced in some form other than writing and an official notice that one party is in breach can be served in the form of a simple letter whereas otherwise a special document called *un exploit d'huissier* (a process-server's writ) would be required.

In most contracts, of course, one or both of the parties is very likely to be engaged in a business. While the normal rules of contract law apply to such agreements, it will usually be easier to enforce remedies against a party who is a *commerçant*. The warranty against hidden defects, implied into every sale by Article 1641 of the *Code civil*, is particularly useful to consumers *vis-à-vis* trading businesses, while the remedies given by the Code to unpaid sellers are essential in situations where a contract fails between two businesses (a commercial contract in the English terminology). These latter remedies include the right to retain the goods if not yet delivered (*droit de rétention*: Article 1612), the right to retake the goods if already delivered (*droit de revendication*: Article 2102(4)), and the right to rescind the contract and claim damages (*droit de résolution*: Article 1654).

Whereas in England there are very few regulations governing the operations of a sole trader, in France such a person must at least register as a *commerçant* in his or her locality. A person who is not a national of an EU country must in addition obtain a trading permit (*carte de commerçant*). As the characterisation of a person as a commercial person depends on the nature of the particular activities in which he or she is engaged, French law makes no distinction between full-time, traditional and infrequent commercial undertakings. But there are extensive special regulations governing capacity to act commercially and admission to commercial professions. Registration in the Register of Commerce and Companies (*Registre du commerce et des sociétés*) is also important and is provided for by a decree of 1967, most recently amended in 1984. Besides creating a central register to supplement the registers kept at commercial courts, this decree takes account of the substantive changes in company and family law. The impact of registration differs depending upon whether the name registered is that of an individual or of a company. Registration of the former has merely a declaratory effect: it raises a rebuttable presumption that the acts of that individual are commercial in nature (Article 41 of the *décret*). If the individual is not registered he or she cannot rely upon his or her status as a commercial person *vis-à-vis* other persons but retains the duty to fulfil the obligations which lie upon him or her as such a person (Article 42). For companies registration has a constitutive effect: it is only then that the company acquires legal personality (Article 5 of the 1966 statute). Since the reforms of 1978 this also applies to *sociétés civiles* (Article 1842 I of the *Code civil*).

Status as a commercial person also has consequences with regard to the duty to keep accounts (Articles 8 *et seq.* of the *Code de commerce*) and insolvency. Indeed, insolvency can occur only in relation to the assets of a commercial person. The *Code de commerce*, in Book 1, contains further provisions on transactions at the stock exchange, commercial pledges, commissions, commercial agents and commercial sales. Much more significant, however, are the special laws which supplement the Code and set up new legal institutions. Most of these are reprinted in the version of the *Code de commerce* published by Dalloz. For insurance law there is a separate *Code des assurances* which is reprinted following Article 1983 in the *Code civil*.

FONDES DE COMMERCE

In France the totality of the assets of a business, with the exception of immovable property connected with the business, is given the collective name of *fonds de commerce*. This embraces a lot more than what is referred to as the 'goodwill' of the business in English law, i.e. the custom of its regular clientèle. The *fonds de commerce* constitutes more than the sum of its various parts and can be sold, leased, pledged or charged just like any particular piece of property within the fund. Indeed, in order to protect creditors of the vendor, sale of a *fonds de commerce* requires compliance with various formalities, such as publication of the sale in legal newspapers and registration of the sale with the Registry of Commerce and Companies and with the tax authorities.

The sale also carries the implications that the vendor will not set up a business in competition with the one he or she has just sold (*clause de non-concurrence*, a restraint of trade clause) and that employees working for the vendor will henceforward be employed by the purchaser. A lease of a *fonds de commerce* (*location-gérance*) means that the lessee takes over the management of the business and pays a commission (*redevance*) to the lessor; no tax is payable on such a transaction, which makes it a popular option for administrators of companies in financial difficulties. It also roughly equates with the operation of franchise agreements in English law.

COMMERCIAL ARBITRATIONS

Commercial contracts differ from non-commercial contracts in that since 1925 they have been allowed to contain clauses which envisage the submission of potential disputes to an arbitrator (*clauses compromissoires*). The commonest variety of arbitration in France is called *amiable composition*, and it differs from arbitration as it is known in England in that its function is to arrive at a conciliation between the parties rather than to apply strict rules of law to the dispute. For this reason, as well as because courts and judges are much more numerous in France than in England, French judges do not see arbitration as an attractive option for contracting parties and are less willing than English judges to uphold arbitration clauses. Such clauses are never allowed, for example, if one of the contracting parties, even to a commercial contract, is a public body.

COMPANY LAW

While general provisions on commercial law are scattered among several pieces of legislation, most of the basic principles governing companies are contained, as already mentioned, in the statute passed in 1966. The general word for a corporate body in France is *société*. As in English law, the main feature distinguishing this form of business organisation from that known as a sole trader (*entreprise individuelle*) is that a *société* has a legal personality separate from that of the people who either own or manage the business. But France does not really recognise an intermediary form of business organisation which is common in England – the partnership. By and large French law deals with partnerships as if they were *sociétés*, most of them, however, not being accorded limited liability.

French law also draws a distinction which is of comparatively little significance in English law, that between commercial companies (*sociétés commerciales*) and non-commercial companies (*sociétés civiles*). The vast majority of companies fall into the former category and Article 1 of the 1966 statute (entitled *loi sur les sociétés commerciales*) makes it clear that the creation of a company in a certain form means that it will automatically be considered as a commercial entity. This applies to all of the types of company described in the next three sub-sections of this chapter. A non-commercial company is usually one that is undertaking a professional activity, such as a firm of architects or lawyers. It is regulated only by provisions in the *Code civil* (Articles 1845–1870), despite the fact that its very *raison d'être* may be the making of profit, and it includes all those corporate bodies which are not otherwise catered for by the law:

> *ont le caractère civil toutes les sociétés auxquelles la loi n'attribue pas un autre caractère à raison de leur forme, de leur nature, ou de leur objet.*

(non-commercial companies are those which are not otherwise categorised by legislation on account of their form, nature or purpose.) (Article 1845)

Such a *société civile* does not need to have a minimum registered capital, but whatever interests (*parts*) do exist in it they cannot be transferred without the consent of all the other interest-holders. One popular variety of *société civile* is the *société civile professionnelle*, adopted today by many firms of lawyers in place of the previous sole trader approach to the practice of law.

Partnerships as companies

The provisions on this variety of company in the 1966 statute (Articles 10–33) are by no means exhaustive. What English law would call partnerships (*sociétés en nom collectif*: SNC) or limited partnerships (*sociétés en commandite*: SC) are also regulated by the supplementary general provisions on companies (*dispositions générales*) in the *Code civil* (Articles 1832 *et seq.*). Although these provisions may not drastically differ in their combined practical effect from those in English law, French law does ascribe legal personality to these entities. Most of them, of course, are small family businesses but there is no limit to the number of members allowed (in English law a partnership cannot usually have more than 20 partners). They must be registered but do not have to have a minimum amount of capital. Members of a *société en nom collectif* will *ipso facto* acquire the status of people engaged in trade (*commerçants*) and they will all be liable to an unlimited extent for the company's debts; the people who manage the company, however, need not themselves be members of it.

Members of a *société en commandite* are either full partners (*commandités*) or limited partners (*commanditaires*). While the former will manage the company and be fully liable for the company's debts, the latter (usually investors) will be 'sleeping' partners with a limited personal liability. If the 'sleeping' partners are not granted shares in the company it is called *une société en commandite simple* (SCS); if shares are granted it is called *une société en commandite par actions* (SCA) and is thereby enabled to grow into quite a large entity. The most prominent SCA in France at the moment is probably Michelin.

To all intents and purposes the form of corporate body known as *une société en participation* is just a variety of the SNC, one where there is a joint venture between established companies for a specific purpose and period. It can be compared with another peculiarly French creation, that of the 'economic interest group' (*groupement d'intérêt économique*: GIE). *The GIE was first provided for by an Ordonnance* in 1967; although it is a legal person with capacity to make contracts and an entry on the Register of Commerce and Companies, it is not a *société*. Its members are themselves businesses which want to work together more economically, without actually merging, to achieve a common goal. The concept proved so attractive to the EC that in 1985 a Regulation was issued by the Council of Ministers allowing for the creation of European economic interest groups so that joint ventures could be undertaken between businesses based in different EC countries.

Private limited companies

The statute of 1966 made significant changes to the law on limited liability companies, of which France knows two main types: *sociétés à responsabilité* limitée (SARL) and *sociétés anonymes* (SA). The former is the commonest form of corporate body, used in about two-thirds of all cases. It is roughly equivalent to the small private company which abounds in England. Especially important are the requirements that such a company must have a minimum paid-up capital of 50,000 francs (about £6,000), raised to this figure from 20,000 francs in 1984 (Article 35), that there be agreement among at least 75 per cent of the members whenever interests in the company are traded with non-members (Article 45) and that the directors (*gérants*) be strictly liable even though the company is the entity being sued (Article 52). The managers of a SARL, like the managers of a *société en nom collectif*, do not themselves have to be members of the company; even if they are members, provided they do not own more than 50 per cent of the company, they can be classified as employees of that company rather than as self-employed.

The *associés* do not have shares (*actions*) in the company but rather part ownership (*parts sociales*), and those who have at least 25 per cent of the ownership are said to possess *la minorité de blocage*. None of the *associés* is classified as a *commerçant* merely on account of involvement in the SARL. The intimate character of such companies is underlined by the rule that if the number of members grows to more than 50 the company must be transformed into a *société anonyme*. This is comparable to the rule of English law that a private company cannot have more than 50 members. In theory none of these members can be made personally liable for the debts of their company, but in both England and France it is customary practice for institutions which lend money to these small private companies to insist upon one or more of the members giving a personal guarantee that the company will repay the loan; if the company defaults then these members can be made to pay instead.

In 1985 it became legally permissible for a limited liability company to be created as a one-person company (*entreprise unipersonnelle à responsabilité limitée*). Parliament wanted to take account of the fact that a considerable number of limited liability companies had been operating for some time as mere shells, with only one active member and one or more 'straw' members. Individual entrepreneurs wanted to have some mechanism whereby they could separate their commercial assets from their personal assets. By Article 36(2) of the 1966 statute a natural person cannot be the sole member in more than one limited liability company; similarly, a one-person limited liability company cannot become the sole member of another such company.

Public limited companies

The main part of the 1966 statute is devoted to what in England are called public limited companies (PLCs) and in France *sociétés anonymes*. Generally speaking these are large companies which sell their shares (*actions*) to ordinary members of the public as investors. They must have at least seven members (there is no upper limit) and a share capital of no less than 250,000 francs (about £30,000). Those which have a minimum share capital of 1.5 million francs (£180,000) are permitted to be listed on the stock exchange (*cotée en Bourse*) and these shares must each be valued at at least 10 francs. They may also raise finance by taking loans from members of the public and issuing debentures in return.

It has been well said that the 1966 statute did not so much completely reform the pre-existing law on *sociétés anonymes* as simply update it. The French Parliament could not bring itself fully to accept the EC's recommended division between management functions and supervisory functions. The statute therefore retains the original principle that management should be in the hands of a board of directors (*conseil d'administration*: Articles 89–117) with one individual as the managing director (*président directeur général*: PDG) and up to 14 other directors. Directors must be shareholders in the company, although the managing director can have up to five non-shareholding directors working as *directeurs généraux*.

In place of these arrangements a general meeting of the company can resolve to adopt a two-tier structure for the company: Articles 119 *et seq.* provide for a board (*le directoire*) and a supervisory body (*conseil de surveillance*). The *directoire* will consist of up to seven members, all appointed by the supervisory body. The *conseil de surveillance* will have up to 12 members, all shareholders appointed at a general meeting and often comprising representatives of the employees. Members of the supervisory body are not under the same strict legal duties as directors on the board. All decisions at a general meeting to change the *statuts* of a *société anonyme* require the support of two-thirds of the members.

Directors can be prosecuted and sued for improper management of a company, and this liability extends to anyone involved in the management whether or not he or she has been formally appointed as a director (*dirigeant ou gérant de fait*). Running the company fraudulently makes a manager liable to large fines and imprisonment for the crime known as *banqueroute*. If a manager's mismanagement leads to the company going into liquidation, whether or not the manager has tried to benefit personally from the mismanagement, he or she may be required to make payments towards reducing the company's deficit and may be made the subject of an order in personal bankruptcy (*faillite personnelle*). Such an order will prevent the manager from undertaking further trading activities for at least five years.

As in England under the Companies Act 1989 and pursuant to the same EC obligation, the 1966 French statute on companies protects persons who lend money to or contract with a company when the company is acting beyond its powers (*ultra vires*). There is a presumption that such loans or contracts are valid unless the company can prove that the lender or contracting party was guilty of fraud. *Sociétés anonymes* must appoint an independent auditor (*commissaire aux comptes*) for a period of six years at a time. This auditor verifies the accounts but must also report any instances of what he or she believes to be criminal mismanagement or taxation irregularity; the auditor's own liability for neglect in this context is more easily established in France than in England.

FORMING A COMPANY

The requirements to be satisfied in French law for the formation of a company are more numerous than those to be satisfied in England. What in English law are referred to as the memorandum of association and the articles of association are in French called *les statuts*. These must be prepared separately for each company, which cannot be taken 'off the shelf' as in England. They must at the very least contain the company's name, the address of its registered office (*le siège social*), its object, its projected life, its type (SNC, SCA, SARL or SA etc.), its registered capital (if any exists at all), the powers conferred on its directors, and details about its shares and how they can be transferred. The identity of the directors is not usually included in the *statuts* but is decided instead at a general meeting of the company's members.

The minimum share capital required (e.g. 50,000 francs for a SARL) must be deposited with a bank and a notice must be placed in an official legal newspaper (the BODACC: *Bulletin Officiel des Annonces Civiles et Commerciales*). Then all relevant documents, including *les statuts* and the names of the company's managers, must be filed with the local *tribunal de commerce* if the company is a *société commerciale*, or with the *tribunal de grande instance* if it is a non-commercial company; the relevant court is that for the locality where the company has its headquarters (*siège*). Details must also be sent to the *Registre du commerce et des sociétés*. In many cases *les statuts* will be drafted for a company by a *notaire*, but this is essential only if the company's assets include land.

A company in the process of being created is termed *une société en formation* and it can be held liable on contracts entered into during this period only if the company, once registered, ratifies the contracts; if no ratification is forthcoming the individuals who made the contract, are personally liable. The objects clause in the company's *statuts* may, as in English law following the Companies Act 1989, be worded in a general manner so as to allow all manner of activities to be conducted. Having identified the kind of market in which the firm wishes to compete, the clause might end with words such as, '*La société a également pour objet toutes activités connexes ou similaires*' ('The company also has power to engage in all connected or similar activities').

INSOLVENCY LAW

There have been large-scale reforms to French insolvency law in the past decade, just as there have in English law. While there was an extensive reshaping of the law in 1967, there was felt to be a need for a further restatement of the law by two statutes passed in 1984 and 1985. The 1984 statute (*Prévention et règlement amiable des difficultés des entreprises*) concentrated on preventing and regulating the financial difficulties encountered by companies, while the 1985 law (*Redressement et liquidation judiciaire des entreprises*) altered the procedures to be adopted when a company actually becomes insolvent. Both of these reforming statutes were to some extent founded on the measures taken slightly earlier in English law. But no change has been made to the fundamental principle in French law that the economic entity which is the company itself must be kept separate from the owners of that entity (in English law this divide is referred to as the veil of incorporation). As in English law, a distinction is drawn between the personal bankruptcy of individuals (*faillite*) and the insolvency of companies (*liquidation judiciaire*). Surprisingly, it was not until 1989 that French law first granted any systematic relief to individuals who become bankrupt.

Insolvencies involving persons engaged in commerce are dealt with in France by the *tribunaux de commerce*; legal persons who are not engaged in commerce are dealt with instead by the *tribunaux de grande instance*. The aim of both the 1967 and the 1984 and 1985 statutes on insolvency was to preserve the functioning of the enterprise in question, but whereas the 1967 statute sought to achieve this through three separate sets of proceedings the later reforms reduced these to one single set. They also provided for preventative measures to be taken to try to ward off an impending insolvency. One of these is called *la procédure d'alerte*. This permits the president of the local *tribunal de commerce* to order the management of a company to come to court to explain what measures they propose to take in order to improve the financial position of their company. The power can be invoked only if the company's annual financial statement shows a loss which is more than one-third the size of the company's worth. A comparable procedure is where the management itself asks the court to appoint an official to strike a deal between the company and its creditors; this official is called *un conciliateur*.

If preventative measures fail, and the business has fewer liquid assets than debts, the company is deemed to be unable to pay its debts (*cessation de paiements*) and to be liable to be wound up (*réhabilitation*). Winding-up proceedings can be initiated by an application from the company itself, from one of the creditors or from the state prosecutor's office (*ministère public*); even the court can set the ball rolling. Nothing turns on where the insolvency petition originates but in all situations the trade unions involved in the company (acting through the *comité d'entreprise*: *see* Chapter 11) must be notified in advance of the court hearing and given the chance to make representations.

Winding-up proceedings begin with the court issuing a rehabilitation order; amongst other things this order will specify the date on which the business ceased to be able to pay its debts. The period between *cessation de paiements* and the issue of the rehabilitation order is known as *la période suspecte*. It cannot be longer than 18 months. During this time the business may not seek to make the general position of its creditors worse by granting what English law refers to as a fraudulent preference in favour of particular creditors; agreements entered into can be re-opened if they are suspect in this way.

If the position of the business is already hopeless the rehabilitation order will be followed almost immediately by a liquidation order. Otherwise there will be what is usually a six-month 'observation period' (Article 8 of the 1985 law on insolvency), during which administrators appointed by the court (*administrateurs*), together with the managers of the company, examine the economic position of the company and make recommendations to the court as to how the company can continue to operate in the future. For smaller companies – those employing fewer than 50 people and with an annual turnover of less than 20 million francs (about £2.4 million) – the court has a discretion whether to appoint an administrator, and in the absence of such a person the company itself will try to devise a plan for preserving its business (Articles 137–147). The observation period lasts initially for 30 days but can be extended by up to four months.

In all cases the creditors of the business have to claim what is owed to them within two months of the rehabilitation order. They will have a representative (*représentant des créanciers*) who verifies which claims by creditors are sustainable and consults with the creditors when the administrator makes proposals for the survival of the company. The final word on which creditor claims to allow rests with the local judge designated by the *tribunal de commerce* as the overall supervisor of the proceedings (*juge commissaire*), though there can be a further appeal to a *cour d'appel*. It is the *administrateur* who makes proposals to the court concerning the future viability of the business, but it is the *juge commissaire* who deals with all the interim disputes prior to the submission of the administrator's report and who authorises all dealings other than in the ordinary course of business. It is also this *juge commissaire* who receives offers of buy-outs, perhaps from the current staff of the business.

During a period of *réhabilitation* the management of the company is conducted by the same managers as before unless the court orders the removal of particular managers or the substitution of the administrator. Contractual obligations incurred by the company prior to the date of the rehabilitation order can be affirmed or disclaimed by the administrator (and if disclaimed they will form part of the company's unsecured debts) but contractual obligations incurred after that date must be met prior to the claims of the earlier creditors.

After the observation period has elapsed the court will decide whether the company can continue as a viable economic entity. If it decides that it can, perhaps by being restructured and selling off some of its assets, or by being completely transferred to new owners, an official will be appointed to ensure that the so-called *réhabilitation* operates smoothly (*un commissaire à l'exécution du plan*, a person who may well be the same as the former *administrateur*). Once a court decides that the company can no longer continue in operation, a liquidator (*liquidateur*) is appointed to convert the business's assets into cash and to pay off the debts.

As in England (and again in compliance with EC law), the first call on whatever cash is available to pay debts can be made by employees, though only as regards their wages for the previous 60 days. Then the costs of the administration itself must be paid. Next come the contractual claims affirmed by the administrator during the rehabilitation period. A creditor can enforce a security interest in the business's assets only if this has been registered, as most claims by the tax authorities would be. But even these claims must take second place to claims by lessors of capital goods (*crédit bail*) and to claims by suppliers of goods governed by a retention of title clause (*clause de réserve de propriété*), provided those goods have not yet been irretrievably mixed with others or bought in good faith by a third party.

As regards personal bankruptcy for debts incurred while not engaged in trading activities, it was only when a statute was passed on 31 December 1989 that individuals in France began to be entitled to some protection against complete ruin at the behest of creditors. There are now two types of proceedings which can be invoked, one a purely administrative procedure (*règlement amiable*), where the debtor reaches a composition with his or her creditors and has this approved by the local administrative commission for bankruptcies and by the local *tribunal d'instance*, and the other where the *tribunal d'instance* itself will reschedule the bankrupt's debts and issue a court order accordingly.

COMPETITION LAW

Competition law in France lacked a coherent basis until quite recently. After several years of state intervention a move was finally made in 1986 towards a freer market economy – in line with the EC's policy of completing the single European market by the end of 1992. The *Ordonnance* of 1986 dealing with freedom of prices and competition repealed a 1945 *Ordonnance*, which was having the effect of stifling competition by permitting state controls to be placed on prices. A decree four weeks later fleshed out some of the details of the 1986 *Ordonnance*; both pieces of legislation, together with the relevant EC law on this topic, are conveniently reprinted in the Dalloz version of the *Code de commerce* under the rubric *concurrence* (competition).

Article 1 of the 1986 *Ordonnance* explicity states that the prices of goods, products and services are to be freely determined by the market (*librement déterminées par le jeu de la concurrence*). Only in situations where prices cannot easily be affected by the market, perhaps because there is a virtual monopoly involved, can the government regulate prices, and only after consulting with both the *Conseil d'Etat* and a special body created by the 1986 *Ordonnance* called the *Conseil de la concurrence*. Likewise, the government can fix limits on prices for up to six months in times of crisis or disaster, though again only after consulting the *Conseil d'Etat* and a body called the *Conseil national de la consommation* (*see* Chapter 8). This latter power was used to regulate the price of petroleum products for five weeks following the invasion of Kuwait by Iraq in 1990.

Articles 7 and 8 of the *Ordonnance* are the national French equivalent to Articles 85 and 86 of the Treaty of Rome, i.e. they prohibit

(a) all agreements between undertakings and all concerted practices which have as their object or effect the prevention, restriction or distortion of competition within the market; and

(b) the abusive exploitation of market power by a dominant undertaking or group of undertakings, or of another's position of economic dependence.

Article 9 provides that any agreement or contractual clause relating to a practice prohibited under Articles 7 or 8 is null and void.

Article 10 exempts some agreements and practices from control but does not adopt the so-called block exemptions which are provided for in Regulations issued by the European Commission under Article 85(3) of the Treaty of Rome. These Regulations cover exclusive distribution and exclusive purchasing agreements, patent and know-how licensing agreements, product specialisation agreements, research and development agreements, franchise agreements and – the only block exemption relating to a particular industry – agreements for the exclusive distribution of motor vehicles. The exemption allowed for by Article 10 of the *Ordonnance* requires an undertaking to demonstrate that the effect of an apparently prohibited practice will be to promote rather than inhibit economic progress (*assurer un progrès économique*) and that it will allow consumers an equitable share of the resulting benefit. Given these provisions, and those in Article 1, the 1986 *Ordonnance* really represents a measured reform rather than an out and out rejection of the principles accepted previously.

The 1986 law obliges trading enterprises to observe provisions intended to guarantee information and protection to customers. Article 28 imposes a positive obligation on every seller of goods or provider of services to indicate by packaging, labelling or some other appropriate method the price of the goods or services, the extent of the seller's or provider's contractual liability and the particular terms of the contract. Article 29 prohibits certain sales techniques (e.g. pyramid selling or the use of loss-leaders – *prix d'appel*), while Article 30 disallows a refusal to deal with a consumer unless he or she takes something else as well. While it would be difficult to claim that these French provisions are more extensive than those applying in England, it is certainly true that the sanctions available to the French courts in the event of their being breached are more severe. The courts may fine the guilty parties (and in advertising cases the fine may be as much as one half of the cost of the whole misleading advertising campaign), send the persons responsible to prison for up to two years or allow injured parties, whether competitors or customers of the defendant, to sue in the civil courts for damages.

As mentioned already, besides the part to be played by ordinary criminal and civil courts in the enforcement of competition law, there is now a special body whose function is to give advice on competition matters to the government, Parliamentary committees, professional associations, trade unions, consumer groups, chambers of commerce, etc. and to decide whether the competition rules laid down in 1986 are being complied with. This body is called the Competition Council (*Conseil de la concurrence*). It had a predecessor called the Competition Commission (*Commission de la concurrence*). The English equivalent, although its powers are by no means identical, is the Office of Fair Trading. The *Conseil de la concurrence* comprises 16 members, with the President and two Vice Presidents serving in a full-time capacity and its decisions being appealable to the *cour d'appel de Paris*. Hearings are held in private but the Council can be addressed by any person whom it believes will be able to contribute useful information (Article 25). The Council can pronounce sanctions and injunctions against offending practices and can even begin criminal prosecutions against violators of the rules (Articles 11–12). An enterprise can be ordered to pay up to 5 per cent of its annual turnover, and a non-enterprise up to 10 million francs (about £1.2 million) (Article 13). Individuals who have been fraudulently involved in anti-competitive practices can be sent to prison for between six months and four years and fined between 5,000 and 500,000 francs (£600 to £60,000) (Article 17).

The *Conseil de la concurrence* also shares responsibility with the Economy Minister for controlling company mergers and break-ups (Articles 38–44). In this field it operates in a similar way to Britain's Monopolies and Mergers Commission. A merger is subject to the Council's control as soon as it affects at least 25 per cent of the internal market or leads to an economic concentration (*concentration économique*) of at least 7,000 million francs (with at least two enterprises involved having turnovers of more than 2,000 million francs). But the Council itself cannot initiate an investigation: it must first be requested to do so by the Economy Minister, who has a discretion in this regard. Nor is there any duty to give prior notice of an impending merger. Such notices are rare in France and sometimes it can be difficult to get information concerning a possible merger. Articles 45–52, however, provide that civil servants have the power to conduct relevant inquiries in this context. If the information revealed leads to the conclusion that the critical market share is affected, the Council will decide whether this will damage the competitiveness of the market, though even if the Council concludes that it will this does not necessarily mean that the merger will be forbidden because the final decision rests with the government Minister. Very few cases examined result in a merger being forbidden, and in one of the earlier examples of this happening the *Conseil d'Etat* later quashed the decision because it was based on procedural defects.

When it comes to protecting commercial activities against unfair competition French law has a wider range of remedies available than does English law. Besides the controls contained in the law of 1986 French law recognises several other restrictions. Many of these have been devised by the courts on the basis of the simple wording of Article 1382 of the *Code civil*, the general provision imposing *responsabilité civile,* already discussed in Chapter 9. One manifestation of this judicial inventiveness is what the French call *imitation* – passing-off in English law. If a trader misuses the name, product or *modus operandi* of a competitor, in such a way as to cause confusion in the mind of the public, the competitor can sue for damages and seek a court order requiring the defendant to alter what is being done. Similar remedies are available if someone publishes misleading information about a competitor or about the competitor's products or services (*dénigrement*), or if someone tries to lure staff away from a competitor in order mainly to acquire the expertise of that member of staff (*débauchage*). The English equivalent to the former would be slander of goods; the only equivalent to the latter would be actions to prevent the breach of a restraint of trade clause. It is apparent that French law is more protective than English law of commercial interests which are affected by someone else's economic activity. The *laissez-faire* philosophy so prominent in the 19th century still holds considerable sway in England.

TAXATION

The French legislation on taxation is conveniently collected in the *Code général des impôts* and its companion *Livre de procédures fiscales*. As in England, there is of course a basic distinction between direct and indirect taxation. For individuals the main form of direct taxation is income tax (*impôt sur le revenu*); for businesses it is corporation tax (*impôt sur les sociétés*). The latter is levied primarily on profits, excluding those made outside France. However, many types of companies, despite having separate legal personality under French law, are disregarded by the tax authorities altogether, the taxes being levied instead on the individuals who make up the company. Thus the *associés* of a *société à responsabilité limitée* will have their share of the company's profits added to their own income before income tax is levied on the total, and the same applies to members of *sociétés civiles* or of *groupements d'intérêt économique*. Members of some companies, in particular *sociétés en nom collectif* and *sociétés en commandite simple*, can declare whether they wish their company's profits to be subjected to corporation tax or to income tax.

The most significant variety of indirect taxation is the equivalent of England's VAT – *taxe sur la valeur ajoutée* (TVA). Although national rates fluctuate, the French standard rate is usually above that in England and it is levied on items which are zero-rated in England such as food and books. Companies must also pay indirect taxes in the form of registration fees (*droits d'enregistrement*) when they are initially formed, when their shares are transferred (with some exceptions), when their *fonds de commerce* (explained above) is sold or when they are wound up.

FURTHER READING

There is probably more available in English on French commercial law than there is on any other aspect of French law, even though some of it is by now somewhat out of date. A good synopsis is contained in Chapter 15 of *Amos and Walton's Introduction to French Law* (3rd edn, 1967), but this excludes an exposition of the 1966 statute on companies. More comprehensive and up-to-date coverage is contained in Alexis Maitland Hudson, *France: Practical Commercial Law* (1991). Many of France's leading cases on commercial law are now reprinted in English, a year or two after their publication in French, in *European Commercial Cases*, a series published by Sweet & Maxwell since 1978. Its companion series since 1988 has been *Commercial Laws of Europe*, a periodical collection of relevant legislative texts. The 1986 *Ordonnance* on freedom of prices and competition is reprinted in English at [1988] 1 CLE 241.

For specialised accounts of French company law see J.-P. Le Gall and P. Morel, *French Company Law* (2nd edn, 1992); S.N. Frommel and J.H. Thompson (eds), *Company Law in Europe* (1975), Chapter 5; P. Meinhardt, *Company Law in Europe* (3rd edn, 1981); and *Jura Europae: Company Law* (looseleaf). This last publication is regularly updated and is very practically orientated; it contains model 'constitutions' (*statuts*) for the most important types of companies. Also well worth consulting, not least because it is so new, is Julian Maitland-Walker, *Guide to European Company Law* (1993).

Amongst the best books in French on general commercial law are *Contrats civils et commerciaux* by F. Collart Dutilleul and P. Delebecque (2nd edn, 1993); *Contrats civils, commerciaux* by B. Gross (1993); *Droit commercial* by P. Didier, 3 vols, (1992–93); *Actes de commerce, commerçants, activité commerciale* by A. Viandier (1992); *Traité de droit commercial* by G. Ripert and R. Roblot, vol 1 (14th edn, 1991); *Manuel de droit commercial* by A. Jauffret and J. Mestre (20th edn, 1991); and *Droit commercial: Commerçants et entreprises commerciales, Concurrence et contrats du commerce* by R. Houin and M. Pédamon (9th edn, 1990). Extracts from important cases are helpfully collected in *Grands arrêts du droit des affaires*, edited by D. Vidal (1992). For coverage of company law refer to *Droit des affaires: L'entreprise commerciale* (1993) by Y. Chartier; *Droit des sociétés* by Y. Chaput (1993); *Droit commercial: Sociétés commerciales* by P. Merle (3rd edn, 1992); and *Droit des sociétés* by M. Cozian and A. Viandier (1992). Books on insolvency law include *Droit des procédures collectives* by J.-F. Martin and S. Leyrie (1991) and *Traité théorique et pratique des procédures collectives* by B. Soinne (6th edn, 1993). Competition law is succinctly explained in *Le droit de la concurrence* by Y. Chaput (2nd edn, 1991). On tax law see *Droit fiscal* by L. Trotabas and J.-M. Cotteret (7th edn, 1992). A good European overview is provided in the remarkable *Droit commercial européen* by B. Goldman, A. Lyon-Caen and L. Vogel (5th edn, 1993).

CHAPTER 11

Labour law

THE HISTORY OF EMPLOYMENT PROTECTION IN FRANCE

The issues which have led English legislators to enact laws protecting employer and employee interests have led the French law-makers to do the same. There is a remarkable similarity between the two legal systems in this area, no doubt largely brought about by European Community Directives and International Labour Organisation Conventions. French employment law, like the English, is very much a product of the late 19th and 20th centuries. At the time of the French Revolution society was not yet fully conscious of the social problems connected with employment, indeed the so-called *loi le Chapelier* of 1791 forbade the formation of workers' associations because they were another example of powerful corporations. Basing itself on the premise of individual freedom of contract, the *Code civil* of 1804 contained just two provisions concerning service contracts (Articles 1780–1781); these simply said that an employment contract must be based either on time worked or on the task to be undertaken and allowed for a presumption that an employer must always pay a wage to an employee.

The first legislation protecting employees was a statute in 1841 concerning the employment of children: factories employing more than 20 workers were prohibited from employing any children aged under eight, and children younger than 16 could not be employed for more than 12 hours per day. The Revolution of 1848 sought to implement a coherent programme of social reform but this came to nothing. In 1864, during the reign of Napoleon III, the prohibitions on strikes and on the creation of associations (*le délit de coalition*) were repealed, though this measure was so limited in its effects that in reality freedom to associate was not guaranteed. Modern labour law did not really begin until the Third Republic (1871). The statute of 1884 is still today the foundation stone of trade union protection. Legislation in 1892 and 1900 regulated working hours, and in 1898 workmen's compensation for accidents was introduced. In 1936 the Popular Front government improved collective labour rights by enhancing bargaining rights and redundancy protection. The Preamble to the 1946 Constitution recognised the right to strike, to join a trade union and to collective negotiation. During the post-War Fourth Republic the right to worker participation in management decisions (*cogestion*) was acknowledged through the establishment of *comités d'entreprise* (workers' committees) and *délégués du personnel* (staff representatives). But most of the recent changes in labour law have concentrated on protecting individual employment rights, such as the provisions on a national minimum wage (*salaire minimum de croissance*: SMIC), which in 1970 replaced earlier provisions dating from 1950.

In 1982, a series of statutory reforms introduced by Monsieur Auroux, the Minister for Labour in the socialist government of the time, brought about numerous improvements to both individual and collective employment rights. The reforms underline the point that French employment law, like that in England, is not just about protecting employees but also about industrial relations. Legislation was passed on part-time work (*le travail temporaire*), on fixed-term employment contracts (*les contrats de travail à durée déterminée*), on a shorter working week (39 hours) and on annual holiday entitlement (five weeks). The bringing forward of the normal age for retirement, the possibility of early retirement and the introduction of a training programme for 16- to 18-year-olds were further measures aimed primarily at fighting unemployment. Annual collective bargaining for large organisations was ensured and firms were obliged to set up committees dealing with matters such as hygiene, safety and conditions of employment. Fortunately for employees, no major part of this reform package was undone when the government of France became Gaullist again between 1986 and 1988 or after March 1993.

THE SOURCES OF EMPLOYMENT LAW

The most authoritative source of French employment law is of course the Constitution. The next most important sources are the international agreements to which France is a party, these being mostly either Conventions agreed by the International Labour Organisation (*l'Organisation Internationale du Travail*: OIT), or Directives and Regulations issued by the European Community. The OIT, based in Geneva, was created in 1919 but now forms part of the United Nations.

However, in practice the main source of employment law in France is legislation. Over the years statutes have whittled away the freedom of contract notion so as to give greater protection to employees, and since 1910 the various legal provisions have been collected together in the *Code du travail*. This is now divided into nine books. Book 1 deals with contracts relating to employment, including collective agreements (*contrats relatifs au travail*), Book 2 with working conditions (*réglementation du travail*), Book 3 with workforce recruitment (*placement et emploi*), Book 4 with employee representation (*les groupements professionnels, la représentation, la participation et l'intéressement des salariés*), and Book 5 with dispute resolution procedures (*conflits du travail*), the court of first instance for individual employment disputes being the *conseils des prud'hommes* (*see* Chapter 2). Book 6 covers work inspections, Book 7 contains numerous provisions relating to particular kinds of employment such as in the energy and transport industries, Book 8 is confined to the law of French territories overseas, and Book 9 regulates the training of employees. In the current Dalloz version of the Code more than 1600 pages are consumed setting out these provisions and annotating them. There then follow almost 400 further pages in an Appendix where further legislation affecting the nine topics in the main body of the Code is reproduced.

Within the Code itself the nine books are each divided into three sections, the sections being grouped together in Parts. Each separate provision is given a letter indicating which Part it belongs to and a number referring to the Book, Title and Chapter where it can be found. Part 1 of the Code reproduces relevant statutes (*lois*), prefixing them with 'L'; Art. L 145-7 is therefore a reference to the seventh article in Chapter 5 of Title 4 of Book 1 in Part 1. Part 2 reproduces *décrets en Conseil d'Etat*, prefixing them with 'R' (for *règlements*). Part 3 contains simple *décrets*, prefixing them with 'D'. Every article, or group of articles, carries an indication of its derivation, i.e. a reference to the original legislation which inserted it into the *Code du travail*. While considerable patience and skill are required to find one's way round the *Code du travail*, it is nevertheless immensely helpful to have all the relevant legislation within the covers of one book. Most published versions are well indexed and cross-referenced. They also include a chronological table showing the reader where to find particular pieces of legislation which have been inserted into the Code. At the moment the oldest such legislation is the 1864 *loi* which removed the prohibition on forming unions (*coalitions*). Well over one half of all the legislation dates from 1980 or thereafter; indeed, in the 1993 version published by Dalloz there are no fewer than 152 references to pieces of legislation from the 1990s!

Although the *Code du travail* has been frequently revised, it still does not include all of the laws relevant to employees. For matters on which there is little or no legislation, such as strikes and employers' liability, or on which the existing legislation is unclear, such as the meaning of '*rupture abusive*' (unfair dismissal), the jurisprudence emanating from the *chambre sociale* of the *Cour de Cassation* is of prime importance. Legislation tends to set a minimum level of protection for employees but collective agreements, as well as agreements within a particular workplace, can enhance this protection. The picture is comparable to the 'floor' of rights which is guaranteed by legislation to employees in English law, though of course in the past 15 years or so the size and thickness of this floor have been diminished somewhat by government legislation.

Additional sources of law in France, as in England, are the collective agreements reached between employee and employer organisations, the customs and practices of trades and professions, and the employment contracts between individual employers and their employees. As mentioned, disputes regarding individual employment matters are initially heard by the *conseils des prud'hommes*. Having been first established in 1806, their members being elected in equal numbers from the ranks of employers and employees and sitting in groups of four (a rare example of a *tribunal paritaire*), these bodies now deal with more than 150,000 cases per year, about a third of which are taken further on appeal to the *cour d'appel*. As their title implies, the *conseils des prud'hommes* are under a duty to try to reconcile the parties before proceeding to adjudicate upon the dispute (*bureau de conciliation avant bureau de jugement*), but these days only about 10 per cent of cases are successfully conciliated. Disputes involving collective employment matters are dealt with by the *tribunaux de grande instance*. Criminal matters, of course, are dealt with by the *tribunaux de police* or (if the infringement is more serious) by the *tribunaux correctionnels*. Even the administrative courts may deal with employment matters if, for example, an employer or employee wishes to challenge a decision taken by an inspector (*inspecteur du travail*).

EMPLOYMENT-RELATED ORGANISATIONS

Apart from the role played by particular employers and employees in the negotiation and performance of individual employment contracts, French law recognises significant roles for a variety of organisations. On the employers' side most firms belong to one of two groupings, either the *Conseil national du patronat français* (more or less equivalent to the Confederation of British Industry and quite liberal in its attitudes) or the *Confédération générale des petites et moyennes entreprises* (comparable to Britain's Chambers of Commerce and grouping together the smaller and medium-sized enterprises).

On the employees' side France has a large number of diverse associations which exist to protect the interests of their members. Trade unions have been lawful since the so-called *loi Waldeck-Rousseau* of 1884. Moreover, the Preamble to the 1946 Constitution, incorporated by reference into the Constitution of 1958, states that every person can defend his or her rights and interests by trade union activity and can belong to the trade union of his or her choice. The French trade union movement is, of course, from the workers' viewpoint at least, a movement struggling to put in place social rights. Traditionally, rather than operating on the basis of consensus it has tended to put conflict before co-operation. This is partly explained by historical factors: industrialisation took longer to become established in France than in other European countries. Even the language used expresses the prevailing ethos: while trade unionists in other countries are 'members' of their union and usually refer to one another as 'colleagues', in France the unionists are 'comrades' (*militants*, from the Latin word for a soldier).

Today French trade unions are numerous and staunchly aligned along ideological and political lines, but their role in public life has altered. While formerly they may often have indulged in relatively fruitless oppositionism, the state has now moved to involve them as 'social partners' in the plans for macro-economic and sectional development (*planification*). This is aimed at facilitating a transition from participation based on demands to one based on discussion, co-operation and focused action. Social partners also have a role in the management of the social security system, and the collective agreements reached by them are often the main basis for conditions of service in the workplace. They participate, too, in the Economic and Social Council (*Conseil Economique et Social*), which is provided for by Articles 69 to 71 of the 1958 Constitution. This Council can give advice on relevant draft statutes, since all proposed laws pertaining to an economic and social programme must be submitted to it for its opinion.

At present there are five large trade union confederations and a host of particular unions which are not affiliated to a confederation. The *Confédération générale du travail* (CGT) is the oldest and largest of the confederations, dating from 1895 and now having about 850,000 members; it is largely communist in its ideology. In 1947 a breakaway group formed the *Force Ouvrière* (CGT–FO) because they wanted to eschew the communist tendencies of the CGT and revert to traditional non party-political trade unionism and socialism; today the CGT–FO has about half a million members. The *Confédération française des travailleurs chrétiens* (CFTC) was formed in 1919 with a distinctly Christian ethos, but in 1964 it also split into two, with 200,000 members choosing to stay in a confederation which retained the original name but more than twice that number opting to go with the *Confédération française démocratique du travail* (CFDT), an organisation claiming to be more democratic and secular. The *Confédération générale des cadres/Confédération française de l'encadrement* (CGC–CFE) represents professional and managerial levels (*cadres*); formed in 1946 it now has about 200,000 members. The five confederations are officially recognised as having certain prerogatives which their member unions can exercise, such as the right to engage in collective bargaining. At the moment only about 15 per cent of employees are members of a trade union but the confederations nevertheless tend to enjoy large support in workplace elections and in their bargaining strategies. Industrial unrest in France during 1993, among aviation workers for example, once again demonstrated the power of the unions even though, unlike their English counterparts, they have not had to withstand a barrage of 'reformist' legislative provisions during the past 15 years.

Collective agreements

Only trade unions recognised as having a representative capacity can enter into collective agreements with an employer or group of employers (*conventions collectives*). To a greater extent than in English law, the agreement constitutes a source of law in France and it binds not just members of the union or unions party to the agreement, but also members of other unions in the same workforce and employees who are not members of any union. This is the so-called *erga omnes* principle.

Traditionally collective agreements have been viewed as zero-sum bargains, with one side winning on a point and the other side losing (*négociation distributive*). More recently collective agreements have been based on the win-win principle, with one side making a concession on one point in return for a concession from the other side on a different point (*négociation de concession*). The agreements are reached on an industry-wide basis rather than on a company-by-company basis.

Within each company there are at least three ways in which the employees can be collectively represented in dealings with the management. First, in firms with more than 10 employees there may be an annual election of *délégués du personnel* (staff representatives). The legislative provisions governing their role are Articles L and R 421 to 426 in the *Code du travail*. These persons have the task of representing the workforce when negotiations are being conducted with the management over such issues as levels of pay, rest periods, working hours and holidays. They can also take complaints to the Employment Inspectorate (*Inspecteur du travail*). Secondly, in firms with more than 50 employees there must be an election every two years for *un comité d'entreprise*, the size of which will depend on the number of employees. The main function of the *comité* is to discuss how the firm should be managed and to arrange social and cultural events. Each member of the committee has a deputy (*suppléant*) and the managing director (*chef d'entreprise*) is *ex officio* a member, as is the trade union representative (see below) if the firm has fewer than 300 employees. The staff representatives and members of the *comité d'entreprise* must meet with the employer at last once a month. The relevant provisions are grouped in Articles L, R and D 431 to 439 of the *Code du travail*.

The trade union representative (*le délégué syndical*) constitutes the third type of representative within a workforce, his or her function being to speak for the relevant trade union when it is dealing with the managing director (*see* Articles L 412-11 to 412-21 and R 412-1 to 412-6 of the *Code du travail*). Roughly speaking one representative is appointed for every 1,000 employees. The representative is entitled to time off work with pay in order to carry out his or her functions: this amounts to 10 hours per month for firms with between 50 and 150 employees, or 15 hours for firms with between 150 and 500 employees. If an employer fails to allow workers' representatives to carry out their functions this constitutes a criminal offence (*délit d'entrave*) and is punishable with a fine of up to 20,000 francs (about £2,400) or even, in serious cases, with imprisonment of between two months and one year (Articles L 481 to 483). An example of this would be where the employer fails to allow employee representatives an appropriate space in which to carry out their activities.

ENTERING EMPLOYMENT

A person can become a fully protected employee (*salarié*) once he or she reaches the age of 16 (the end of compulsory schooling), but even before then, from the age of 15, a person can enter a contract of apprenticeship (*apprentissage*). Such contracts, which are regulated in detail by the provisions in Title 1 of Book 1 of the *Code du travail*, must be in writing and officially registered. From the age of 14 a school pupil can undertake light work (*des travaux légers*) but only during school holidays. In all these cases the wages paid to the young person must relate to the figures laid down in the regulations on the national minimum wage (SMIC). To encourage employers to take on young people aged 16 to 25 the French government reduces, or in some cases eliminates altogether, the contributions employers have to make for their employees to the social security fund (*cotisations sociales*).

The hiring of new employees is referred to as *l'embauche* or *le recrutement*. Publications which carry job advertisements must provide details of the advertiser both to the Employment Office of the *département* in question and to the National Employment Association (*Agence nationale pour l'emploi*: ANPE). If an application form for a job asks questions directly concerned with the applicant's race, ethnicity, nationality, religion, gender, pregnancy or family status, this constitutes a criminal offence on the part of the employer unless he or she can show that the question is directly relevant to the job concerned (*see* Chapter 6). Firms which employ more than 20 people must reserve a 6 per cent quota of jobs for persons who are disabled (*handicapés*) (Article L 323-1); in English law the quota is 3 per cent. But instead of actually employing disabled people the employer can satisfy the legal requirements by adopting an approved action programme for the advancement of disabled persons, or by contributing to a fund for the development of their employment opportunities. Non-EC nationals working in France require either a one-year residence permit stamped '*salarié*' (worker), or a 10-year residence permit automatically conferring the right to work. Within a month of a foreign employee's entry into France the employer must pay a fee to the *Office des migrations internationales*. Employing a non-EC national who does not have the relevant work permit is a criminal offence.

Anti-discrimination laws in France ultimately derive from the provision in the 1958 Constitution which guarantees equality before the law. This has been supplemented by the incorporation into French law of Convention No. 111 of the International Labour Organisation and by the Equal Pay and Equal Treatment Directives of the EC (75/117/EEC and 76/207/EEC). It is fair to say that today discrimination on grounds of race, religion, sex or trade union membership is contrary to French *ordre public* and the new *Code pénal* is quite explicit in its condemnation of such practices. As an example of the approach manifested by the *Code du travail* we can cite part of Article L 122–25:

> *L'employeur ne doit pas prendre en considération l'état de grossesse d'une femme pour refuser de l'embaucher, résilier son contrat de travail au cours d'une période d'essai ou . . . prononcer une mutation d'emploi. Il lui est en conséquence interdit de rechercher toutes informations concernant l'état de grossesse de l'intéressée . . . La femme candidate à un emploi ou salariée n'est pas tenue . . . de révéler son état de grossesse.*

(An employer must not take into consideration the pregnancy of a woman when refusing to recruit her, terminating her contract of employment during a probationary period or . . . announcing a change in her work. The employer is consequently forbidden to seek any information regarding the woman's pregnancy . . . A female candidate for a job or a female employee is under no duty . . . to disclose whether she is pregnant.)

In this context fewer cases have been taken to the European Court of Justice against France than against England, but both countries are bound by that court's interpretation of the relevant European standards. National courts can apply a contrary provision of national law only if this is necessary to comply with the country's obligations under a Convention concluded prior to the entry into force of the Treaty of Rome.

Persons who have been made redundant for economic reasons, or who have left work because of a pregnancy or who have been called to do their military service, have the right to be re-employed when the reason for their absence disappears (*priorité d'embauche*).

CONTRACTS OF EMPLOYMENT

There is no statutory definition of a contract of employment in French law but, as in England, the courts see the main attributes as being the performance of services on the instructions of another and in exchange for remuneration. An employee is distinguished from a person who provides a service at the request of another by the fact that he or she is subordinate to the directions of the employer; this is referred to as *subordination juridique*. To avoid doubt the *Code du travail* expressly designates the supply of services by such persons as sales representatives, journalists, performing artists, fashion models, caretakers (*concierges*) and child minders (*assistantes maternelles*) as the performance of a contract of employment (Articles L, R and D 751 to 773).

French law is like English law in that a contract of employment does not normally have to be in writing, but of course disputes will be avoided, or more easily resolved, if the principal terms and conditions are set out in a written document. Contracts which are for a fixed term (*à durée déterminée*) do need to be in writing but the term involved, with some exceptions, cannot exceed 18 months (Article L 122–1–2). Every contract must state how long it is to last, the date on which it is to begin operating, the place where the work is to be carried out, the hours of work, the rate of pay, the employee's duties and the relevant collective bargaining agreement, if one exists. Most contracts operate for a trial period (*une période d'essai*), during which the employee is on probation. Unless the contract is for a fixed term the employer can extend the trial period if the contract provides for this; if the employee does not agree to the extension the contract is terminated (*résilié*). Any termination of the contract by the employer during a trial period does not constitute dismissal (*licenciement*) unless it is for reasons unconnected with the employee's performance of his or her duties; in such a case the employee can claim compensation.

If performances under a contract of employment for a fixed term continue to be exchanged even after the expiry of the term, French law will infer the existence of a replacement contract on the same conditions as the earlier one but of indefinite duration. In any event, an employer is generally not permitted to enter into consecutive fixed-term contracts with different employees for the same position: a period equal to at least one-third of that of the first fixed term must elapse before any such second contract can be agreed.

Obligations under a contract of employment

One of the clearest obligations on an employer is to remunerate his or her employees for work done. As in England, each time an employee is paid there must be an itemised pay statement (*bulletin de paie*) indicating how the pay has been calculated. Since the late-1970s even most manual workers in France (*ouvriers*) have been paid on a monthly basis (*mensualisation*), thereby reducing the importance of any distinction that might be drawn between *travail manuel* and *travail intellectuel*. Work paid for without an itemised pay statement is likely to be classified as *travail noir* or, if a self-employed person fails to declare earnings, as *travail clandestin*.

Any 'material' alteration (*révision*) to a contract of employment is possible only with the consent of the employee. But the employer preserves a prerogative to modify some aspects of the employment relationship in order to ensure the continuing profitability of the business. This distinction between *éléments substantiels* and *éléments modifiables* lies at the bottom of many labour disputes, and to avoid such disputes arising many contracts now make express provision for the employer's power to alter some important terms. These provisions include clauses on mobility and on performance-related pay. As regards the place where the work is to be performed, a unilateral alteration can be made to this without the employee's consent only if it does not entail a much longer journey to work from home or does not make it impossible for the employee to take his or her children to or from school. Likewise, a change to the hours a person is asked to work is 'material' if it is impossible to make the new time-table fit with that of the employee's spouse or children. If an employee is demoted (*déclassé*), or if his or her pay is cut (*réduction de rémunération*), this is tantamount to outright dismissal.

It is increasingly common for contracts of employment in France to include a restraint of trade clause (*clause de non-concurrence*). These can protect an employer's interest in matters which are not otherwise protected by the law on intellectual property, matters such as customer lists, organisational arrangements and management techniques. They can operate not just during the contract of employment itself but also thereafter. There is nothing in the *Code du travail* itself to regulate *clauses de non-concurrence*, but Article 121–1 provides that contracts of employment are subject to the generally applicable rules of law: '*Le contrat de travail est soumis aux règles du droit commun*'. In French as well as English law, such clauses are basically valid provided they are reasonable, though in France the general consensus seems to be that the permitted maximum duration of the restraint is two years and that an employee should receive special remuneration for complying with the clause, especially when the contract is otherwise terminated. Tradition has it that this special remuneration should equal the employee's previous month's salary. The *conseil des prud'hommes* will strike down a clause which it thinks goes too far in protecting an employer's interests.

Misconduct by an employee can lead to disciplinary action, including dismissal, if there is a lack of good faith on the employee's part. As noted in chapter 8, Article 1134 of the *Code civil* requires all contracts to be performed in good faith (*doivent être exécutées de bonne foi*). A lack of good faith will also disqualify an employee from any entitlement to remuneration for work performed under what turns out to be a void contract.

SAFETY AND DISCIPLINE WITHIN THE WORKPLACE

Every employer who employs 20 or more persons must have works rules (*un règlement intérieur*) (Article L 122–33). These should deal with matters of hygiene, safety and discipline and should be established only after consultation with the works council (*comité d'entreprise*). The Employment Inspectorate (*Inspecteur du travail*) is empowered to make sure that the works rules comply with legislative requirements. A statute of 1982 obliges every firm with more than 50 employees to elect a health and safety committee (*comité d'hygiène, de sécurité et des conditions de travail*: CHSCT). This committee must meet at least three times per year and has the general responsibility for ensuring that the rules on health and safety are complied with within the workplace. It must conduct regular inspections of the premises and investigate any accidents which occur.

As regards discipline, the works rules must set out a hierarchy of punishments which can be administered for misdemeanours. These range from a warning (*l'avertissement*) to suspension (*la mise à pied*), demotion (*la rétrogradation*) and dismissal (*le licenciement*). The appropriate punishment obviously depends upon factors such as the past disciplinary record of the particular employee, the length of time the employee has been employed by this employer, the nature of and difficulties attendant upon the employee's current job and the consequences of the breach of discipline on the other employees and on the firm itself. Suspension is permissible only when the employee has been seriously at fault (*en cas de faute grave*); for dismissal something even more serious is required (*faute lourde*), such as theft or breach of trust. An employer cannot fine an employee or deduct money from his or her wages; this is also outlawed in English law by the Wages Act 1986.

Before any employee is disciplined he or she must be called to a preliminary interview, given an indication of the reasons for the proposed disciplinary action and provided with a written notice of the disciplinary action finally taken. The employee can always appeal, even against a mere warning, to the *conseil des prud'hommes*, and punishments administered for one breach of discipline cannot be taken into account when a punishment is being administered for another breach of discipline if the latter occurs more than two years after the former.

EMPLOYEE RIGHTS

Hours of work and remuneration

In general employees must not be asked to work longer than 39 hours per week or 10 hours in any one day. There must also be a rest period of at least 24 hours each week; usually this is on a Sunday, though in recent times many shops have ignored this requirement and trade unions have had to go to court to protect their members' rights (with judges issuing a monetary *astreinte* to compel the shops to comply with the law). Employees can be required to work overtime (*des heures supplémentaires*) but only after there have been proper consultations with staff representatives; for overtime worked over and above a 39-hour week a wage increase of 25 per cent per hour must be paid, and this goes up to 50 per cent for work beyond 47 hours. For firms with more than 10 employees time off in lieu must be accorded to those who work more than an extra 130 hours in any one year (at the rate of 50 per cent for the hours exceeding 130). No employee must work for longer than 46 hours for 12 consecutive weeks, a restriction which applies even to those employees who have more than one job: employers are under an obligation to ensure that they do not employ someone who works these excessive hours.

All employees are of course entitled to be paid for the work they do. For amounts larger than 10,000 francs per month (about £1,200) the payment must be by cheque or bank transfer. It is not uncommon in France, especially at Christmas time, for employees to be paid a bonus salary for a fictitious thirteenth month. For workers who become unemployed (other than through voluntary resignation) there is unemployment benefit (*l'assurance chômage*), which is administered by regional offices called *les ASSEDIC* (*associations pour l'emploi dans l'industrie et le commerce*); the amount of the benefit depends partly on the previous earnings of the applicant and, as in England, the applicant must register as someone seeking work (with the *Agence national pour l'emploi*: ANPE) and demonstrate that he or she is actively doing so. There is a complementary scheme called *le régime de solidarité* (roughly speaking, income support) to help in cases where the applicant, being young, has not yet found employment or, being long-termed unemployed, is no longer entitled to unemployment benefit. The maximum period during which unemployment benefit can be claimed is three years. The legislative provisions concerning workers not in employment (*travailleurs privés d'emploi*) are grouped in Articles L, R and D 351 to 353 of the *Code du travail*.

Maternity leave

A woman is entitled to at least 16 weeks of maternity leave (*congé de maternité*), six of the weeks prior to the confinement and 10 weeks subsequent to the confinement, though if the employee already has three or more children her maternity leave is extended to 24 weeks. If she does not wish to return to work after her maternity leave she must inform her employer of this at least two weeks prior to the end of her leave; even then she can apply to return to work within the following year and if a job is available she must be given priority (*priorité d'embauche*). This right to priority also exists if either of the child's parents decides to take up to three years' unpaid childcare leave (*congé parental d'éducation*), but only if the employer has more than 10 employees. Similar rights are given to fathers as well as to mothers of children whom they adopt (*congé d'adoption*). A female employee cannot be dismissed from employment on account of being pregnant, a protection which continues for a month after she has given birth. If during her maternity leave she is dismissed for conduct occurring prior to the beginning of her leave, the dismissal cannot take effect until at least four weeks have elapsed after the birth. For the Code's provisions on maternity, see Articles L 122–25 to 122–32 and R 122–9 to 122–11.

In England a father cannot claim any entitlement to childcare leave at all but a mother is entitled to 40 weeks' maternity leave (extendable by four weeks if she is ill) provided that she has been in the employment of the same employer for more than 16 hours per week during at least the two-year period preceding the eleventh week before the expected birth of her child. From October 1994 this two-tier period will be reduced to six months. During her maternity leave a woman is entitled to statutory maternity pay (paid by the employer but reclaimed from the state) for 18 weeks, though her own contract of employment may require the employer to pay more than this. Women who have not been employed for the required period receive a lesser welfare benefit in the form of statutory maternity allowance. The Trade Union Reform and Employment Rights Act 1993 gives *all* working mothers an entitlement to a minimum of 14 weeks' maternity leave.

Sex discrimination and sexual harassament

Both the *Code du travail* and the *Code pénal* contain provisions which expressly outlaw sex discrimination (e.g. Articles L 123–1 to 123–7 and Articles 225–1 to 225–4 respectively). As far as civil liability is concerned, a woman would have to rely upon Article 1383 of the *Code civil*, which says that a person is liable for the loss he or she causes by negligent or wilful conduct (*par sa négligence ou par son imprudence*): *see* Chapter 9. There is no comprehensive legislation in France comparable to England's Sex Discrimination Act 1975 or Race Relations Act 1976, nor are there bodies with powers similar to those of the Equal Opportunities Commission or the Commission for Racial Equality. But in 1983 a statute did create a *Conseil supérieur de l'égalité professionnelle entre les femmes et les hommes* (Articles L 330–2 and R 331 of the *Code du travail*). This is a intra-governmental body involving the Ministries responsible for women's rights, employment and training, and its task is to help define and implement policies affecting equality between the sexes in the area of employment.

As far as the more specific topic of sexual harassment is concerned (*harcèlement sexuel*), various well-established provisions of the *Code pénal* can be invoked, such as those dealing with assault or indecent behaviour (*see* Chapter 6), and the *Code du travail* sees dismissal of an employee who has resisted sexual advances as unjustifiable because it is not based on a 'real and serious' ground (*see* below). But French law does not categorise sexual harassment itself as a manifestation of sex discrimination and it defines harassment as merely a type of abuse of authority, ignoring the varieties of harassment perpetrated by colleagues or non-employees. This approach is perpetuated in a 1993 penal statute specifically enacted on the topic, which makes sexual harassment by supervisors a criminal offence in the following terms:

> *Le fait par quiconque abusant de l'autorité que lui confèrent ses fonctions d'user des pressions afin d'obtenir de sa part des faveurs de nature sexuelle, est puni d'un an d'emprisonnement et de 100.000 F d'amende.*

(An act by anyone who abuses the authority conferred by his or her position with a view to obtaining sexual favours is punishable with one year's imprisonment and a fine of 100,000 francs [about £12,000].)

An amendment to the *Code du travail* was also made by a statute of 2 November 1992, and here the definition of sexual harassment is slightly more wide-ranging. Article L 122–46 provides that no employee can be disciplined or sacked as a result of being subjected to *agissements de harcèlement* (incidents of harassment) in the form of any kind of orders given, threats made, duress imposed or pressure exerted with a view to the receipt of sexual favours. Nor can an employee be disadvantaged because of having witnessed or reported such incidents. By Article L 122–47, every employee committing this kind of harassment is liable to be disciplined and Article L 122–48 imposes a duty on every managing director (*chef d'entreprise*) to take all necessary steps to prevent sexual harassment occurring. The 1992 law also allows each firm's health and safety committee (CHSCT) to make proposals for preventing harassment in the workplace (Article L 236–2).

Sick leave

An employee in France is entitled to sick leave if he or she is ill (*congé de maladie*). The contract of employment is suspended during the employee's absence (Article L 223–4) and he or she is paid a daily social security allowance by the state (*indemnité journalière*), which may be supplemented by payments made by the employer under the terms of the employment contract. Within three days of the illness beginning the employee must send a doctor's certificate to the employer. As in English law, only if the period of sick leave is very long and causes serious inconvenience to the employer will the latter be justified in dismissing the employee.

If an employee is injured at work, or *en route* to or from work, he or she must notify the employer within 24 hours. In turn the employer must notify the local social security office within 48 hours of learning of the accident's occurrence. If the works' doctor certifies that the employee is no longer able to undertake his or her previous job the employer must offer the employee alternative work commensurate with the terms and conditions of his or her previous employment.

Paid leave

By statute all employees are supposed to have five weeks' paid holiday (*congés payés*) each year (in fact 30 days, but unlike in England Saturday is counted as a working day) (Article L 223–2). The holiday year is taken as running from 1 June of one year to 31 May of the following year. In addition, employees are permitted to take 11 public holidays per year (*jours fériés*: 1 January, Easter Monday, 1 May, 8 May, Ascension Day, Whit Monday, 14 July, 15 August (*l'Assomption*), 1 November (*la Toussaint*), 11 November, 25 December), but with the exception of 1 May they are not entitled to be paid for these days. Supplementary days off are permitted for events such as marriages and family deaths. Contracts may of course allow for more generous holiday entitlements than these statutory minima. Service as a *conseiller prud'hommal* or as a trade union official also justifies extra days off.

Dismissal

An employee can be dismissed in France if he or she has been seriously at fault, if there are economic reasons requiring the dismissal or if the employee and employer just do not get on. Mere *faute légère* is not a ground for valid dismissal. For there to be a justifiable dismissal for fault the employee must have been responsible for grave misconduct (*faute lourde ou grave*), and in cases where the relationship between the employer and employee has broken down there must be a genuine reason for the dismissal (*cause réelle et sérieuse*). In both these types of situation a statute of 1973 requires the employer to have a preliminary interview with the employee (*entretien préalable*); it must be made clear to the employee that the pupose of the interview is to discuss the employer's intended dismissal of the employee and the employee is permitted to be assisted at the interview either by another member of staff (often a trade union official) or, since a statute of 1991, by an adviser from outside the firm (*conseiller extérieur*). At the meeting the employer must state his or her reasons for the intended dismissal and the employee must be given the opportunity to explain his or her version of events. If the employer decides to go ahead with the dismissal a letter must be sent two days after the interview. If the letter does not stipulate the reasons for the dismissal the employee can ask for these to be sent in writing; the employer must comply with this request within 10 days or else a legal presumption will arise that the dismissal is unjustified. The interview procedure must be used even in cases where the employer has summarily dismissed the employee for particularly bad behaviour. If the conditions just mentioned are not satisfied in a particular case an employee can claim unfair dimissal (*licenciement abusive*). An employee who feels obliged to resign because of harassment (*harcèlement*) or lack of support (*quarantaine*) can claim what an English lawyer would call constructive dismissal.

Dismissal can of course also occur if a person is made redundant (*licenciement pour motif économique*). This is defined by a statute of 1989 as follows:

Constitue un licenciement pour motif économique le licenciement effectué par un employeur pour un ou plusieurs motifs non inhérents à la personne du salarié, résultant d'une suppression ou d'une transformation d'emploi ou d'une modification substantielle du contrat de travail, consécutives notamment à des difficultés économiques ou à des mutations technologiques.

(Redundancy occurs where an employer dismisses an employee for one or more reasons not connected with the employee himself or herself but flowing from a reduction or alteration in the work or from a substantial change to the employment contract, resulting in particular from economic problems or technological advances.)

As in England, there are complex requirements to be fulfilled regarding consultation with unions, notice to employees and redundancy compensation. Furthermore, transfer of the employer's business into other hands will not be a legal justification for the termination of existing employment contracts unless there is also a good economic reason for such termination (Article L 122–12 of the *Code du travail*). One such reason would be where a public body decides to procure services from a different firm (*rupture de marché en cours*), although as in England, under the Transfer of Undertakings (Protection of Employment) Regulations 1981, there are protective provisions for cases where the transfer is a nominal one. Article L 122–12 of the *Code du travail* therefore represents a significant exception to the general principle of privity of contract laid down in Article 1165 of the *Code civil*: '*Les conventions n'ont d'effet qu'entre les parties contractantes*' (Contracts affect only the parties to them).

Constitutional freedoms

French employment law differs significantly from English employment law in that it is affected by provisions in the country's written Constitution. The 1958 Constitution, as explained in Chapter 3, incorporates by reference the Preamble to the 1946 Constitution. In explicit terms that Preamble staunchly affirms a person's right to work, right to join a union, right to strike and right to participate in the running of a business:

Chacun a le devoir de travailler et le droit d'obtenir un emploi. Nul ne peut être lésé, dans son travail ou son emploi, en raison de ses origines, de ses opinions ou de ses croyances. Tout homme peut défendre ses droits et ses intérêts par l'action syndicale et adhérer au syndicat de son choix. Le droit de grève s'exerce dans le cadre des lois qui le réglementent. Tout travailleur participe, par l'intermédiaire de ses délégués, à la détermination collective des conditions de travail ainsi qu'à la gestion des entreprises.

(Every person has a duty to work and the right to obtain employment. No person can suffer loss in his or her work by reason of his or her origins, opinions or beliefs. Every person can defend his or her rights and interests through trade union activities and can belong to the union of his or her choice. The right to strike can be exercised within the framework of the statutes regulating it. Every worker participates, through delegates, in the determination of working conditions as well as in the management of the firm.)

However, no court in France has ever taken these statements as conferring justiciable constitutional rights; they have preferred to portray them as mere aspirations or exhortations. Much more attention is paid to the provision in Article 34 of the 1958 Constitution to the effect that it is the prerogative of Parliament and not the government to lay down the fundamental principles of labour law (*les principes fondamentaux du droit du travail, du droit syndical et de la Sécurité sociale*). In a case concerning the socialist government's statute on redundancies in 1989, the *Conseil constitutionnel* accepted the Opposition's argument that the statute needed to be amended so as to ensure that individual members of trade unions give fully informed consent before a union can decide to take legal action on their behalf. In a 1979 case regarding the right to strike within the broadcasting services, the *Conseil constitutionnel* stressed that the 1946 Preamble protected the right to strike only 'within the framework of the statutes regulating it'; it therefore upheld a private member's Bill which aimed to ensure the maintenance of minimum television and radio services at all times, the justification being '*la sauvegarde de l'intérêt public*' (safeguarding the public interest). The most important constitutional case in this area is that of 1982 on trade union immunity from civil actions: the *Conseil constitutionnel* held that a government Bill went too far with the immunity it conferred because the Bill paid no regard to the seriousness of the losses in question. Today a 1985 statute governs the position but it merely protects *l'exercice normal du droit de grève* (the normal exercise of the right to strike); it would appear that this does not excuse breaches of the criminal law or other serious abuses of the right to strike, but it is difficult to be more precise.

FURTHER READING

There are useful accounts of the political role of French trade unions in *France Today* by John Ardagh (1990), pp. 98–118, in *The Government and Politics of France* by Vincent Wright (3rd edn, 1989), pp. 274–79, and in *Social Change in Modern France: Towards a Cultural Anthropology of the Fifth Republic* by Henri Mendras and Alistair Cole (1991), pp. 80–90. For a 'dictionary' approach to labour law, see *European Employment and Industrial Relations Glossary: France* (1993). Comprehensive coverage is provided by Despax and Rojot, *Labour Law and Industrial Relations in France* (1987), while more specific treatment can be found in 'Dismissal Law in France', Chapter 4 in Napier, Javillier and Verge, *Comparative Dismissal Law* (1982). Journal articles include Glendon, 'French labour law reform 1982–83: The struggle for collective bargaining' (1984) 32 Am Jo Comp L 449;

Forde, 'Trade union pluralism and labour law in France' (1984) 33 ICLQ 134; Forde, 'Bills of Rights and trade union immunities: some French lessons' (1984) 13 Ind L J 40; and Forde, 'Liability in damages for strikes: a French counter-revolution' (1985) 33 Am Jo Comp L 447.

For good accounts of modern individual employment law in French see Gérard Coutourier, *Droit du travail* (2nd edn, 1993), vol. 1; *Le droit du travail en France: Principes et approche pratique du droit de travail* by Denis Gatumel (4th edn, 1993); *Droit du travail* by B. Teyssié (1992) vol. 1; *Droit du travail* by G. Lyon-Caen and J. Pélissier (16th edn, 1992); *Droit du travail* by J. Rivero and J. Savatier (1991); and *Le droit du travail* by Michel Despax (7th edn, 1991). *Droit du Travail: Droit vivant* by Jean-Emmanuel Ray (3rd edn, 1993), is written primarily for people besides lawyers who have to implement the various rules and regulations. A succinct book on where to find the relevant legislation and case law is *Les sources du droit du travail* by Bertrand Mathieu (1992). In 1993 Michel Coffineau submitted a report to the Prime Minister entitled *Les Lois Auroux, dix ans après*, but this is mostly about the effects of the laws on collective employment rights. Dalloz publishes a four-volume, looseleaf, *Répertoire de droit du travail*; this is divided into 160 sections totalling approximately 2,350 pages.

CHAPTER 12

Property law

INTRODUCTION

There are basic differences between the French and English approaches to property matters. The two systems do not use the same concepts or structures. Nevertheless, we can once again note that in many instances the effects of the law are the same in both jurisdictions.

Despite the highly structured nature of French law, and of the *Code civil* in particular, property law in France is not as systematically organised as an outside observer might expect. Book 2 of the *Code civil* is entitled '*Des biens et des différentes modifications de la propriété*', but after some initial articles which distinguish between immovable property and movable property (Articles 516–536) and go on to deal with the consequences of ownership of property (Articles 544–577) the Book sets out rules concerned mainly with immovable property. There are a lot more such rules contained in legislation which has not been incorporated into the *Code civil*, in particular the 1955 decree on the registration of interests in land (*décret portant réforme de la publicité foncière*), though for convenience this is reprinted after Article 2203 in the Dalloz version of the *Code civil*. There are also various pieces of legislation governing the construction of buildings; these are available from some publishers as the *Code de la construction et de l'habitation*.

In France property law is studied and written about as a discrete legal subject. The legal system still maintains the basic Roman division between the law of persons, the law of property and the law of obligations. English law, when it speaks of property law at all, usually has in mind land law. England has very few books or courses on the law relating to personal property, most of this being covered in books or courses on tort law, commercial law, restitution law or equity. Moreover, the very existence in English law of both legal and equitable interests in property is something totally alien to the French legal mind; French law knows nothing of trusts. Nor, unlike English land law, does French law recognise the concept of an estate, as opposed to an interest, in property. In France a person is either an absolute owner or not an owner at all. While there can of course be other rights held by persons other than the owner, rights such as life interests in property or the right to make use of property, these do not alter the fact that somewhere there must be a person who can be called the absolute owner.

However, England and France share the view that if property is to be divided it is much more convenient for that division to be made in relation to immovable property than to movable property. Consequently, in both systems it is rare to find interests less than ownership affecting movables. England does of course have the notion of a 'bill of sale', which is a 'chattel' mortgage over personal property, but this is rarely created today. French law, by Article 2119 of the *Code civil*, makes it impossible to create such mortgages (though there are one or two exceptions): '*Les meubles n'ont pas de suite par hypothèque*'.

In France property is either *un bien corporel* or *un bien incorporel*. The former obviously embraces all physical things, whether movable or immovable, while the latter includes not just non-physical things, like patents, copyright and shares, but also rights less than ownership in physical things. Rights less than ownership are collectively referred to as *démembrements de la propriété*. Some things, however, are not property at all: '*Il est des choses qui n'appartient à personne et dont l'usage est commun à tous*' (There are things which belong to no one and which everyone can use) (Article 714). These include the water in the sea or rivers and the air we breathe. If a piece of property has no owner the *Code civil* confers ownership on the state (Article 713), unless there is a particular law dealing with the situation (as there is for abandoned or lost property which is later found).

OWNERSHIP

Article 544 of the *Code civil* defines ownership (*la propriété*) as:

> *le droit de jouir et disposer des choses de la manière la plus absolue, pourvu qu'on n'en fasse pas un usage prohibé par les lois ou par les règlements*

> (the right to enjoy or dispose of things in whatever way one pleases, provided one does not use them in a way which the law prohibits).

This rather absolutist conception has undergone substantial modification since 1804. Even at that time it had to be read subject to other provisions in the *Code civil*, such as those dealing with life interests (*usufruit*: Articles 578–624), the occupation of land (*usage et habitation*: Articles 625–636), easements (*servitudes*: Articles 637–710), pledges (*nantissement*: Articles 2071–2091; a pledge of movable property is called *gage* while that of immovable property is known as *antichrèse*), and acquisitive prescription or squatter's rights (*la préscription*: Articles 2219–2283). On the other hand the definition in article 544 makes no reference to two other basic features of ownership in France – that an owner is entitled to the property to the exclusion of all others and that ownership endures in perpetuity.

French law differentiates between *droits réels* and *droits personnels*, the former being property rights which are valid against the whole world and the latter being rights which can be claimed only against certain individuals. The two categories are roughly equivalent to the English concepts of rights *in rem* and rights *in personam*. *Droits réels* allow the reclaiming of property from whomever happens now to be in possession of it, the so-called *droit de suite*. The epitome of a *droit réel* is of course ownership, but further examples include life interests (*usufruits*), use (*usage et habitation*), easements (*servitudes*) and mortgages (*hypothèques*). *Droits réels* are chiefly protected in law through the doctrine of notice: once the right is notified then it binds other persons. *Droits personnels* are rights arising out of the law of obligations, in particular the law of contract and tort. That the distinction between *droits réels* and *droits personnels* does not lead to further consequences is due largely to the status given by French law to the principle that the parties' agreement governs the destiny of property. For, unlike the law of some other European systems (though not England's), French law does not recognise the concept of a transfer of movable property as something separate from the contract by which the transfer is agreed. As Article 1583 puts it, a sale is complete between two parties, and ownership passes to the buyer *vis-à-vis* the seller, as soon as an agreement has been reached on the thing to be sold and on the price, even though the thing may not yet have been delivered or the price paid.

POSSESSION

Possession of movable property is also guaranteed through giving notice of the possession, but only if the possession is not intermittent (though no specific period of continuous control is required), not secret and not ambiguous. As Article 2232 puts it: '*Les actes de pure faculté et ceux de simple tolérance ne peuvent fonder ni possession ni prescription*' (Merely being able to do something, or having something tolerated, cannot ground possession or acquisition of ownership). Article 2233 adds that the possession must have been peaceful: '*Les actes de violence ne peuvent fonder non plus une possession.*' One is reminded of the Latin adage in English property law that for property to be acquired through prescription the possession must have been *nec vi nec clam nec precario* (not violent nor secret nor intermittent).

A person is in possession of property if he or she is both able and willing to exercise control over the property, but in addition he or she must intend to retain possession on his or her own behalf. Anyone who is merely in temporary control of the property, such as a lessee, bailee or licensee, is not in possession and is labelled a mere retainer of the property (*détenteur précaire*). This is made clear in the provisions in the *Code civil* on the acquisition of property through being in control of it for a certain period

(Articles 2228–2235). Indeed Article 2228 defines possession as '*la détention ou la jouissance d'une chose ou d'un droit que nous tenons ou que nous exerçons par nous-mêmes, ou par un autre qui la tient ou qui l'exerce en notre nom*' (retention or enjoyment of a thing or of a right which we hold or exercise ourselves or which some other person holds or exercises on our behalf). Only someone in possession can acquire ownership by prescription. Similarly, a person can acquire ownership of the fruits of property only if he or she is in possession of that property in good faith (Article 548).

Possession of immovable property carries with it the right to take advantage of the special possessory actions which are available only in relation to that kind of property (*actions au possessoire*). The main such action is called *complainte* and it must be brought within a year of the alleged dispossession. A tenant, because his or her interest is in the eyes of the law movable property, cannot bring a possessory action unless the dispossession was achieved by force; in that case the action taken is termed *réintégrande*. The defendant to a possessory action cannot assert his or her own title to the property – such a claim must be dealt with in a separate legal action.

Good faith acquisition of movable property

The willingness of French law to allow a possessor to prevail even as against persons with real rights over the property is enshrined in the well-known French legal maxim '*en fait de meubles, la possession vaut titre*' (Article 2279). This is the vehicle by which French law protects people who acquire movable property in good faith. Its location in the section of the Code dealing with prescription highlights the fact that it is basically a rule of procedure: claims for restitution of property cannot be successful against a person who is in proper possession of that property. A good faith possessor of movable property benefits from an almost irrebuttable legal presumption confirming his or her ownership of the property.

The acquirer of the property must be in good faith and have physical control over the property (*possession réelle*). For cases where a person is under an obligation to deliver property to two people in succession, Article 1141 lays down the following criteria:

celle des deux qui en a été mise en possession réelle est préférée et en demeure propriétaire, encore que son titre soit postérieur en date, pourvu toutefois que la possession soit de bonne foi

(the person who has got possession of the property is to be given preference and will remain the owner of the property, even if his or her entitlement arises at a later time than another person's, provided that the possession is in good faith).

But Article 2279 goes on to make it clear that good faith acquisition of property is not possible in situations where a person loses property against his or her will (through its being stolen or lost). French law then permits the original owner to recover the property if he or she pays to the possessor the purchase price originally paid for the property by the possessor, provided this was paid at a public market or auction or to a dealer. The owner's claim must also be made within three years, rather than within the normal 30-year limitation period. This principle in Article 2279 also applies to documents the ownership of which passes by delivery, such as bank notes, some cheques and bills of lading (*titres au porteur*); it does not, however, apply to other incorporeal movables such as patents and copyright.

Possession leading to ownership

As mentioned, one of the most important features of possession is that it can lead to the acquisition of title by prescription or, as English lawyers sometimes refer to it, by adverse possession. As regards immovable property the possession must have endured for 30 years, unless it was obtained *par juste titre* (under a just title), that is, by a legal act which purported to convey full property (*translatif de propriété*). In this latter case Article 2265 makes a curious distinction: if the true owner lives within the jurisdiction of the *cour d'appel* where the land is situated then ownership is acquired by a possessor after 10 years, but if the owner lives outside that jurisdiction then it is acquired only after 20 years. In English land law, of course, title can be acquired if there is adverse possession for just 12 years, provided the true owner at no time makes a claim to it during that period.

Security interests

The consent principle, it is possible to say, allows for the recognition of the retention and transfer of property for security purposes even in the absence of direct possession. However retention of title (*réservation de propriété*), which French law portrays as a conditional sale, came to be viewed as a security device only in 1980, when Parliament made it clear that it was not anti-competitive by nature. This roughly coincides with the discovery of the potential of reservation of title clauses in English commercial law (see the *Romalpa* case, 1976). As in the law of Scotland, French law does not otherwise permit the creation of security interests *per se*, a fact which may be due to its failure to distinguish sharply between acts which are obligational in character and those which are essentially proprietary.

ACQUISITION OF INTERESTS IN LAND

If interests in French land are to be enforceable against third parties they must be registered, a process which can be expensive, especially if the land is to be used for commercial rather than residential purposes. As in England, such interests are created by a two-stage process, first by a contract for the sale of the land and then by an actual transfer of the land. The former does not need to be *un acte authentique* drawn up by a notary (though it usually is) but the latter, and any accompanying mortgage agreement, does. The period between the signing of the contract and completion of the transfer is used by the purchaser's notary to investigate the vendor's title and to make inquiries about the development plans for that area (*certificat d'urbanisme*). A particular danger, and one that is virtually impossible for the purchaser to guard against, is the right of pre-emption which vests in local communes and in the tax authorities.

The contract of sale itself is enough to transfer ownership in land (and indeed all other things) as between the vendor and purchaser. This is made explicit in Article 1583 of the *Code civil* (mentioned earlier) as well as elsewhere. It represents the standard position in English law only as far as the transfer of title to movable property is concerned. In France a good title to movables is acquired *vis-à-vis* the rest of the world only if possession of the thing is actually delivered, and a good title to immovable property *vis-à-vis* the rest of the world requires the prior registration of the purchaser's interest in the land register (*le fichier immobilier*).

A purchaser can withdraw from the contract at any time prior to transfer, but if he or she does so for an insubstantial reason a deposit already paid will not be recoverable. If a vendor withdraws without good reason (e.g. if he or she tries to gazump the purchaser) an amount equal to twice the deposit will be required to be paid to the purchaser. On the other hand, if the vendor later discovers that the land has been sold at less than five-twelfths of its actual value he or she can rescind the sale (Article 1674). This is called *rescision pour lésion* and is available for a two-year period after the sale (Article 1676).

The registration system in France is one which records the transactions in land rather than the actual ownership of land: in English terms there is a register of deeds but no register of title. The intention is that in due course a register of title will be created, but this is taking as long to achieve as the equivalent plan in England. Even the register of deeds was not provided for in the *Code civil* itself but by a statute passed in 1855, as amended by a decree exactly a century later. Almost all transactions concerning interests in land can now be registered, including leases for periods longer than 12 years and the vendor's own claim against the new owner for the purchase price (*le privilège du vendeur*). Those transactions registered first take priority over those registered later, though even if it is not registered a transaction remains valid (provided it was for value) against other persons who have no registrable interest (such as the vendor's eventual heirs). Even if a purchaser registers his or her interest, knowing that an earlier unregistered transaction exists, this is no bar to the priority of the registered interest (Article 1071). In English land law the principles are similar.

Contracts for the sale of a building which is not yet fully constructed are governed by Articles 1601–1 to 1601–4 of the *Code civil* (inserted by two statutes passed in 1967) and by provisions in two decrees of 1978 which now form part of the *Code de la construction et de l'habitation*. These laws stipulate matters such as the size of stage payments and the retention of 5 per cent of the purchase price until the purchaser is satisfied with the work done. The usual practice is for the parties to draw up a preliminary contract prior to the execution of the actual *acte de vente*.

Ownership of flats

The purchaser of land will acquire what in England would be called either a freehold title (*pleine propriété*) or co-ownership on a long leasehold (*co-propriété*). The latter is used particularly within blocks of flats, a much more usual form of residence in France than in England, particularly in large cities and tourist resorts. In these blocks the common areas such as halls and lifts will be owned jointly by all the inhabitants rather than by a landlord, though in both cases, of course, a managing agent (*syndic*) will often be engaged to maintain those areas in good repair. Whereas most of the law governing *pleine propriété* is contained in the *Code civil*, the law on co-ownership (sometimes referred to in English as condominia) is enshrined in a statute of 10 July 1965 and a *décret* of 17 March 1967, as amended. The relevant legislation is reproduced in the Dalloz edition of the *Code civil* within the Title on easements (*servitudes*), after Article 664.

A notarial act is required for the creation of *co-propriété* (the document being called *un règlement de co-propriété*) and it must be publicly registered. The *règlement de co-propriété* is a sophisticated document which recites in some detail the rights and obligations of the flat-owners *inter se*. The individual flat-owner's interest is referred to as *un lot*. Before alterations are made to the building, majority agreement thereto must be reached at a meeting of all the co-owners (*syndicat*); voting rights at such meetings (which may be exercised by proxy, a useful facility for owners who otherwise live abroad) are determined in accordance with the share of each co-owner in the common areas – in turn these shares are calculated by relating the surface area and location of each flat to the size and variety of the common areas, the result being expressed in thousandths or some other fractions (*millièmes* or *tantièmes*) and the share being referred to as *une quote-part*. This calculation also determines the proportion of service charges to be paid by each flat-owner.

While the *syndicat* has significant power to regulate the way in which a block of flats is internally managed, it has no power to control the sale of any particular flat, as regards either the price or the identity of the purchaser. But the *syndicat* does serve the purpose of fairly distributing responsibilities among all the residents; this makes the situation somewhat different from the standard English practice – thankfully not as universal as it once was – of a distant owner of the block confronted by a group of residents, all with long leases.

Tenancies

In France a lease of land is termed *un bail* (plural *baux*), while in England the term 'bailment' is restricted to the hiring of movable property. A lessor is *un bailleur* and a lessee is *un preneur*. In both countries the lessee's interest is not, technically speaking, an interest in land but a merely personal contractual right. However, Article 1743 of the *Code civil* stipulates that if the lessor sells the land the purchaser cannot expel the lessee until the specified date for the termination of the lease comes around.

Since the 1920s, in France as in England, protection has been granted to tenants of business premises in certain circumstances. Provided that the tenant is engaged in a business (*un commerçant*), that the premises are being used for the purposes of that business and that the tenancy is for longer than two years, the tenant can take advantage of a 1953 decree (included in the *Code de commerce*). This entitles the tenant to have the tenancy renewed (usually for periods of nine years at a time) unless the tenant has seriously breached the original agreement. If the landlord refuses to renew the lease he or she must pay compensation for the loss suffered by the tenant, which may include an allowance for the disappearance of the business's goodwill (*fonds de commerce*). The landlord can avoid paying compensation if he or she needs to recover possession of the premises so that they can be demolished, but then reasonably equivalent replacement premises must be provided to the outgoing tenant.

Within the duration of a business lease the tenant must comply with any restrictions on the use of the premises; alterations to the use, including the exercise of business activities supplementary to those originally agreed ('*déspécialisation*'), require the consent of the landlord (although, as in English law, this cannot be unreasonably refused) and can mean an increase in rent. The tenant can sell his or her leasehold interest to a third party without the landlord's consent, but only if the business is sold as a going concern. Sub-letting is usually prohibited and any breach of this will permit the landlord to terminate the lease. The tenant usually also has the option of terminating the arrangement (*donnant congé*) at the end of every three-year period (on giving six months' notice). It is also at those intervals that rent reviews occur. The change in rent will often be calculated in accordance with a clause in the lease itself (*une clause d'échelle mobile*); failing agreement between the parties, the issue can be decided by a local Commission or eventually by a local court, and such judicial involvement can be compulsory if the index-linked change leads to a rent which is 25 per cent higher or lower than the original rent. The percentage change in rent must be within the limits laid down with reference to the official index of construction costs (*indice trimestriel du coût de la construction*: INSEE).

PLANNING

Responsibility for planning controls is largely in the hands of *communes*, most of which have published a land use plan for their area (*plan de l'occupation du sol*). The *commune* will require to be satisfied, for example, that any new development will not lead to waste disposal problems. At the departmental level further controls are imposed on the siting of industrial plants. An intention to set up a minor plant simply needs to be declared, although the *préfet* can subject the declaration to conditions. Major plants require full prior authorisation (*autorisation préalable*), which entails a public inquiry as well as an environmental impact survey (*étude d'impact*), both of these having to be paid for by the person applying for planning permission.

As in the United Kingdom, the influence of EU standards is becoming ever more important in French environmental law. Quite apart from the criminal and civil liabilities which may arise under the variety of special statutes on this topic (most of which are collected together in the *Code rural* and *Code de l'urbanisme*), there remains a basic liability under Article 1382 of the *Code civil* for causing loss through pollution (*see* Chapter 9).

INTELLECTUAL PROPERTY

Like English law, French law recognises and protects a variety of rights over industrial and artistic inventions, and in 1992 a statute consolidated the relevant statutory provisions (not yet the *règlements*) in a *Code de la propriété intellectuelle*. The two most commonly encountered forms of this are *brevets* (patents) and *propriété littéraire et artistique* (copyright). *Brevets* within France itself are applied for to the *Institut National de la Propriété Industrielle* and applications which are granted are then publicised in an official journal, the *Bulletin Officiel de la Propriété Industrielle*. To qualify for protection an invention must display the same characteristics as a patent in English law, i.e. it must be novel, the result of inventive activity and capable of industrial application. Again as in England, protection is normally granted for 20 years, but there is a special type of protection, lasting for just six years, which is granted to inventions in a field where it would be undesirable to stifle further inventive activity along the same lines for a longer period (*certificat d'utilité*). Patents can also be granted under Conventions which afford international protection. Both the United Kingdom and France are parties to the EC's Patent Convention (1975) and to the Convention signed in Paris the same year.

The holder of a patent can grant a licence to another person to exploit the patent. Both of these parties can then sue anyone who is apparently infringing the patent. The remedies available include damages (amounting to the plaintiff's lost profits), injunctions and destruction of offending articles.

As in other contexts, if an infringement continues despite the issuing of an injunction the court can order a daily penalty to be paid (*astreinte*). The courts competent to deal with patent disputes are the *tribunaux de grande instance*.

The *Institut National de la Propriété Industrielle* is also responsible for the registration of trademarks in France and these are again publicised in the *Bulletin Officiel de la Propriété Industrielle*. Protection endures for 10 years, but this may be indefinitely renewed so long as the trademark is used at least every five years. As well as marks indicating the manufacturer of goods, French law permits distributors and providers of services to register marks. For all these marks the remedies for infringement are similar to those available in patent cases. Infringement occurs, as in English law, if the defendant's mark causes confusion in the minds of the general public. Similar protection is available, as we have seen in Chapter 10, to a person whose business prospects are damaged because of a rival firm's unfair use of similar symbols or names (even if not registered as trademarks).

Copyright is the subject of a statute passed in 1957 (*sur la propriété littéraire et artistique*), which is reprinted in most editions of the *Code civil* at the end of the first Title of Book II. France is also a party to international conventions, in particular the Geneva Convention of 1952 and the Berne Convention of 1974: foreign artists are therefore protected in France just as they are in England. However, Article 1 of the 1957 statute immediately makes apparent a difference between English and French law in this context: whereas English law protects only the economic exploitation of copyright material, French law also protects the copyright holder's artistic rights (*droits moraux* as opposed to *droits patrimoniaux*). This means that the writer of a novel, for example, can prevent it being adapted as a play or film. *Droits patrimoniaux* can be sold, or transferred to a licensee, but *droits moraux* are inalienable. Nor can an artist of any description 'enslave' him- or herself to, say, an agent or manager by promising to sell all of his or her future works to that person. As in English law, such contracts would be struck down as being in unreasonable restraint of trade. Even when an artist sells just one work, if it later transpires that this work is much more successful than originally expected (to be exact, 2.4 times more successful: Article 37 of the 1957 law) then a court can order the purchaser to pay the artist a supplementary amount. This is an example of the doctrine of *lésion*.

Article 2 of the 1957 statute says that virtually anything can be protected by copyright:

> *Les dispositions de la présente loi protègent les droits des auteurs sur toutes les oeuvres de l'esprit, quels qu'en soient le genre, la forme d'expression, le mérite ou la destination.*

> (The provisions of this statute protect the rights of authors over all works of their imagination, whatever their nature, form, merit or intended audience.)

Article 3 then goes on to list some of the more common types of work which are protected, and this was supplemented by a statute passed in 1985 which added items such as circus acts, cartoon films, photographic works and computer software. Generally speaking copyright is protected for up to 50 years, though computer software is protected for only 25 years and musical compositions for 70 years. *Droits moraux* are protected forever. The civil remedies available again equate with those open to holders of patents and trademarks. But the criminal courts can impose sanctions too; they can sentence infringers to fines of between 6,000 and 120,000 francs (about £720 to £14,400), to prison terms of up to two years and transfer to the copyright holder of all the defendant's profits.

FURTHER READING

An excellent starting point for a description of French property law is still, despite its age, the account in Chapters 5 and 6 of Amos and Walton's *Introduction to French Law* (3rd edn, 1967). There are also helpful chapters on industrial and intellectual property (Chapter 1), real property (Chapter 8) and environment and planning (Chapter 13) in *France: Practical Commercial Law*, by Alexis Maitland Hudson (1991). Two practical guides on dealing with land in France are Henry Dyson, *French Real property and Succession Law: A Handbook* (1988) and W.H. Thomas, *Buying Property in France* (1991).

Regulated as it is by the *Code civil*, French property law is discussed in the large works devoted to an exposition of that Code. Amongst the most recent of these are C. Atias, *Droit civil: Les biens* (1993); F. Terré and P. Simler, *Droit civil: Les biens* (4th edn, 1992); and J. Carbonnier, *Droit civil: Les Biens* (1992). On specific topics, see F. Givord, C. Giverdon and P. Capoulade, *La copropriété* (4th edn, 1992); J. Schmidt-Szalewski, *Droit de la propriété industrielle* (2nd edn, 1991); J. Foyer and M. Vivant, *Droit des brevets* (1991); A. Bertrand, *Le droit d'auteur et les droits voisins* (1991); Kischinewsky-Broquisse, *La copropriété des immeubles bâtis* (4th edn, 1989); R. Dumas, *La propriété littéraire et artistique* (1987). In the *Que Sais- Je?* series, see B. Edelman, *La propriété littéraire et artistique* (2nd edn, 1993); J. Morand-Deviller, *Le droit de l'environnement* (2nd edn, 1993); and J.-M. Wagret, *Brevets d'invention et propriété industrielle* (4th edn, 1992).

CHAPTER 13

Family and succession law

HISTORY AND SOURCES OF FAMILY LAW

Family law was an area of law drastically affected by the Revolution of 1789. Prior to then the law of France very much supported the idea of the family, though in doing so it conferred extensive powers on the male head of the family, the person whom the Romans called the *paterfamilias*. The *droit intermédiaire* improved the lot of wives and of illegitimate children but made divorce extremely easy to obtain; in 1792 the number of divorces was more than one-third the number of marriages. The *Code Napoléon* restored the family as a centrepiece of social life, and in particular protected the institution of marriage. It limited divorce (and divorce was banned altogether in 1816), confirmed the authority of the husband over his wife, shut out illegitimate children and did not recognise adopted children as full and equal members of their new family.

Divorce was not made legally possible again until 1884 (by the *loi Naquet*); illegitimate children were not afforded more rights until 1912; adopted children were not given an enhanced status until 1923; wives did not begin to shake off the authority of their husbands (*prédominance maritale*) until 1938; fathers continued to have more say over the up-bringing of children than mothers did until as late as 1970. In the last two decades further reforms have considerably changed the character of family law: the disadvantages attached to illegitimacy were almost completely removed by laws enacted in 1972 and 1993, divorce was made much more easy to obtain in 1975 (so that by 1992 the proportion of divorces to marriages was almost identical to that of 200 years earlier), and complete equality between husbands and wives as regards property rights (*régimes matrimoniaux*) was achieved in 1985.

Alongside the modernising of the law there has been an updating of the terms used in the law. Marriage is no longer characterised by *cohabitation* but by *communauté de vie*; a divorce petitioner no longer asks for *une pension alimentaire* (maintenance) but for *une prestation compensatoire* (financial provision); unmarried couples no longer indulge in *concubinage* but in *cohabitation*; even the word *avortement* (abortion) has been replaced with *interruption volontaire de grossesse* (voluntary pregnancy termination).

The main source of law on the family is, of course, the *Code civil*. 'Les *personnes*' in French law also covers legal capacity, disappearances, names, domicile, guardianship, etc. All subsequent statutes affecting the area are now a part of that Code, and various other legislative provisions are usually included in printed versions. Many of the reforming laws were first drafted by Professor Jean Carbonnier, who has also written extensively on civil law in general and on family law in particular. It can be reasonably asserted that the reforms of recent years do hang together; they were, of course, preceded by various sociological studies tending to demonstrate the need for change. Case law also plays a significant role in this field, especially as several decisions of the highest courts have in effect distorted the literal meaning of the legislative texts. Today the provisions of the *Code civil* dealing with family law are distributed as follows in Titles 5 to 11 of Book 1: marriage (Articles 144–228), divorce (Articles 229–310), the parent-child relationship (*filiation*, Articles 311–342), adoption (Articles 343–370), parental authority (Articles 371–387), minors and their guardianship (Articles 388–487), and guardianship of adults (Articles 488–514). Also relevant are Articles 7–33, which deal with the enjoyment and removal of personal rights under the civil law (*droits civils*).

Marriage

As is its wont with some basic concepts, the *Code civil* does not actually supply a definition of the term 'mariage'. Nor does it say anything about periods of engagement (*fiançailles*). Nevertheless, in another startling instance of judicial law-making, French judges in the 19th century, from 1838 onwards, were prepared to hold that a woman who was let down by her fiancé could obtain compensation from him if it was a case involving *rupture fautive* (blameworthy rupture). This had also been possible prior to the Revolution. But the judges did not allow compensation merely for a breach of promise of marriage: they allied the remedy more to the law on tortious liability than to the law on contractual liability, though they did not insist that the engagement be proved by a written document. Compensation was commonly awarded in cases where the deserted applicant had borne a child fathered by the respondent. Cases such as this can still occur today; oddly enough it does not seem possible for a jilted man to claim, only an abandoned woman. Today, status as a fiancé(e) can be said to have two further consequences: it can justify an inquiry into whether the man involved is the father of the woman's child and, most strangely to English ears, it can justify the celebration of a posthumous marriage if one member of the engaged couple happens to die before the agreed marriage can take place (Article 171 of the *Code civil*, as amended in 1959); in this latter eventuality a Presidential dispensation must be obtained and there must be a serious reason for the marriage (*motif grave*), such as the fiancée's pregnancy; once it has been contracted the *mariage posthume* is immediately treated as dissolved because of the death of one party, but Article 171 makes it clear that the surviving spouse cannot inherit from the dead spouse if he or she dies intestate and no *régime matrimonial* (marriage settlement) is regarded as having existed between the spouses.

The *Code civil* contains one clear provision on broken engagements. By Article 1088, any presents given to or between the fiancés must be restored, the condition subject to which they were originally given (the marriage of the donee(s)) having failed to materialise. However, an engagement ring need not be restored if the donor of the ring broke off the engagement in a blameworthy manner (*a commis une faute*), unless the ring happens to be a family jewel (*un bijou de famille*) for then the family's claim is seen as taking priority.

In 1993 the *Conseil constitutionnel* confirmed that freedom to marry is a basic constitutional principle which must not be jeopardised by a *loi*. Nevertheless, it remains clear that for a marriage to be validly contracted in France a variety of conditions must be satisfied. In the first place the parties must be male and female: homosexuals or lesbian marriages are not possible. There has not yet been a case where a person who is known to have undergone a sex-change operation has sought to contract a marriage; it is to be hoped that French law will be more tolerant in this respect than English law has been (*Corbett v Corbett*, 1971). Secondly, a man has to be 18 before he can marry and a woman has to be 15 (Article 144 of the *Code civil*); the *procureur de la République* can lower these age limits if there is a strong reason for doing so, such as the pregnancy of the woman, but generally they are strictly adhered to. A woman aged 15, 16 or 17 must obtain the consent of a parent or guardian (article 148). In English law, of course, the age limit for both parties is 16. Thirdly, each party must undergo a medical examination no sooner than two months before the marriage: if this medical certificate is not produced the marriage cannot be validly celebrated. Fourthly, there must be a free, conscious and unconditional consent to the marriage on the part of each party (*consentement conscient, libre et éclairé*). Physical duress (*violence physique*) would negate such apparent consent, as would a genuine mistake (*erreur*), but fraud (*dol*) would not. French law is more willing than English law to accept that a mistake can nullify a marriage – in France there are cases where women were allowed to get out of marriages contracted during the First World War to men who turned out to be German nationals and a marriage contracted with a man when the woman did not know he had been through a divorce. But a person cannot have a marriage declared null just because he or she, or the other party, was on his or her deathbed at the time it was celebrated (*mariage in extremis*), nor, in most cases, is a marriage null merely because the parties had an ulterior motive for going through with the ceremony. However, if the motive is completely unconnected with the usual features of married life then the marriage can be declared null.

In order to counter the phenomenon of marriages of convenience (*mariages blancs*) contracted in order to acquire French nationality (for anyone marrying a French national can declare him or herself to be French from then on), Parliament amended the relevant provision in the *Code civil* (Article 21) in July 1993 so as to make the effectiveness of the foreigner's declaration dependent upon the parties living together for two years after the marriage; similarly, the *Conseil d'Etat* confirmed in a decision in 1992 that a foreigner can be denied a residence permit (*carte de séjour*) if the marriage was purely one of convenience (*Abihilali*). In August 1993 the *loi Pasqua* banned all persons living in a polygamous state in France from acquiring a residence permit; the *Conseil constitutionnel* upheld this provision because polygamy is alien to the French way of life. English law is more pluralistic in this regard, for it not only allows polygamously married people to live in England but also gives them access to the courts.

A fifth requirement for a valid marriage is that the parties must not be too closely related, nor of course already married. They cannot marry if one is directly descended from the other, or if they are brother and sister; nor if they are directly related by marriage (e.g. a man cannot marry his own daughter-in-law). Nieces and nephews can marry their uncles and aunts only if a dispensation is obtained from the *procureur de la République*. There are no restrictions on full cousins marrying each other.

There are also some formal requirements for a valid marriage. A notice of intended marriage (*projet de mariage*) must be posted in the local town hall for 10 days (Articles 63 and 64). The parties must be present in person before a state official to notify their agreement to marry; there must be at least two witnesses to confirm the identity of the parties and to verify that the ceremony has taken place. The state official pronounces the couple married (*unies par le mariage*). The ceremony must take place in a *commune* where at least one of the parties has been living for no less than a month.

Cohabitation

It is of course as common for unmarried people to live together in France as it is in England, and both legal systems have had to decide what rights and duties should be imported into such *unions libres*, sometimes still referred to as *concubinage*. At present it is estimated that there are approximately one million unmarried couples living together; it is no longer possible, as Napoleon is alleged to have said, for the law to ignore their position (*'la loi se désintéresse d'eux'*). However, it has stopped short of characterising such personal arrangements as contractual. There is no uniform theory applying to them: the legal rules vary according to the context. Thus, in criminal law and taxation law (*droit fiscal*) unmarried partners do not enjoy any of the privileges, or share any of the disadvantages, of husbands and wives. But in landlord and tenant law an unmarried partner is in the same position as a married person when it comes to succeeding to a tenancy: Article 14 of the 1989 statute on residential leases accords this right '*au profit du concubin notoire ou des personnes à charge qui vivaient avec lui depuis au moins un* an' (in favour of a cohabitee or dependent person who was living with [the former tenant] for at least a year). English landlord and tenant law is similar (see *Dyson Holdings Ltd* v *Fox*, 1976).

Social security law in France permits unmarried partners to claim welfare benefits dependent on the other partner's contributions, provided only that the partners are *vivant maritalement*; it is worth noting that a 1993 statute allows even homosexual partners this right. But conversely, France denies some welfare benefits to a person (e.g. single parent allowance) if the applicant is cohabiting with someone else. Normally a cohabitee has no claim to financial compensation if the relationship breaks down, but France goes further than England in saying that if the breakdown is attributable to the fraudulent behaviour of one of the partners and if the other partner suffers material loss as a result then some monetary award can be claimed. This is seen as a tortious claim (under Article 1382 of the *Code civil*). A partner who can show that he or she contributed to the other's financial success (other than by merely doing the housework) may be allowed a claim, when the relationship collapses, on the principle that a denial of compensation would constitute *enrichissement sans cause* (unjust enrichment). Occasionally the French courts will imply a commercial partnership agreement between the cohabitees (*société de fait*). In 1970, in another good example of French judicial creativity, the *Cour de Cassation* (sitting as a *chambre mixte*) allowed a woman to claim compensation from a defendant who had negligently killed the man with whom she had been living; indeed, in one or two later cases the courts have allowed both the man's wife and his mistress to sue!

If the female cohabitee has a child then both partners are legally entitled to exercise parental authority over the child if they agree to that or, even if they do not agree, if they are living *en commun* and they officially recognise the child before it reaches its first birthday.

Nullity

Decrees of nullity are as rarely sought in France as they are in England (just a handful each year). In the vast majority of instances divorce decrees will give the parties what they want. Nevertheless, the law on nullity helps to define what exactly constitutes a valid marriage in the first place. It also sets out the consequences of non-compliance with the requisite formalities. In this connection France draws a distinction between requirements which are mandatory (*empêchements dirimants*) and those which are not (*empêchements prohibitifs*).

In the former category are the requirements that the parties be of different sexes, that each of them has freely consented to the marriage and that there takes place a ceremony. In the latter category – defects which do not of themselves make the marriage null – are accidental failure to publicise the intended marriage and a third party's lack of consent to it. But even mandatory requirements do not always make a marriage null in the eyes of the whole world: often it is only the parties themselves who are entitled to plead the defect in order to escape from the marriage, as when the alleged defect is the lack of one partner's original consent. Article 184 of the *Code civil* lists six defects which can be cited even by third parties in order to claim the invalidity of a marriage: one party's lack of physical capacity to consummate the marriage (*impuberté*), one party's inability to consent to the marriage, one party's bigamy, an incestuous relationship, deliberate failure to publicise the intended marriage, and failure to marry in a permitted location or in front of a qualified official. The 1993 statute on nationality has in effect added a seventh cause for nullity – contracting a marriage for some purpose entirely extraneous to the institution, such as the acquisition of the other person's French citizenship (Article 190–1 of the *Code civil*).

If a decree of nullity of marriage is issued by a court it makes the marriage void from the moment it was supposedly celebrated: the decree operates retrospectively, whereas a divorce decree operates only prospectively. This means that any matrimonial property régime entered into by the parties has no effect: any reallocation of property takes place as if the parties were simply cohabiting. Nor does either party have any right to succeed to property on the death of the other. However, any children of the relationship are not labelled illegitimate as a result of the decree, and if one or both of the parties entered into the marriage in good faith, being unaware of the ground for nullifying the marriage, it retains its consequences *vis-à-vis* that or those parties (*mariage putatif*). This could entitle the mistaken party, for example, to claim a financial provision order (*prestation compensatoire*) from the other, a point first admitted by the *Cour de Cassation* in 1990. In 1993 an amendment was passed to the 1972 statute on parent–child relationships so as to equate the position on the exercise of parental authority after a nullity decree with that following a divorce decree.

Judicial separation

A spouse who does not wish to obtain a divorce but wants legal permission not to live with the other spouse can apply to a court for a decree of judicial separation (*séparation de corps*). The grounds upon which such a decree can be issued are the same as those for divorce and therefore will not be set out here but in the next section. The decree means that neither party is under an obligation to live with the other, but nor can they marry anyone else. There is a continuing duty to provide mutual help to each other, which will allow one party to claim maintenance payments from the other (*l'obligation* or *la pension alimentaire*). As in the case of nullity and divorce, a wronged party can claim compensation (*dommages-intérêts*) from the other (Articles 266 and 1832 of the *Code civil*). If one spouse obtains a decree against the other (as opposed to a joint application for a decree by consent) then the former would retain succession rights against the latter's property if the latter were to die, but not *vice-versa*.

Divorce

The rate of divorce in France has crept steadily upwards in recent years, though there has been a certain levelling off since 1985; in 1990 there were over 104,000 decrees. As in England, there has been a considerable liberalisation of the laws in the past 25 years; the main statute in this regard was enacted in 1975, six years after England's Divorce Reform Act 1969. In effect it provided for divorce in four different situations:

(a) where one or both parties have been at fault;
(b) where the marriage has, as English law puts it, irretrievably broken down (*rupture de la vie commune*);
(c) where the parties jointly petition for a divorce;
(d) where one party petitions for a divorce and the other does not object to a decree.

The first two situations usually lead to defended divorce petitions (*divorces contentieux*); the last two result in undefended petitions (*divorces gracieux*).

In a joint petition for divorce one lawyer can act for both parties but the judge is charged with ensuring that the agreement to divorce is a genuine one, which he or she achieves by interviewing both spouses separately and then together. The judge can alter the terms of the agreement in order to give better protection to children involved. The petition cannot be lodged sooner than six months after the marriage has occurred (in English law the waiting period is one year) and once the judge has initially approved the agreement the parties must return to court between three and nine months later to have the agreement confirmed; this is comparable to the distinction in English law between a decree *nisi* and a decree absolute. In both legal systems there is now a trend towards a 'clean break approach' in divorce (*une fois pour toutes*) but the French *Code civil* does provide for the terms of an agreed decree to be modified at a later time '*si l'absence de révision devait avoir pour l'un des conjoints des conséquences d'une exceptionnelle gravité*' (if a failure to modify would have exceptionally serious consequences for one of the parties) (Article 279). In 1990, about 41 per cent of all divorces granted were granted on this ground.

In cases where one party applies for a divorce and the other does not object to it, there is no agreement as such to be provisionally and then finally approved; in theory – rarely in practice – the judge can refuse to pronounce a divorce. The petitioner (*le demandeur*) lodges a memorial (*un mémoire*) detailing the facts which in his or her view make a continuation of married life together intolerable; the respondent (*le défendeur*) lodges a second memorial putting forward his or her own version of the facts. The judge then calls the parties and their lawyers together to try to effect a reconciliation. If this fails the court later decides whether to grant a decree, which is almost inevitable if neither party is contesting its suitability. Technically, however, the decree is granted on the basis of joint fault (*aux torts partagés*). In 1990, this ground accounted for about 14 per cent of all divorce decrees.

For cases of genuine *faute* the relevant provision is now Article 242 of the *Code civil*:

> *Le divorce peut être demandé par un époux pour des faits imputables à l'autre lorsque ces faits constituent une violation grave ou renouvelée des devoirs et obligations du mariage et rendent intolérable le maintien de la vie commune.*

> (Divorce can be requested by a spouse on account of the other spouse's actions if these actions constitute a serious or repeated violation of the duties and obligations in a marriage and make living together intolerable.)

This provision replaces two of the three separate types of fault recognised by the pre-1975 law, namely adultery (*adultère*) and unacceptable behaviour (*injure*). Most commentators seem to think that intolerable acts do not cover anything beyond what would previously have been designated as unacceptable behaviour, although as society changes the law's view as to what is acceptable or tolerable obviously changes too. Today there appears to be little difference between the ease with which a divorce can be obtained on these grounds in both France and England. In both countries adultery remains the commonest basis for alleging an intolerable matrimonial relationship, though France still adheres a little more strictly to the notion that if one spouse condones or connives at adultery this will prevent that spouse from later claiming a divorce. The third type of fault recognised before 1975 was conviction of a crime leading to *une peine afflictive et infamante* (a serious and infamous punishment). Today this is covered by Article 243 of the *Code civil*, which provides that a spouse can request a divorce if the other spouse has been sentenced to a long term of imprisonment for a *crime* or a *délit*.

No divorce can be granted on grounds of fault if the spouses have become reconciled since the acts in question occurred (*la réconciliation*), but the temporary resumption of cohabitation (*la vie commune*) does not of itself amount to reconciliation if it occurs only because there was nowhere else for one or other of the spouses to live, or because of the need to ensure education for the children (Article 244). Proof that the petitioner has him-or herself also been at fault does not prevent the court from considering the petition but may lead it to conclude that the respondent's actions were not serious enough to justify granting the petition; indeed the respondent can rely upon the petitioner's own faults in order to submit a counter-petition (*une demande reconventionnelle*); if both petitions are accepted then the court declares a divorce on the basis of *torts partagés* (joint fault). This ground for divorce is still the most commonly cited in France: in 1990, approximately 45 per cent of decrees were based upon it.

Divorce on the ground of irretrievable breakdown of marriage is governed by Articles 237–241 of the *Code civil*. The breakdown must have resulted in the spouses living apart for at least six years, although such a breakdown is presumed if the mental health of one spouse has been so seriously affected over a six-year period that a *communauté de vie* no longer exists between the spouses and has no reasonable prospect of being re-established in the future. Prior to 1975 French family law did not favour allowing a divorce in such circumstances: it took more seriously than it does today the spouses' mutual pledge to stay with each other for better and for worse (*pour le meilleur et pour le pire*).

In this type of case the petitioner must indicate to the court the means by which he or she will perform his or her legal duties to the respondent spouse and to any children of the marriage, and if the respondent is able to establish that granting a divorce would have exceptionally serious consequences for him or her or for the children (*des conséquences matérielles ou morales d'une exceptionnelle dureté*), especially in view of the respondent's age and the length of the marriage to date, the court can reject the petition. Not surprisingly, this ground for divorce is today fairly unusual in France: it arose in just 1 per cent of the cases decided in 1990.

Financial provision

French law obliges three categories of person to make financial provision for others (*l'obligation alimentaire*):

(a) one spouse with respect to the other spouse;
(b) parents with respect to their children (Articles 203 and 205); and
(c) sons-in-law and daughters-in-law with respect to their fathers-in-law and mothers-in-law (unless the daughter or son who is the reason for this in-law relationship has died) (Article 206).

In all cases the obligation is a reciprocal one (Article 207). Moreover, the estate of a deceased spouse owes a similar obligation to the surviving spouse. In theory, therefore, France is wedded to the notion of the family unit, with mutual interdependence, though Article 208 makes it clear that the duty to pay is a relative one only:

Les aliments ne sont accordées que dans la proportion du besoin de celui qui les réclame, et de la fortune de celui qui les doit.

(Maintenance is due only in proportion to the needs of the person claiming it and to the means of the person owing it.)

Moreover, if one party seriously fails to perform his or her maintenance duty towards another, the court can take this into account when deciding whether that other is reciprocally bound to provide maintenance (Article 207), a provision exempting many children from the duty of having to look after their elderly parents who deserted them earlier in life.

The interspousal duty of maintenance can be properly considered only as part of the more general subject of matrimonial property regimes (Articles 1387–1581 of the *Code civil*), although the former is an inescapable consequence of marriage whereas the latter is very much a matter of choice for the husband and wife. When people get married today, French law will assume that they wish to own subsequently acquired property jointly: this regime of *communauté des biens* will be imposed in the absence of convincing evidence that a different regime was preferred by the parties (Article 1393, referring to Articles 1400–1491). There are some fairly standard alternative regimes but freedom of contract is again the overriding principle here and the courts will be very loathe to interfere with whatever bargain the husband and wife have struck:

> *La loi ne régit l'association conjugale, quant aux biens, qu'à défaut de conventions spéciales, que les époux peuvent faire comme ils le jugent à propos, pourvu qu'elles ne soient pas contraires aux bonnes moeurs ni aux dispositions qui suivent.*
>
> (Statute law only applies to marriages, as far as property is concerned, in the absence of special agreements between the spouses, which they can make as they deem appropriate provided they are not contrary to custom and practice or to the following provisions.) (Article 1387)

The following two articles make it clear that in whatever agreement the spouses make they cannot qualify (*déroger*) the duties and rights flowing from the marriage or alter the order in which successors inherit property on an intestacy (*see* below). But if a marriage breaks down the courts are now prepared to accept not only that the better-off spouse should make financial provision for the worse-off spouse as far as the future is concerned (*la pension alimentaire*), but also that a spouse who has rendered services for the other in the past without being remunerated in any way for them is entitled to submit a claim for compensation based on the principle *enrichissement sans cause* (*see* Chapter 9). The latter sum, it is now recognised, should be calculated not as of the date when the enrichment was conferred but as of the date when the post-breakdown settlement is being arranged. As yet, however, the performance of ordinary housework has not been categorised as enrichment for this purpose: the services rendered must have gone beyond the obligation to contribute to the ordinary burdens of running a home (*au-delà de ses obligations de contribuer aux charges du ménage*). A *pension alimentaire* can be index-linked as well, either by agreement between the spouses or by order of the judge (Article 208).

If a spouse refuses to comply with a court order on maintenance the other spouse can apply to have the debtor's goods seized (*saisie*), or for a court order requiring third parties who owe money to the other spouse (e.g. an employer) to pay the money directly to the creditor spouse – attachment of earnings in the English jargon.

THE PARENT–CHILD RELATIONSHIP

In France, as in the United Kingdom, while the birth-rate has been falling in recent years the proportion of illegitimate births has been rising; in France about 30 per cent of all births are to parents who are not married. But the legal consequences of this phenomenon are not at all as significant as would have been the case even 20 or 30 years ago, because practically all the legal disadvantages attached to being illegitimate have now been removed from the statute book. A statute of 1972 established the principle that illegitimate children should in general have the same rights and duties as those who are legitimate, this now being enshrined in Article 334 of the *Code civil*: '*L'enfant naturel a en général les mêmes droits et les mêmes devoirs que l'enfant légitime dans ses rapports avec ses père et mère.*' A father's relationship with, and responsibility towards, an illegitimate child can be established either by his voluntary recognition of paternity in the form of an *acte authentique* (an authenticated document usually drawn up by a *notaire*) (Articles 335–339) or by the judgment of a court (Articles 340–341), although this latter method of establishing paternity was not permitted in French law until 1912. The statute of 1972 also allows a child who cannot prove his or her paternity, or someone on the child's behalf, to claim maintenance (*une action de subsides*) against a man who has had sexual relations with the child's mother during the period when the child might have been conceived (Article 342). As in English law, it is possible for an illegitimate child to be legitimated, either through the marriage of his or her parents or through a court order (*par autorité de justice*). The latter has been possible only since 1972 and is remarkable because it means that a child can now be legitimate even though his or her parents remain unmarried to each other. The 1972 statute also extended legitimation by marriage to children born of adulterous relationships (*enfants adultérins*), a group which had previously suffered discrimination because of the alleged affront to the first marriage which a subsequent marriage would imply.

As regards adoption, under the original *Code civil* this was possible only in respect of adults. In 1923, partly because of the number of children orphaned in the First World War, the institution was extended to persons under 21. Today there are two types of adoption available in France, both granted by an order of the *tribunal de grande instance*: *adoption simple* and *adoption plénière* (Articles 343–370). The former (which remains surprisingly popular, with about 2,500 cases per year) does not alter the connection which the adopted person (*l'adopté*) has with his or her natural family (*famille d'origine*) but does create a new relationship with the adopting person (*l'adoptant*); in particular, the succession rights flowing from the connection with the natural family remain unchanged but the adopted person acquires additional succession rights *vis-à-vis* the adopter. *Adoption plénière* is full-scale adoption of the type familiar in English law. An adopter in this situation must be aged over 30 or else have been married for more than five years, and the person he or she is adopting should be at least 15 years younger; if the person being adopted is the child of the adopter's spouse the adopter can be of any age (Articles 343–344). The adopted person must be less than 15 years of age, unless he or she is already the subject of *une adoption simple* and if aged 13 or more his or her consent is a prerequisite to the adoption. The consent of the child's natural parents is also required and once given can be withdrawn during the following three-month period. The chief effect of the adoption order is to substitute the new family for the original family: the adopted person acquires full succession rights as if he or she were a legitimate child of the adopter(s). Again, this is the same position as in English law.

After the ending of a marriage the court will decide which parent is to have *l'autorité parentale* over the children of the marriage. Before 1970, the tendency was to allow the less blameworthy of the two spouses to retain the right to determine the way in which the children should be educated and raised, with the other spouse being accorded the periodic right to visit or correspond with the children. A statute of 1970 suggested that in the vast majority of cases the right to control the upbringing of the children should vest in the spouse legally entrusted with looking after them (*garde*), but this naturally resulted in the disempowerment of many men since most children, especially younger ones, are put into the custody of their mother. In 1987 the *loi Malhuret* rearranged matters so as to make it the norm to award joint authority to both parents (*autorité conjointe*), regardless of where the children have their habitual residence, and this approach was consolidated in a further reforming statute in 1993. In practice, of course, the welfare of the child is the most important consideration, though this is not made as explicit in French law as it is in English law, especially following the enactment of the Children Act 1989.

THE FEATURES OF FRENCH SUCCESSION LAW

French law on the inheritance of property is contained in the first two parts of Book 3 in the *Code civil* (Articles 718–1100). To a large extent these provisions are rooted in the *droit ancien*, but the influence of the French Revolution is also apparent, especially in the provisions on dispositions in favour of grandchildren and nephews and nieces (Articles 1048–74). The French law also remains different in some important respects from other civil law systems in Europe. Particularly noteworthy are the Code's treatment of surviving spouses (*conjoints survivants*) and illegitimate children (*enfants naturels*), its splitting of parents' rights between the maternal line and the paternal line (*fente successorale*), its rules concerning the liability of heirs (*responsabilité*) and its protection of certain inalienable rights (*la réserve héréditaire*). Few people in France make a will, which means that the rules on intestate succession play a significant role in the distribution of property on death. These rules will be considered before we look at the rules governing the making of wills. The French use the terms *succession ab intestat* or *succession légale* to describe intestate succession, and *succession testamentaire* to describe testate succession.

The legal position of an heir

Although a different attitude was adopted prior to the Revolution, France now adheres to the doctrine of universal succession, whereby all of a deceased's property is included in the fund for distribution (*l'unité du patrimoine*). In England, by contrast, a distinction is made between personal property and real property (i.e. between goods and land).

In France, at the moment of the death of the deceased (the French speak of *le décès*, *le défunt* or *le 'de cujus'*) all of his or her property vests in the heirs (*héritiers* or *successeurs*), this being known as *saisine* (*le mort saisit le vif*). *Saisine* confers immediate ownership on the heirs as well as the right to take possession of the deceased's property without fulfilling any further formalities. There are no such things in French law as the appointment of a personal representative on an intestacy, or the granting of probate after a will: the deceased's estate will usually be administered in an *ad hoc* fashion by a *notaire* rather than in a highly organised fashion by a personal representative or an executor. As we shall see, however, certain court procedures must be followed in particular circumstances.

When an heir is confronted with a deceased's estate he or she can choose to accept the property in one of two ways, the difference lying in the consequences regarding the heir's liabilities. If there is a 'simple' acceptance of the inheritance then, along with the property, the heir acquires a liability for all the deceased's debts. The heir, or an administrator on the heir's behalf, must pay off the debts in accordance with prescribed regulations. These liabilities can be avoided, however, if the heir accepts the inheritance 'under benefit of inventory' (*sous bénéfice d'inventaire*: Articles 793–810), a device known to late Roman law. Indeed, this procedure must be adopted if the heir is under 18 years of age or otherwise legally incapable. It entails the heir making a declaration before the *tribunal de grande instance* for the area where the deceased died. The heir is then allowed three months in which to make an inventory of all the deceased's movable property, and a further 40 days in which to decide whether still to accept the inheritance. Acceptance will keep the deceased's property separate from the heir's own property and will restrict the heir's liability for the deceased's debts to the amount received in the inheritance.

Alternatively, an heir may decide to renounce the inheritance altogether (Article 784), an attractive proposition if the deceased's estate is clearly insolvent. The deceased's remaining heirs can then apply to a court for authority to accept the inheritance instead (Article 788) and the renouncing heir is relieved of any responsibility for administering the estate or for paying off the deceased's debts. He or she cannot even be made to account for (*rapporter*) gifts made by the deceased before death, a duty which English law refers to as 'bringing into hotchpot' and which applies in France unless the heir can show that the donor's intention was to make the gift in addition to whatever the donee might eventually receive as an heir (*par préciput et hors part*). Otherwise the gift is presumed to be an advancement to the heir (*avancement d'hoirie*). Once he or she has renounced, the heir's share of the estate, such as it may be, passes instead to his or her co-heirs as if he or she did not exist. If no one at all wishes to accept the inheritance, not even the state, the local *tribunal de grande instance*, on the application of interested parties such as creditors, can appoint an administrator of the property (*curateur*); these rare situations are referred to as *successions vacantes* (Articles 811–814).

Co-heirs are liable for the deceased's debts *per capita*, provided the debt is divisible (Article 1220). This means that the creditor carries the risk of a co-heir not being able to pay, which can be all the greater since the law often envisages property being distributed among several heirs. But a creditor can require the heir to divide his or her property into two parts and thereby have the payment of the deceased's debts given preference over the payment of the heir's own debts (*séparation du patrimoine*: Article 878). As regards the preservation of movable property this claim for separation must be made within three years of the deceased's death (Article 880). There is no time limit as regards immovable property, but if the creditor wants to preserve his or her prior claim over it the claim must be registered within four months (Article 2111).

'Classes' and 'degrees' of successors

The basic principle in French succession law is that relatives of the deceased have prior rights of succession. The 1804 *Code civil* gave no inheritance rights whatsoever to spouses, and their position today remains inferior. Relatives' rights depend to a greater extent than in other European countries on the degree of relationship between the relative and the deceased. Prior to the French Revolution a system of primogeniture prevailed, meaning that eldest sons inherited everything.

According to the *Code civil* there are four 'classes' (*ordres*) of heirs, the first taking priority over the second, the second over the third, and the third over the fourth. Within each class relations of the first degree (*degré*) take priority over relations of the second degree, the second over the third, and so on. Members sharing the same degree of relationship inherit the deceased's property equally. The relation between a parent and his or her child is one degree for this purpose, so that there are two degrees between a grandparent and grandchild, four degrees between cousins (*cousins germains*: Child A – Parent A; Parent A – Grandparent B; Grandparent B – Parent C; Parent C – Child D), and six degrees between second cousins (*cousins issus de germains*). This is the ancient Roman method for categorising relatives. Persons who can inherit are referred to generally in France as *les successibles*.

No one can inherit, however, unless he or she was alive at the time of the deceased's demise. To deal with cases where the *de cujus* and a potential heir have been killed in the same incident, the *Code civil* raises a series of rather arbitrary legal presumptions (Articles 720–722). For instance, if one of the persons killed was under 15 years of age and the other was over 60 years of age, the former is presumed to have survived the latter; if both persons are aged between 15 and 60 but are of different sexes, the male is presumed to have survived the female if there is less than a year's difference in age between them. In most situations, however, the courts are able to see something in the surrounding circumstances of the fatal incident which helps them to decide who survived without having to resort to these presumptions. If no conclusion is possible as to which person survived the other then each person's property is dealt with as if the other did not survive.

The first class of heirs comprises descendants of the deceased – children, grandchildren and great-grandchildren – each of whom take a proportionate share regardless of gender, age or whether they are the offspring of different marriages or born out of wedlock (Article 745). Most adopted children are also included. By way of exception to the principle that heirs take priority in accordance with the degree of relationship they have with the deceased, if a descendant dies before the deceased then his or her share of the inheritance passes to his or her children or, if there are none, to the grandchildren, and so on: the *Code civil*, like ancient Roman law, recognises that the right to an inheritance can vest in a substitute heir (*représentation*: Articles 739–744). Thus, if a man dies leaving a daughter and two grandchildren fathered by his son (who himself has already died), the daughter will inherit one-half of the property and the two grandchildren will each inherit one-quarter. This is known as *partage par souche*.

The second class of heirs consists of the parents and the brothers and sisters of the deceased (*ascendants et collatéraux privilégiés*: Articles 746–749), with substitution of heirs again being permitted in favour of the children and grandchildren of the brothers and sisters (Articles 742). The way in which the property is distributed among this class depends upon whether the parents are still alive. If they are both still alive then together they receive one-half of the deceased's property, the other half going to the deceased's brothers and sisters. If only one parent is alive then the brothers and sisters get three-quarters of the property.

The third class of heirs is made up of ascendants other than parents. The 'nearer' ancestor (e.g. grandfather) takes priority over those who are more remote (e.g. great-grandmother). The fourth class consists of collateral relatives other than brothers and sisters, i.e. all those people who are related to a common ancestor, though as a general rule French law allows this ancestry to be traced back only to the sixth 'degree' (Article 755). It therefore includes uncles, aunts, great uncles, great aunts, first cousins and second cousins. Only if the deceased was incapable of making a will, perhaps through mental illness, can the next-of-kin be traced further back, to the twelfth degree. In both the third and fourth classes substitution of heirs is not permitted.

This classification of heirs has to be understood subject to the principle that if the deceased is survived by relatives on his or her mother's or father's side but not by any children, grandchildren or great-grandchildren then his or her property must be divided accordingly (*fente successorale*: Article 733). For example, if the deceased dies leaving a paternal uncle and a maternal great-uncle, these two persons must share the deceased's property equally. This is a rule deriving not from Roman law but from the customary law of Northern France in force prior to the Revolution. The same principle applies as regards half-blood relationships. Children who share the same father and mother are referred to as *frères germains*; children who share only the same mother are called *frères uterins*, and those who share only the same father are called *frères consanguins*. So, if a person dies leaving only a full sister and a half-brother, the full sister will inherit through both the maternal line and the paternal line while the half-brother will share the inheritance only through one of these lines; hence the full sister will take three-quarters of the property and the half-brother will take one-quarter.

Illegitimate children have had enhanced inheritance rights since a law was passed to that effect in 1972. Until then they received only one-half of the share of a legitimate child if they were co-heirs with such a child. Now they have basically the same rights as legitimate children, provided paternity has been established by formal recognition or by a court judgment (Articles 756–757). An illegitimate child can himself or herself confer inheritance rights on his or her relatives (Article 758). However, the 1972 law retains in place some preferential rights for spouses and legitimate children *vis-à-vis* children of adulterous relationships (Articles 759–760). These children are also disadvantaged with regard to agricultural land and the matrimonial home (Articles 761 and 832). A parent can also exclude the child of an adulterous relationship from inheritance rights by giving away property out of his or her estate while still alive.

Surviving spouses

The original denial of, and continuing limitations on, the inheritance rights of spouses are a corollary to the highly questionable preference given by French law to the rights of blood relatives. However, some degree of compromise is achieved by the legal rules concerning matrimonial property régimes. There is a presumption in French law that a matrimonial property régime is dissolved by the death of one of the spouses (Articles 1441 and 1442), which goes some way towards justifying the inheritance rights now recognised as vesting in spouses. Added to this is the so-called *institution contractuelle* or, to give it its official title, *une donation de biens à venir* (Articles 1081–1090). This peculiarly French device, being partly a gift, partly a contract and partly a will, enables a spouse in an ante-nuptial agreement to transfer to the other spouse the whole or part of his or her estate when he or she dies, subject of course to the *réserve héréditaire* (*see* below). A person can also make provision for his or her spouse in an ordinary will, but again the spouse cannot enjoy any entitlement to the *réserve* which the testator must exclude from his or her will. French law also recognises the concept of a gift between spouses of present *and future* property (*donation entre époux*: Article 1093); many spouses take advantage of this in order to regulate their affairs when the first of them dies. When examining the inheritance rights of spouses, we must bear in mind as well that France has developed an extensive social security system and that for many families this system (and the concomitant rights to a pension) is now more important than any inheritance rights they might happen to have under succession law.

If the deceased is survived by one or more children or remoter issue, the surviving spouse obtains a life interest (*usufruit*) in one-quarter of the deceased's property. Until a reforming law of 1972, children of the deceased's former marriage took equally with the surviving spouse of the current marriage, so that if there were four such children the surviving spouse would receive only one-fifth of the deceased's property. Today it does not matter whether the deceased's children are legitimate, or illegitimate or whether they are children of the deceased's current marriage or a previous marriage. If the deceased leaves no children but only parents, brothers and sisters, or children from an adulterous relationship, the spouse receives a life interest in one-half of the property. Even then the spouse must account for gifts made to him or her by the deceased and can keep these as additional property only if able to prove that the deceased stipulated that this was to happen. The other heirs can insist on the spouse's life interest being converted into an annuity provided it is supported by sufficient securities. Only if there are no co-heirs does the spouse receive full ownership of any of the deceased's estate: one-half if there are ascendant relatives (e.g. a parent or grandparent) on either the maternal or the paternal side; the whole if there are no such relatives. However, even in this situation, if the deceased leaves a child conceived in an adulterous relationship, the inheritance rights of the surviving spouse are reduced by one-half.

No person can inherit as a surviving spouse if he or she was divorced from the deceased prior to the deceased's death, or if he or she was the respondent to a petition for judicial separation brought by the deceased at some earlier time. The same rule applies, of course, if the marriage in question is declared null.

Also, no one can inherit property if he or she is 'unworthy' (*sanction de l'indignité*: Articles 727–730). This situation arises when the person has been convicted of killing or of attempting to kill the deceased, when he or she has made an allegation of capital murder against the deceased, or when he or she is aware of the identity of the deceased's murderer but refuses to reveal it. (Inter-spousal murders in France are, regrettably, just as common as in England.) Likewise, no one can be a substitute heir for someone who is 'unworthy' and a substitute must not himself or herself be 'unworthy'. When English courts are faced with such scenarios they usually invoke the maxim *ex turpi causa non oritur actio* (no claim can be based on turpitude).

If a person dies leaving no living relatives up to the sixth degree and no surviving spouse then his or her property passes to the French state as *bona vacantia*. This mirrors the residual role of the state in English law and is referred to in France as *succession en déshérence*. But the state in France is not granted *saisine*, i.e. the automatic right to take possession of the property. Instead it requires a court order (*envoi en possession*: Article 724). The preferred view in France is that the state takes the property not as a residual heir but as a sovereign power. This means that if a foreigner dies in France without leaving heirs, his or her property will go to the French state and not to whomever his or her 'personal law' determines. It is a generally recognised rule of private international law that succession to a person's movable property should be determined by that person's 'personal law', but France sees this as being the person's national law (*lex patriae*) whereas English law sees it as being his or her domiciliary law (*lex domicilii*): *see* Chapter 14.

CO-HEIRS AND CO-OWNERSHIP

As regards co-heirs, reforming statutes since 1976 have made considerable dents in the principle that if there is more than one heir they should all take the inherited property in equal but undivided shares (*copropriété*). By Article 815 no heir can now be compelled to remain in co-ownership (*nul ne peut être contraint à demeurer dans l'indivision*) unless a delay on dividing the property has been imposed by a court or by agreement between the parties (*les indivisaires*). A court order can endure for two years but can be imposed only if prior division of the property would run the risk of depreciating its value.

If, contrary to the wishes of one co-heir, the remaining co-heirs wish to remain in co-ownership beyond two years, the court can convert the former's notional share of property into a real share, provided the property is divisible; alternatively the co-heir can insist upon being paid the monetary value of his or share by the co-heirs who are unwilling to divide the property. If a person wishes to sell his or her share of the property the other co-heirs have a preferential right of purchase. Article 815 allows for further divisions in favour of definite groups of people (a surviving spouse or a child under the age of majority) and in respect of definite pieces of property, such as agricultural goods and premises used as residences or businesses.

French law currently distinguishes between 'simple co-ownership' (*indivision simple*: Article 815 *et seq.*) and 'agreed co-ownership' (*indivision conventionnelle*: Article 1873). Under the former arrangement every increase or decrease in the property's value is shared equally between the co-heirs, and any dealing with the property must have the consent of all the co-heirs. One of them may be given authority by the others to manage the inherited property on behalf of the whole group and the President of the *tribunal de grande instance* can prescribe or authorise the taking of such necessary measures as are in the common interest of all the co-heirs. As regards *l'indivision conventionnelle*, Article 1873 permits a contract to prohibit the division of inherited property, either forever or for a specified period up to five years. The Code's provisions on termination of such contracts, and on their management, demonstrate that they are closely allied to the agreements creating civil law corporations, which are regulated by the *Code civil* in the immediately preceding paragraphs. Any division of inherited property operates retrospectively, but acts validly carried out prior to the division remain fully effective (Article 833).

WILLS

The most basic notion in both English law and French law concerning dispositions on death is the principle of testamentary freedom. A testator is free to dispose of his or her property much as he or she wishes. This helps to explain the prohibitions on joint wills (Article 968) and on testamentary contracts (*pactes sur succession future*: Article 1130), both of which are permitted only exceptionally. It also justifies the principle that substitution of heirs (*représentation*) is not permitted in the cases of testamentary succession. However, arrangements can be made for the *inter vivos* distribution of property in anticipation of death (Articles 1075–1080) and, unlike in English law, property not dealt with in the will is inherited as if there were an intestacy; in English law the residual legatee under the will takes the remaining property.

To be valid a French will (or indeed any later codicil to a will) must be in one of three prescribed written forms. It cannot be purely oral, even in the most extreme conditions, although if a written will is accidentally destroyed its contents can be proved by oral evidence. The first type of will, and by far the most common, is the holograph will (*le testament olographe*), unknown in English law. This is a will which the testator entirely hand-writes, dates and signs (Article 970). It should be deposited with a *notaire* for safe-keeping and, when the testator dies, it should be presented to the President of the local *tribunal de grande instance* so that an official note of its existence can be made (*un procès-verbal*). The second type is an authentic will (*le testament authentique*), which is a will drawn up by a notary in accordance with the testator's instructions and in the presence of two witnesses or of a second notary. The *notaire* and the witnesses must sign the document after the testator. As in English law, a beneficiary under the will cannot be a witness, but France extends this prohibition to relatives of beneficiaries and to clerks of the notary. The third type of will – *le testament mystique ou secret* – is an amalgam of the other two: the will is written by the testator or at his or her dictation and is then presented to a notary and two witnesses in a sealed envelope which is then signed by all four parties. The second and third types of will, because of the compulsory involvement of a notary, are comparatively expensive and unpopular; the second type has the added disadvantage of lack of privacy at the time of its creation.

To be legally capable of making a will a person must be of sound mind (*sain d'esprit*), not under someone's undue influence and over 16 years of age (Articles 901 and 903). A weak-minded person who is under the guardianship of a judicial counsellor (*conseil judiciaire*) can make a will under the counsellor's guidance. Members of the armed forces on active service and persons on a sea voyage are allowed to make wills in a different form but these cease to be valid six months after the end of the service or the voyage (Articles 981 and 984). Similarly, it appears that French nationals living abroad can make wills recognised as valid by French law provided they adhere to the requirements of the local law (Article 999).

The provisions in a will can be wholly or partly revoked by another will (of whatever type), by a separate document prepared by a notary, by the will being torn or burnt, or by the *inter vivos* disposal of some property specifically dealt with in the will. France does not have the English rule whereby the later marriage of the testator automatically revokes his or her former will but, it does revoke the will of a person who has later been sentenced to life imprisonment.

Persons designated as beneficiaries under French wills are not called *héritiers* but *légataires*. The single term *legs* is used to cover what in English law may be a monetary legacy, a bequest of personalty or a devise of realty. A specific legacy (*legs particulier*) actually confers ownership on the legatee, as does *saisine* in cases of intestacy. A general legacy (*legs à titre universel*) is one whereby the testator confers a right to a definite part of the deceased's estate, such as all the movable property or one-third of the immovable property (Article 1010). It carries with it the duty to pay off a proportionate amount of the deceased's debts (Article 1012), whereas a specific legatee will only suffer a reduction in the amount received (Article 1024). A third type of legacy is called *un legs universel*; this in effect appoints one or more residual legatees to take any property not otherwise the subject of a legacy (Article 1003) and it imposes an obligation to pay the deceased's debts as well as the other legacies.

No will can transfer property to a person who has not been conceived at the time of the testator's death (Article 725): this is the French equivalent to

England's rules on perpetuities. Nor can a person receive property if he or she is serving a period of life imprisonment, and ministers of religion or doctors who have looked after a testator cannot inherit under a will made during the period of such ministrations (Article 909). Many companies and charities cannot accept a legacy (or indeed an *inter vivos* gift) unless they first obtain official governmental authorisation.

A legacy, moreover, can be made conditional upon the fulfilment of some request, though conditions which are impossible or contrary to law or good morals can be ignored (Article 900). More specifically, no legacy can be made subject to the condition that the legatee look after the property and transfer it on his or death to a third party: these so-called *substitutions fidéicommissaires* were common in the *ancien régime* as a means of tying up property in the same family but, subject to certain exceptions, they were abolished by the *Code civil* (Article 896). Any attempt to create one today would cause the legacy to lapse (*caduc*). This would also occur if the legatee dies before the testator or before the fulfilment of a request by the testator, or if the legatee chooses to renounce the legacy or is designated as an ingrate (*ingrat*). *Ingratitude* arises when the legatee has attempted to kill the testator, or has gravely insulted the testator or the testator's memory (Articles 954–955 and 1047).

Usually the person given responsibility for administering the will is the general legatee or the heir who takes on the remaining intestacy, or at any rate the notary instructed by such legatee or heir. It is possible, however, for the testator to appoint an executor (*un exécuteur testamentaire*), though this person does not act in the same way as an executor in English law. He or she can have his or her expenses covered out of the estate but cannot be remunerated for the task. The chief functions of any such executor are to make sure the will's provisions are complied with by preparing an inventory of the deceased's property and paying the legacies. He or she can sell movables if this is required in order to provide enough cash for the legacies (Article 1031) and the testator can confer the additional power to sell immovables. The executor is not personally liable for any of the deceased's debts – the creditors must still sue the heir or the universal legatee – but if he or she refuses to accept the appointment as executor then any benefit conferred on him or her by the will is lost.

A particular type of testamentary disposition is permissible between an ascendant and his or her descendants (usually between a mother or father and their children). Known as *un testament-partage*, it represents partly a disposition by will and partly a division of property on an intestacy (Articles 1079–1080). It takes effect on the donor's death but occurs *inter vivos*, so that each of the donor's heirs who would take on an intestacy knows in advance how much he or she can expect to receive on the donor's death (though this must not be less than his or her share of the reserved property – *réserve héréditaire*).

Reserved property

The *Code civil* seeks to protect close relatives of the deceased by preventing the deceased from disposing of a proportion of his or her property as he or she thinks fit. The testator can will away only the 'disposable' part of his or her property (*le quotité disponible*). French law actually confers on the reserved heirs a proprietary right to the so-called reserved property, not just a personal claim to the equivalent value of that property, and the reserved heirs actually have *saisine*, which entitles them to possession as well as ownership of the testator's property, including all the fruits of that property, from the date of the deceased's death.

Only the ascendants and descendants of the deceased ever have reserved rights, not collateral relatives or the deceased's spouse. Descendants' rights take precedence over those of ascendants. If there is only one descendant (i.e. a son or daughter) the reserve is one-half of the deceased's estate. If there are two children the reserve is two-thirds; if there are three or more it is three-quarters. If a descendant has predeceased the *de cujus* then his or her share of the reserve is taken in a substitute capacity by his or her own children. If the deceased leaves no descendants then one-quarter of his or her estate is reserved for each of his or her parents, if they are alive.

By Article 920 the person entitled to the reserved property can apply to have dispositions set aside if they were not made for any consideration or if there is not enough property left in the estate to satisfy the *réserve*: legatees will have their legacies reduced proportionally (Articles 926–927) and after that donees *inter vivos* must return their gifts until the reserve is re-established, the most recent donees having to make restitution first (Article 923). This process is known as *réduction des libéralités*.

FURTHER READING

Good French books on family law include A. Bénabent, *Droit civil: La famille* (5th edn, 1993); P. Malaurie and L. Aynès, *Droit civil: La famille* (4th edn, 1993); A. Weill and F. Terré, *Droit civil: Les personnes. La famille. Les incapacités* (5th edn, updated 1993); P. Courbe, *Le divorce* (1993); P. Dupont-Delestraint and P. Courbe, *Les personnes. La famille. Les incapacités.* (14th edn, 1992); J. Carbonnier, *Droit civil*, vol. 1, 'Les personnes' (18th edn, 1992) and vol. 2, 'La famille. Les incapacités' (15th edn, 1991). For a more socio-legal approach, see Irène Théry, *Le démariage: justice et vie privée* (1993), and for a practical guide Suzanne Lannerée, *Le divorce* (1992). In the *Que Sais-Je?* series there are *La médiation familiale* by L. Topor (1992) and *La filiation et l'adoption* by M.-L. Rassat (2nd edn, 1992). On property regimes consult G. Cornu, *Les régimes matrimoniaux* (6th edn, 1992) and F. Terré and P. Simler, *Les régimes matrimoniaux* (1989).

The best general treatment of French succession law in English, though it is now out-of-date on matters such as the rights of illegitimate children, is in Chapters 13 and 14 of *Amos and Walton's Introduction to French Law*, by F. Lawson, A. Anton and N. Brown (3rd edn, 1967). There are also very readable accounts in Chapters 16 to 20 of *French Real Property and Succession Law* by Henry Dyson (1988); the same author has published a much abbreviated version in the *Solicitors' Journal* ((1987) 131 Sol Jo 493). Also useful are two pieces by D. G. MacDonald Allen: 'Making a Will in France' and 'Dying Intestate in France', (1983) 127 Sol Jo 181 and 850.

For books in French, see A. Sériaux, *Les successions. Les liberalités* (2nd edn, 1993); P. Malaurie and L. Aynès, *Droit civil: Les successions. Les libéralités* (2nd edn, 1993); M. Grimaldi, *Droit civil. Successions* (1992); F. Terré and Y. Lequette, *Droit civil: Les successions. Les libéralités* (2nd edn, 1988).

CHAPTER 14

Private international law

INTRODUCTION

Perhaps the most obvious development of recent years in French and English private international law has been the convergence of the two systems owing to the countries' membership of the European Community. Non-EC treaties, such as those produced at the Hague, have also played an increasing role in harmonising the choice-of-law rules. Nevertheless, particularly in the area of family law, there is still room for conflicts of laws between the two countries. These could be solved by bilateral treaties between the United Kingdom and France, but the adoption of such treaties would tend to undermine the multilateralist approach favoured in Brussels, the Hague and Rome.

France has a long and distinguished record in the field of private international law and it is a subject which today is much studied in university law departments. Among the well-known early writers in the field were Dumoulin (1500–1566) and d'Argentré (1519–1590), and these were followed in the 19th and early 20th centuries by scholars such as Bartin, Pillet, Niboyet, Arminjon and Batiffol. A good deal of general theorising still takes place, so that the relevant textbooks tend to devote more space to a discussion of the underlying rationales for particular rules than to a discussion of the operation of the rules themselves. Moreover, in France the subject itself embraces much more than it does in England. It includes not only choice-of-law rules (conflicts of laws properly so called – *conflits de lois*) but also nationality law, laws regulating the position of foreigners in France and rules on jurisdiction in international cases (*conflits de juridiction*).

While legislation is the main source for the law on nationality, case law and academic opinion (*jurisprudence et doctrine*) are the main sources for the rules on choice-of-law. Bilateral and multilateral treaties, which by Article 55 of the French Constitution have a status superior to purely domestic law, are increasingly important sources for the rules on the position of foreigners and jurisdiction. Sometimes such treaties also lay down special legal solutions for international cases (as in matters to do with the transport of goods or the protection of intellectual property rights) and the Conventions agreed at the Hague Conferences on Private International

Law often contain choice-of-law rules which for the most part are to be applied regardless of the end-result in a particular case.

LAWS ON NATIONALITY AND FOREIGNERS

The *Code civil* of 1804 did not use the term *'nationalité'*; instead it spoke of *'qualité de français'*. By Article 10, every child born of a French man was said to be French, even if born abroad; conversely a person born of a foreigner in France was not said to be French but Article 9 allowed him or her to claim French nationality within a year of reaching his or her majority provided he or she was by that time domiciled in France. After several intervening reforms the law on nationality was eventually remodelled by the *Code de la nationalité française*, promulgated by an *Ordonnance* of 19 October 1945 and amended on many subsequent occasions. The relevant articles in the *Code civil* were fully repealed. In the 1970s and 1980s reform of nationality law was again often on the political agenda, new proposals being brought forward with practically each new government. The Gaullist government which came to power in 1986 tabled a Bill which tended to make it more difficult for children to acquire French nationality if they were born in France to parents who were not born in France. The proposals caused such a political stir that the Bill was put 'on ice' and a 19-member Commission was set up (*La Commission de la nationalité*) to look again at the issue. This Commission reported in January 1988 (*'Être Français aujourd'hui et demain'*) but none of its 60 recommendations saw the light of day until the Gaullists were back in power in 1993. The three main thrusts of the report and of the 1993 statute were that granting nationality must not itself be a substitute for the integration of foreigners into French society; that granting nationality should help to develop the consciousness of a French identity; and that being a national must increasingly mean being a member of a 'nation' with shared values. In July 1993 the *Conseil constitutionnel* approved the proposed new law, save for a few provisions which it queried on technical grounds. The statute inserted a new Title 1 into the *Code civil* (Articles 17 *et seq*).

The amended provisions in the *Code civil* still rely both upon the *ius sanguinis* principle and the *ius soli* principle. That is to say, children can acquire French nationality either because one or both of their parents is French (*attribution par filiation*), or because they themselves were born in France (*attribution par la naissance en France*). The former rule applies regardless of whether the child is legitimate, illegitimate or adopted, but it admits of an exception in a situation where only one of the parents is French: if the child in such cases is not born in France then he or she is allowed to repudiate French nationality during the six months preceding the attainment of majority (i.e. his or her eighteenth birthday), or (a change introduced by the 1993 law) during the 12 months following that birthday, always provided that by this time the non-French parent has not also acquired French nationality. The rules concerning birth in France say that French nationality is conferred on a child, first, if one of his or her parents was also born in France (*le double droit du sol*), secondly, if the child's parents are unknown or stateless (*parents inconnus ou apatrides*), or, thirdly, if no other country is prepared to confer its nationality on the child.

Children born in France who do not satisfy these conditions (e.g. children of first generation immigrants) will acquire French nationality on their sixteenth birthday only if at that date they reside in France, they have had a habitual residence in France during the previous five years *and* they demonstrate a willingness to acquire French nationality (*manifestation de volonté*) (Article 21-7). This last requirement does not necessitate an oath of allegiance to France (as is required in the United States of America when a person becomes naturalised): it is enough if the young person performs a simple act such as applying for a resident permit (*carte de séjour*) or answering a straightforward question in writing (Article 21-9). On the other hand, a young person can be denied French nationality if he or she has been sentenced for certain offences committed when over the age of 18; these offences include terrorist crimes, drug trafficking and serious assaults.

Since the law was amended in 1973, marriage to a French national has not of itself had any effect on a foreigner's nationality. Now, after further reforms, first in 1984 and then in 1993, once the marriage has survived for two years (formerly six months), the foreigner can declare that he or she is taking French nationality, provided the spouses are still living together and the French spouse has not lost his or her French nationality in the meantime (Article 21–2).

A further method of acquiring French nationality is, of course, through naturalisation. For this to occur six conditions must usually be satisfied: the candidate must be at least 18 years of age, be ordinarily resident in France, have been habitually resident in France for the previous five years, not have been sentenced for serious offences, be of good character ('*de bonnes vie et moeurs*') and be able to demonstrate that he or she is now assimilated into French society (e.g. by proficiency in the language).

As regards the legal position of foreigners, the most important provision is Article 11 of the *Code civil*, according to which foreigners in France have the same rights as those which are guaranteed to a French national in the foreigner's country. This 'reciprocity' provision is in fact interpreted to mean that foreigners have whatever rights are not expressly denied to them by French law, though judges brought about this liberalisation only after Parliament had specified the rights which foreigners are *not* allowed to enjoy, whether in civil law disputes or in public law matters (e.g. they have no right to vote and no right to make state officials accountable for their actions). Particularly important are the regulations concerning entry into professions, such as those dealing with the right to work or the right to trade (*carte de commerçant*). But the EC's Treaty of Rome has necessitated some drastic changes in this context. The principles governing the single European market, and the rights to establish oneself and to provide services, have not yet led to the removal of all restrictions on foreigners, but the permits which are still required are now granted automatically to nationals of other EC states. For certain professions, however, there are still specific difficulties to do with the nature of the activity. As mentioned in Chapter 2, this applies to the practice of law.

CHOICE-OF-LAW RULES

French choice-of-law rules have a lot in common with those operating in other civil law systems. While the rules are certainly rules of French law, the international dimension to this subject has always led to countries borrowing from one another. As examples we need cite only the contractual doctrine first devised by the Frenchman Dumoulin and the theory concerning the 'seat of legal relationships' originally propounded by the German Roman law expert, von Savigny. Today French private international law distinguishes between three sets of choice-of-law rules: those dealing with personal and family matters, those dealing with property rights, and those dealing with legal obligations such as contracts and torts (including matrimonial property régimes). For each of these contexts it adopts different 'connecting factors' (*points de rattachement*); these are, in turn, a person's nationality, the physical location of property and the place where a legal relationship is created.

General principles

The *Code civil* does not contain many articles devoted to choice-of-law, fewer even than exist in the codes of other civil law systems. As a result case law and academic doctrine have played a very significant role in the development of this area of law in France. Article 3(1) of the *Code civil* simply states that laws concerning the 'policing' and security of the state are binding on all those persons who live in France (*Les lois de police et de sûreté obligent tous ceux qui habitent le territoire*). This is an oblique way of saying that foreign laws cannot be applied in France if they offend against basic French public policy (*ordre public*). But the content of this public policy has had to be established through case law and the courts have been quite restrictive in their interpretation. Another bar to the application of foreign law has been the doctrine on evasion of law (*fraude à la loi*), which applies whenever one or more parties deliberately attempts to avoid the application of French law by exploiting choice-of-law rules. A famous example of this occurred in the *Princesse de Beaufremont* case. In the 1870s the Princess wanted a divorce but at that time France did not allow such a thing. She consequently moved to Germany, became a naturalised German citizen, obtained a divorce there and remarried a Prince in Berlin. Both the divorce and the remariage were ruled invalid by the French courts.

The classic problems of *renvoi* and characterisation (*qualification*) have been much analysed in France, the solutions ultimately preferred being the double *renvoi* theory and characterisation in accordance with the forum's principles (*lege fori*). Double *renvoi* means that, if a French choice-of-law rule points to the law of country X, which in turn points either back to French law or on to the law of country Y, French courts will 'accept' the *renvoi* and apply either French law or the law of country Y as the case may be (see the *Forgo* case, 1878, and the *Patino* case, 1963). In addition, the French court will seek to interpret the connecting factor used in the choice-of-law rule of country X (e.g. domicile) in the same way as a court in country X itself would do (an exception to the general approach to problems of characterisation). France has not adopted the 'total' *renvoi* theory, which would require a French court to decide the case exactly as the courts would do in the country to which the French choice-of-law rule first points; to adopt this approach would be to cede to a foreign country all responsibility for deciding the case. English private international law also accepts the theory of double *renvoi* but rejects total *renvoi*, which unfortunately means that the two countries could well differ as to how the same case should ultimately be decided: if an English woman dies domiciled in France, a French court will apply French law to the questions connected with inheritance of her property because, although it first refers to English law as the deceased's *lex patriae*, it accepts the *renvoi* from England because English law would apply French law to these questions in its capacity as the deceased's *lex domicilii*, but if the case arises first in an English court it will apply English law because it too would accept the *renvoi* from France as the *lex domicilii*; the outcome of the case will therefore depend on where the case is brought, a result which it is the very *raison d'être* of private international law to avoid.

The French view of characterisation (i.e. whether to classify an issue as belonging to one area of law, such as contract, or to another, such as tort) derives largely from the work of Bartin at the end of the 19th century, and in particular from his analysis of the *Bartholo* case (1889). Two British nationals, having lived and married in Malta, had moved to Algeria, at that time a French colony. When the husband died his widow claimed one-quarter of his immovable property situated in Algeria: she argued that this was her right under Maltese law, which governed the matrimonial property régime applying between her husband and herself. Mr Bartholo's other heirs, however, argued that her claim to the immovables was an issue relating to inheritance and therefore subject to French law, as it was in a French colony that the property was situated. The courts in Algeria, like Bartin, supported classifying the issue in accordance with French national categories, i.e. as an issue in succession law. French courts now regularly characterise an issue in this way (*qualification lege fori*): the approach was confirmed in the *Caraslanis* case in 1955, where the French courts held that the marriage of a Greek man in France did not have to entail a religious ceremony as required by his *lex patriae*. But subsidiary matters (*questions préalables*) are characterised in accordance with the foreign *lex causae* (i.e. the law to be applied to the main issue), so, for example, while the French choice-of-law rule for property states that it is all to be governed by the law of the country where it is situated (the *lex rei sitae*), it is that foreign law which is left to determine whether the property is to be dealt with as movable or immovable property. Moreover, as in English private international law, French legal concepts are sometimes stretched so as to embrace novel foreign legal institutions: polygamy, for instance, is in both systems recognised to some extent as a form of marriage.

What English conflicts of laws scholars refer to as the 'time factor' the French call '*un conflit mobile*'. This can be a problem in many different contexts, whether it be family law, property law or the law of contract and tort. For instance, a piece of property may be frequently transferred from one country to another and a court may need to decide at which time its location must be specified for choice-of-law purposes. In France it is not possible to identify a fixed approach to the problem: the time chosen will depend on the nature of the choice-of-law rule and on the relevant interests at stake.

In English private international law, a foreign law will not be applied by an English court unless it is both pleaded and proved to the satisfaction of the English judge. The substance of the law is treated as a question of fact on which expert evidence can be adduced. The French attitude is similar but not identical. Foreign law is seen as a fact, so that there can be no appeal against the determination of its content to, say, the *Cour de Cassation*, unless the court has so misinterpreted the foreign law as to distort it completely (*dénaturation*), but a French judge can apply it *proprio motu*, i.e. without being asked to do so. The judge can carry out his or her own research into the state of the foreign law but will usually ask for the foreign law to be proved by way of a document called a *certificat de coutume*, which is often drawn up by expert legal academics in French universities. Applying a foreign law designated by a choice-of-law rule is not, moreover, mandatory: a French judge can conclude that to apply it would be contrary to the public policy embodied in France's own national rule.

Personal and family matters

Article 3(3) of the *Code civil* stipulates that the provisions on personal status and legal capacity apply to French nationals even when they are abroad. Case law has bilateralised this rule so that foreigners in France are also subject to their own *lex patriae*. The *lex patriae* is thus the basic law applied by France to problems arising within personal and familial relationships. The tying of people to their national law is an idea most trumpeted by the

Italian scholar Mancini (1817–1888) in the middle of the 19th century. England and other common law countries, of course, have preferred to use the connecting factor known as domicile, though difficulties in defining that concept, as well as increasing reliance upon international treaties, have led to habitual or ordinary residence replacing domicile as the connecting factor in some choice-of-law rules.

The validity of a marriage is a matter for the *lex patriae* of each of the spouses: the requirements of both systems must be satisfied except to the extent that they are contrary to France's public policy (e.g. a requirement that a divorced person cannot remarry within a certain number of years after the divorce). If the marriage has been celebrated in France the local French requirements must also be satisfied. As regards the form in which a marriage is celebrated, the French adopt the same rule as the English: compliance with the requirements of the *lex loci celebrationis* is enough. An exception is made, however, for some marriages conducted by consular officials: they have the authority to conduct marriages between their own nationals in foreign countries while following their own national requirements. The law which governs the consequences of a marriage being declared null is generally speaking the *lex fori*, though the effect *vis-à-vis* the legitimacy of children of the marriage is a matter for the *lex causae* for that particular issue (*see* below).

Application of a choice-of-law rule pointing to the parties' *lex patriae* has naturally led to uncertainties in cases where parties to a marriage who are of different nationalities have sought a divorce. After many decisions had come down in favour of applying the husband's *lex patriae*, and the *Cour de Cassation* in the *Ferrari* case in 1922 had applied French law to permit a French woman to obtain a divorce from a husband whose national law did not allow a divorce, case law eventually settled for the application of the law of the parties' common domicile (the *Rivière* case, 1953). In these situations French law has therefore moved away from giving a preference to the husband's law without having to treat the matter as raising a constitutional issue based around sex discrimination (as has happened in Germany).

The reform of divorce law in France in 1975 meant that the case law on the relevant choice-of-law rule was replaced by a new version of Article 310 of the *Code civil*. French law must now be applied to a petition for divorce or judicial separation if both spouses are French nationals or have a common domicile in France, or if no foreign law claims to be applicable and French courts have jurisdiction to hear the petition. Article 310 is framed in unilateral terms, but again the courts will tend to apply it by way of analogy in cases where, for example, both spouses share a foreign nationality. Cases not covered by Article 310 at all, such as where the parties have different nationalities and separate domiciles, are left to the courts to decide for themselves. In the vast majority of cases French law will be applied in these exceptional cases, if only by default. In English private international law it is unheard of for a court to apply a foreign law to a divorce petition, even though some nullity suits can be so dealt with. The prevailing view seems to be that it would be against English public policy for an English court to grant a divorce on grounds not recognised by English law. In both systems the consequences of a divorce decree being issued will be determined by the local law as the *lex fori*.

A person's capacity to undertake legal acts, such as a marriage or a contract, is also subjected by French private international law to that person's *lex patriae*. However, an important exception exists for situations where a party dealing which someone who lacks contractual capacity could not reasonably have been expected to know this (the *Lizardi* case, 1861). In that eventuality the *lex loci contractus* applies.

A statute of 3 January 1972 deals with children. Whether a child is legitimate or illegitmate is basically a question to be determined by the mother's *lex patriae* at the time of the child's birth, or by the *lex patriae* of the child if this is more favourable to the child (Articles 311–414 of the *Code civil*). Whether the child can be legitimated or claim maintenance are also matters either for the child's own *lex patriae*, or for that of the man wanting to legitimate the child or against whom the claim for maintenance is made: the child or his or her guardian can choose whichever of these laws is more favourable to his or her position. Since 1972 children in France have also benefited from the 1961 Hague Convention on the Protection of Minors, which gives primary responsibility for the welfare of children to the authorities in the country where the child is habitually resident but which also recognises a limited right of authorities in the child's own nation to take protective measures.

Property questions

The French say that all tangible property is governed by the law of the place where it is situated (*lex rei sitae* or *lex situs*). Article 3(2) of the *Code civil* expressly states this rule in relation to immovable property within France. It has proved controversial when courts have sought to apply it to movable property, not just because of the attraction of the old adage *mobilia sequuntur personam* (movables follow their possessor) but also because of the opportunities it provides for parties easily to change the governing law. Case law nevertheless makes it clear that today the *lex rei sitae* does wholly apply to rights over movable property. Given this dual role for the *lex rei sitae* it is natural, as mentioned earlier, that it is left to that law, rather than to French law as the *lex fori*, to determine whether the property in question is indeed immovable or movable. English private international law, because it has different choice-of-law rules for the two forms of property (the *lex situs* for immovables and the *lex actus* for transactions involving movables, though compliance with the *lex situs* is often regarded as enough), characterises the property *lege fori*. In France the *lex rei sitae* also governs questions such as priority of charges obtained over the property and the property's alienability. In both legal systems ships and planes are usually governed by the law of the country where they are registered (*la loi du pavillon*) and cars are subject to the law of the country where they are 'kept' (*situation effective*).

In France, whether property has been joined with other property, or nationalised, expropriated or possessed, are all matters for the *lex rei sitae* to determine. Otherwise transfers of property are governed both by that law and by the *lex causae* of the transaction itself, usually a contract. So a charge can be created over property only if this is allowable by the law of the place where the property is situated as well as by the law of the contract creating the charge. Likewise, a retention of title clause is valid only if it is acceptable to both the law governing the sales contract in question and the law of the property's current location. The choice-of-law rule can therefore be said to be one of cumulative reference. Choses in action (*biens incorporels*) are for the most part governed by the *lex rei sitae* of the property affected by them; this applies to shares in a company or to interests in a fund (*fonds du commerce*). Claims to copyright are, by the Berne Convention of 1886 and the Geneva Convention of 1952, subjected to the law of the country where the protection is being claimed, except that the law of the country where the copyright originated (*loi du lieu de la première publication*) must be consulted to see if it grants any exclusive rights to the author. By a statute passed in 1964, France will protect original foreign works only if the country in question grants reciprocal protection to original French works. Patents and trademarks are protected by French private international law if the law of the country where the protection is being sought allows it (*le principe de l'indépendance des droits*); like most countries, France also adheres to the Paris Convention of 1883 which permits a patent or trademark registered in one country to be protected in all the other Convention countries too.

French private international law deals with problems concerning the inheritance of property in much the same way as it deals with other proprietary issues, though this time it does distinguish between immovables and movables. Succession to immovable property is governed by the inheritance law of the place where the property is located at the time of the deceased's death, while succession to movable property, perhaps surprisingly, is subjected to the law of the deceased's domicile at the date of his or her death. France has retained this approach to inheritance rights despite the complexities involved in dividing a deceased's estate and the consequent risk of having conflicting decisions from two legal systems.

Contracts and torts

Until recently French private international law subjected contracts and other legal obligations to the law of the place where they were created (*lex loci contractus*). The relevant maxim was *locus regit actum* (the place governs the act). Gradually the rule came to be used only in relation to the form required for such acts, and even then compliance with the local law was not always seen as mandatory. The most relevant factor determining the applicable law was eventually seen to be the will of the parties, certainly for contracts (*loi d'autonomie*). If the parties had not expressly chosen the applicable law then the contract was to be governed by whatever law was most clearly indicated by the circumstances. If there were no special indications, such as the language used in the contract or the jurisdiction specified by the parties as the one where any dispute between them was to be settled, the courts would fall back on the law of the place where the main obligation in the contract was to be fulfilled (in a sales contract this would be the place where the goods were to be delivered) or (if this led to the contract being upheld as valid) the law of the place where the contract was concluded.

France has now ratified the 1980 Rome Convention on Contractual Obligations, which has been in force since 1 April 1991. The intention behind the Convention is to create uniform choice-of-law rules for contractual obligations in all member states of the European Community. Its provisions do not differ significantly from those already applying in France by virtue of the judge-made rules and, because the United Kingdom has also ratified the Convention and incorporated it into domestic law by the Contracts (Applicable Law) Act 1990, an explanation of those provisions can be looked for in any of the modern textbooks on English private international law. The Convention applies to many, but not all, contracts and it is not confined to cases where the contract is somehow connected with another member state of the European Community – the connection can be with any other country in the world. It takes second place, however, to other Conventions dealing with specific types of contracts (such as those on carriage of goods). When two Protocols to the Convention come into force appeal courts in each state will be able to refer questions concerning the meaning of the Convention's provisions to the European Court of Justice in Luxembourg. Meanwhile national courts are able to interpret those provisions in the light of the *travaux préparatoires* preceding the Convention (the Giuliano, Lagarde and Tizzano Reports) and they must follow any previous decision on the point issued by the European Court of Justice (which may even now have to deal with the Rome Convention when hearing a case referred to it under the 1968 Brussels Convention on jurisdiction, described below).

One obvious point is that the Rome Convention applies only to contractual obligations and countries may differ as to what obligations they characterise as contractual. We may have to await the pronouncements of the European Court of Justice before harmony is achieved on this. The French concept of contract is by no means the same as the English concept: it embraces as well, for example, some agreements not supported by consideration, some gifts and some so-called quasi-contractual situations. Moreover, the Convention itself excludes from its operation a variety of issues. It does not apply, for example, to arbitration agreements, most contracts of insurance, contracts creating or dissolving a company, negotiable instruments (such as cheques and debentures) or social and family agreements. Nor does it alter the basic rule prevailing in both English and French private international law whereby matters of evidence and procedure are for the forum hearing the case to decide in accordance with its own *lex fori*, though the required form which a contract must display (e.g. whether it needs to be in writing) would not for this purpose be regarded as merely a question of procedure and the Convention would therefore apply.

Article 3(1) of the Rome Convention states the basic principle to be that 'a contract shall be governed by the law chosen by the parties'. This is in line with the pre-existing French choice-of-law rule, although it is more doubtful whether that rule would have allowed different laws to be chosen for different parts of the contract, as the last sentence of Article 3(1) expressly permits (a procedure known as *dépeçage* – picking and choosing), or whether it would have allowed parties to change their chosen law during the life of the contract, which Article 3(2) permits. However, the Convention guards against excessive law-shopping by providing in Article 3(3) that the parties' choice of a foreign law cannot avoid the application of 'mandatory rules' of another country if that is the country with which the contract has all relevant connections; this is reminiscent of the French *fraude à la loi* doctrine. In France mandatory rules are known as *lois d'application immédiate* or *lois de police*.

There is little difficulty in establishing the chosen law in cases where the parties have made an express choice. In other cases the chosen law will need to be inferred from the circumstances, and for French courts one of the most revealing of these circumstances will be a reference in the contract to the jurisdiction whose courts are to be allowed to settle any disputes arising under the contract (*clauses attributives de compétence* or *clauses de prorogation*). If a choice of law cannot be inferred then the court will apply the law of the country with which the contract is most closely connected (Article 4(1)) and there is a rebuttable presumption that this will be the law of the country where the party who is to effect the characteristic performance of the contract has his or her habitual residence or, if that party is a company, its central administration. This notion of an obligation's 'characteristic performance' is derived from Swiss law, but it is not that far removed from the English law concept of 'the proper law of the contract'.

Special choice-of-law rules, or presumptions, are laid down in the Convention for particular types of contracts. For example, a contract concerning a right over immovable property is presumed to be governed by the *lex rei sitae*, in conformity with the pre-Convention French rule, and a contract with a consumer is governed by the law of the consumer's habitual residence, a rule which is new to most European national laws but which is in line with the EC's policy in favour of protecting consumers. There are also rules of alternative reference for deciding whether a contract has been drawn up in the correct form (Article 9): if concluded between persons who are in the same country, the contract can comply either with the law of the country where it is concluded or with the *lex causae* determined under the Convention for matters other than form; if concluded between persons who are not in the same country, the contract can comply either with the *lex causae* just mentioned or with the law of either of the countries where the parties are located; consumers, however, are entitled to expect the requirements of form of the country of their own habitual residence to be complied with.

Contracts for the sale of goods and contracts for the supply of work are regulated in France by the Hague Convention on International Sales of 1985, replacing an earlier Convention of 1955. It has also ratified the 1980 Vienna Convention on Contracts for the International Sale of Goods. These Conventions rely mostly upon the *lex loci contractus*, this being defined as the law of the country where the order for the goods or work in question has been received.

France largely deals with matrimonial property as if it were a matter of contract law, which is how the *Code civil* portrays it. This approach dates from the opinion of Dumoulin in the 16th century, who imagined an implied contract governing the property. French case law has maintained this rule despite some strong criticism, some of it going back to the era of d'Argentré. The chief factor indicating the 'locality' of the implied contract is the domicile of the spouses, but common nationality or other elements can also play a role.

In the eyes of French private international law, torts are governed almost without exception by the law of the place where the tort was committed, even when the parties share a *lex patriae* which is not the *lex loci delicti*. If the tort has been committed in one country but the damage has materialised in another, French case law tends to favour applying the latter. The *lex loci delicti* is also applied to legal actions taken directly by the victim of the tort against the tortfeasor's insurer. English private international law defers to the *lex loci delicti* to the extent that it requires the tort to be actionable by that law, but it also requires it to be actionable by English law as the *lex fori* (*Phillips* v *Eyre*, 1870) and it is prepared to subject a particular tortious issue to the law of the country which has the most significant relationship with the parties (*Boys* v *Chaplin*, 1969). For two particular types of case France's position is determined by Hague Conventions, which the United Kingdom has not yet incorporated into national law. The first is the Convention on the Law Applicable to Road Traffic Accidents (1971), which mostly opts for the law of the country where the accident occurred (*loi du lieu de survenance de l'accident*) and exceptionally for the law of the country where the car or cars were registered (*loi du pays d'immatriculation*). The second is the Convention on the Law Applicable to

Product Liability (1973). This applies the law of the country where the act which has caused the damage has occurred, but only if this is also the country where the victim habitually resides, where the party responsible is based or where the victim acquired the product. The law of the country of the victim's habitual residence is preferred, however, if this is also the law under either of the last two criteria.

INTERNATIONAL CIVIL PROCEDURE

What the French refer to as a *conflit de juridictions* entails discussion of two separate sets of questions. One has to do with which country's courts have jurisdiction to hear a dispute, the other with whether the judgments rendered in one country will be recognised in another. The *nouveau Code de procédure civile* also contains specific provisions on the international exchange of documents and on the obtaining of evidence abroad (*commissions rogatoires*); these are briefly referred to in Chapter 7.

The *Code civil* deals in a very piecemeal fashion with questions of international judicial competence. By virtue of Article 14 a foreigner can be taken to court in France in respect of contracts concluded in any country with a French national, and by Article 15 a French national can be sued in France on a contract concluded in any country with a foreigner. But case law has expanded upon these basic principles. It has applied them to all disputes involving French nationals. Even more striking is the change which has been effected in relation to disputes between foreigners. In situations where French courts could apply French law they soon began to accept that they had jurisdiction even in situations involving non-French nationals, especially cases concerning property rights or torts, for which in any event the relevant choice-of-law rule pointed to the *lex loci*. Eventually even this rationale for accepting jurisdiction was abandoned and it became enough that the plaintiff had his or her domicile in France. Today the domestic French rules are also applied when the question at issue is in which region of France a court case should be heard.

When it comes to the recognition of foreign judgments, French private international law distinguishes between judgments concerning a person's status or capacity and other judgments. Foreign judgments in the former category are effective in France without having to undergo any special recognition procedure. France does not restrict recognition to cases where the foreign country in question itself recogniaes French judgments, nor does it re-examine the substance of the judgments. But if someone wishes to rely upon a judgment it has to be proved in the same way as if it were a domestic French judgment being enforced (a process known as *jugement d'exéquatur*) and the following conditions must be satisfied:

(a) the foreign judge must have had jurisdiction according to France's own rules on international civil procedure;

(b) the foreign trial must have been conducted in accordance with the basic principles of fairness;
(c) the law applied must have been the law to which French choice-of-law rules would have pointed; and
(d) there must have been no violation of French public policy or evasion of the appropriate law (*fraude à la loi*).

Note must also be taken of the international conventions applicable in the procedural sphere. Of particular importance is the 1968 Brussels Convention on Jurisdiction and Enforcement of Judgments in Civil and Commercial Matters, which is in force in France just as it is in England (by virtue of the Civil Jurisdiction and Judgments Acts 1982) and on which the European Court of Justice has already pronounced many times. As with the Rome Convention, therefore, the provisions of the Brussels Convention are fully discussed in English textbooks. By and large the Brussels Convention requires legal actions to be taken against defendants in the state where they are domiciled, though defines 'domicile' in a way which brings it closer to the notion of habitual residence (s. 41 of the English Act). There are also special bases of jurisdiction, allowing, for example, a defendant to be sued in matters relating to contract or tort in, respectively, the country where the contractual obligation was to be performed or the country where the tort occurred (Article 5). A Dutch case involving a French company which was allegedly discharging 10,000 tons of chlorides into the Rhine every day was taken to the European Court of Justice in 1976; the Court held that the plaintiff could choose to sue either in the country where the wrongful act occurred (i.e. France) or in the country where the damage was suffered (i.e. The Netherlands): *Handelskwekerij Bier* v *Mines de Potasse d'Alsace SA*. A consumer can usually bring a legal claim to the courts of his or her own domicile instead of to the courts of the defendant's domicile. Claims to immovable property must be brought in the country where the property is situated, and some claims concerning companies must be brought in the country where the company has its 'seat' (i.e. where its central management and control are located). The 'exorbitant' claims to jurisdiction in Articles 14 and 15 of the *Code civil* are disapplied, as is the English rule that jurisdiction can be based on service of documents on a defendant while he or she is in England, or on the presence of the defendant's property in England.

On account of the strictness of the Convention's provisions on jurisdiction, it can afford to be much less demanding in the spheres of recognition and enforcement of judgments. The basic rule is that a judgment given by a court which has jurisdiction under the Convention is entitled to automatic recognition and enforcement in all other EC states, with the recognising state unable to re-examine the merits of the judgment. However, the European Court of Justice has held that France's procedure which allows unilateral seizure of a defendant's property after an *ex parte* application to a court (*saisie conservatoire*) is not deserving of recognition abroad because it does not give the defendant an opportunity to be heard (*Denilauler* v *SNC Couchet Frères*, 1980). England and France now recognise and enforce each other's judgments with the greatest of ease under the 1968 Convention; the provisions of the former Anglo-French Treaty on this topic, dating from 1934, are no longer in force. In France all that a judgment creditor need do is to apprise the President of a *tribunal de grande instance* that a judgment has been issued in another EC country in his or her favour and the President will grant an enforcement order (*l'ordonnance d'exéquatur*). On appeal to the *cour d'appel* the judgment debtor can overturn the order only if he or she shows that enforcement would contravene Articles 27 or 28 of the Brussels Convention. These permit a court to deny recognition or enforcement if, for example, it would be contrary to public policy or irreconcilable with an earlier judgment already pronounced between the parties in the court's own state.

FURTHER READING

There is no good modern account in English of French private international law, though obviously a glimpse of the French and other European systems is often apparent in the English textbooks when they discuss cases involving both England and France. Indeed, many of the English *causes célèbres* have arisen out of conflicts with the French system: *Leroux* v *Brown* (1852), *Castrique* v *Imry* (1870), *Godard* v *Gray* (1870), *Schibsby* v *Westenholz* (1870), *Jacobs* v *Crédit Lyonnais* (1884), *De Nicols* v *Curlier* (1900), *Ogden* v *Ogden* (1908), *Raulin* v *Fischer* (1911), *Re Annesley* (1926), *Cammell* v *Cammell* (1965) and the *Compagnie Tunisienne* case (1970). An interesting journal article is T. Guedji, 'The theory of *lois de police*' (1991) 39 Am Jo Comp L 661.

Perhaps the most readable account in French is the textbook by D. Holleaux, J. Foyer and G. de Geouffre de la Pradelle, *Droit international privé* (1987), but see also Y. Loussouarn and P. Bourel, *Droit international privé* (4th edn, 1993), P. Mayer, *Droit international privé* (4th edn, 1991) and (in the *Que Sais-Je?* series) F. Majoros, *Le droit international privé* (3rd edn, 1990). The French bible in the area – the equivalent to the English practitioner's Dicey and Morris – is H. Batiffol and P. Lagarde, *Droit international privé* (8th edn, vol. 1, 1993; vol. 2, 1983). On recent reforms to nationality law, see P. Courbe, *Le nouveau droit de la nationalité* (1994).

INDEX

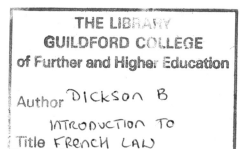